Disability, Self, and Society speaks with authenticity about disability as a process of identity formation within a culture that has done a great deal to de-emphasize the complexity of disability experience. Unlike many who hold the conventional sociological view of disability as a 'lack' or stigmatized identity, Tanya Titchkosky approaches disability as an agentive (not passive) embodiment of liminality and as a demonstration of socially valuable in-between-ness. She argues that disability can and should be a 'teacher' to, and about, non-disabled or 'temporarily abled' society, hence, the vital necessity that disability *stays* with us.

Titchkosky's poignant reflections on disability rely on the thought of Hannah Arendt as well as her personal experience as an individual with dyslexia living with a blind partner; she uniquely draws on her own and others' situations in order to demonstrate the sociopolitical character of disability. A thoughtful and cohesive integration of narrative and theory, *Disability, Self, and Society* presents a critical Canadian contribution to the growing subject of disability studies.

TANYA TITCHKOSKY is Associate Professor of Sociology at St Francis Xavier University in Nova Scotia.

TANYA TITCHKOSKY

Disability, Self, and Society

170201

WITHDRAWN

UNIVERSITY OF TORONTO PRESS
Toronto Buffalo London

© University of Toronto Press Incorporated 2003
Toronto Buffalo London
Printed in Canada

ISBN 0-8020-3561-2 (cloth)
ISBN 0-8020-8437-0 (paper)

Printed on acid-free paper

National Library of Canada Cataloguing in Publication

Titchkosky, Tanya, 1966–
   Disability, self, and society / Tanya Titchkosky.

   Includes bibliographical references and index.
   ISBN 0-8020-3561-2 (bound)   ISBN 0-8020-8437-0 (pbk.)

   1. Sociology of disability.   2. People with disabilities – Social
   conditions.   I. Title.

HV3011.T58 2003   305.9'0816   C2002-903532-5

This book has been published with the help of a grant from the Humanities and Social Sciences Federation of Canada, using funds provided by the Social Sciences and Humanities Research Council of Canada.

University of Toronto Press acknowledges the financial assistance to its publishing program of the Canada Council for the Arts and the Ontario Arts Council.

University of Toronto Press acknowledges the financial support for its publishing activities of the Government of Canada through the Book Publishing Industry Development Program (BPIDP).

To Rod

The body is not a thing, it is a situation ... We shall hold that the body ... exists concretely ... only in the total perspective of existence ... Interpreting the body on a basis of existence ... [its] meaning is seen at once as dependent on a whole context.

Simone de Beauvoir, *The Second Sex*, pp. 38, 67

Contents

Acknowledgments

This book grows out of my desire to connect life and social theory, and this desire has been supported by many. I thank the Social Sciences and Humanities Research Council of Canada for its generous support of my research through a standard research grant. Thanks to Virgil Duff of University of Toronto Press for guiding this project through to completion. Ken Lewis did a great job of copy-editing this book and was particularly sensitive to all of my dyslexic renderings of the written word. Thanks are due to Debbie Murphy and Carla Haley-Baxter, who, despite their busy secretarial service to St Francis Xavier University's Department of Sociology and Anthropology, always found time for me. Professors Janice Newson and Penni Stewart, of York University, have given me much support and encouragement along the way to here, for which I am very grateful. I am indebted to the active student members of the seminar courses and voluntary reading groups with whom various aspects of this book have been put through the discussion wringer. I am especially grateful to Terri Pitts and Barbara Barker, who helped proof-read. Dan and Annette Ahern encouraged me throughout the writing of the book and offered me an unwavering belief that the project would come to fruition. Their sensitivity and humour were invaluable sources of support to me.

Lindsay McVicar responded to much of this work, offering many thought-provoking comments. Dan and Judy MacInnes contributed many good thoughts and shared many good times with me when I most needed them. Judy treated both my writing of the manuscript and its potential publication as an unquestionable matter of fact. I am especially grateful to Dan MacInnes, who was the Chair of the Department of Sociology and Anthropology while I was writing this book. Against many odds, Dan treated me as a *bona fide* and valuable colleague, supported the continuation of my teaching, and encouraged me to teach courses that would enhance my writing. My deepest respect and gratitude I give to Rod Michalko. A life with him in blindness has made for much reading and many wonderful conversations, and has filled them, as well as this book, with vigour and life. I thank him also for maintaining a faith in me that I could not develop or maintain on my own. The provocation of his life, work, and wisdom has taught me the importance of developing a sociological stance that can speak to embodiment and to the moral implications behind being-in-the-world as disabled people.

Various parts of some chapters have been published previously, and I am grateful for permission to use this work in this book. Parts of chapter 2, 'Situating Disability: Mapping the Outer Limits,' first appeared in Mairian Corker and Tom Shakespeare's edited collection *Disability/Postmodernity: Embodying Disability Theory* (2002) as 'Cultural Maps: Which Way to Disability?' Sections of chapter 4, 'The Expected and the Unexpected,' are from my part of a joint publication with Rod Michalko entitled 'Putting Disability in Its Place: It's Not a Joking Matter,' which is a chapter in the collection *Embodied Rhetorics: Disability in Language and Culture* (2001), edited by James C. Wilson and Cynthia Lewiecki-Wilson. Much of chapter 5, 'Disability Studies: The Old and the New,' appeared under the same title in the *Canadian Journal of Sociology*.

DISABILITY, SELF, AND SOCIETY

CHAPTER ONE

Disability: A Social Phenomenon

This book grows out of my experience with two disabilities: blindness and dyslexia. While I live with both, I am only one – dyslexic. For more than ten years now, I have shared my life with fellow sociologist, teacher, and author Rod Michalko. Rod is blind. So, while I live with both blindness and dyslexia, I do so in very different ways. I can choose, for example, to orient to the unique standpoint of Rod in blindness, but I can also choose to disregard it. Dyslexia, however, seems to orient my relations to space and print regardless of my decisions; still, I can choose to disregard and, often, even cover up this difference. Dyslexia and blindness are both typically regarded as disabilities, and both are part of my life. To begin this book, however, I have decided not to disregard Rod's blindness and to commingle it with my dyslexia as a methodological device for making my way through the lived experience of disability and its meanings. The overriding decision upon which this book is based is to stay with the experience of disability as a significant social phenomenon that can reveal and illuminate culture. This orientation means that disability experience is a matter for social inquiry.

Throughout the time of our relationship, Rod has gone 'really blind.' His vision has changed from legal blindness to almost total blindness: light and shadow is what Rod now sees. Whereas Rod has lived with blindness since childhood, it was only a couple of years prior to living with him that I acquired an understanding of my self as dyslexic. Going blind and being identified as dyslexic are radically different from one another. Still, both require a grappling with identity as this is positioned in relation to culture's many different ways of speaking of blindness and dyslexia, of the body, and of its vicissitudes. To live with both is to live with the plethora of ways that culture has of making up the meaning of its people; and, conversely, it is to live with the plethora of ways that people have to make up the meaning of their culture. This book attends to the cultural processes of meaning-making surrounding disability by showing how disability matters. Judith Butler (1993: 32) reminds us that '"to matter" means at once "to material-ize" and "to mean."' The ways in which the matters of dyslexia or blindness are experienced by any of us have something to reveal about the cultural meaning of disabil-ity. It is an abiding assumption throughout this book that culture is dynamic – culture receives its meaning from people, while, at the same time, giving people their mean-ing. Therefore, living with disability provokes a continual wrestling with the question of identity, at both practical and theoretical levels.

Everyone, disabled or not, who interacts with disability is engaged in producing its meaning and its social identity. A 'disability identity' does not belong strictly and only to those of us who are identified as disabled. I experience not only my dyslexia but also Rod's blindness, and I experi-ence what meaning is made of both dyslexia and blindness by others and by me, and all these experiences are configured within a culture that has much to say and do about disability. It is impossible to experience disability outside of our relations with others. Whole cultures and whole societies experience disability, and this too is done within the confines of a commingling of various ways that disability is identified and made meaningful. But my experience of dyslexia and blindness does not determine the meaning of disability since this experience is always informed by, and representative of, the interrelations among my self, others, and our culture. Thus, throughout this book, I write of Rod's blindness, of the disabilities of others, of how non-disabled people experience disability, of how institutions and organizations treat disability, and of disability narratives. In all these ways, disability comes to experience. Yet, I am not appropriating experience; instead, I am reflecting upon the understandings of disability that give rise to my own and my society's experience of it in the first place. If it is true, as Mikhail Bakhtin (1986: 70–1) suggests, that each and every utterance is bounded by the expectation that others will respond, then articulating the experience of disability and attempting to understand it can be conceived of as 're-appropriation.' Re-appropriation means taking back, talking back, and staying with the experience of disability so as to reveal the meaning that has already been granted to disability by culture, by others, and by me. After all, it is the commingling of all of these experiences of disability that produces and reflects cultural and societal responses to it.

Henri-Jacques Stiker says in *A History of Disability* (1999: 14, 18), 'A society reveals itself by the way in which it treats certain significant phenomena,' and this is why he characterizes his research goal as, at most, 'to enlarge the understanding that we already have.' Disability is certainly a significant social phenomenon, and it is so in a variety of ways. It is significant numerically in that many people are disabled and many more will become so. According to the

Canadian government (*In Unison*, 2000), 4.2 million people
are disabled in Canada; according to the U.S. Census Bureau, 54 million people are disabled in the United States
(Fleischer and Zames, 2001: xvi); and according to the
International Disability Foundation there are more than
half a billion disabled people in the world and this number
is rising (Priestley, 2001: 3). While disability touches the
lives of many people, Stiker implies that the ultimate significance of this social phenomenon lies in the quality of
the appearance of disability issues and in society's treatment of its disabled people.

Social inquiry into the treatment of disability includes
how disability is experienced through the ways in which a
culture excludes and includes disability matters within daily
life, in knowledge and image production, and in the arrangement of the environment. All of the ways in which
disability takes shape and is treated, are in themselves interesting. We all can take some interest in how governments or social workers or store clerks, or film-makers and
novelists, have treated disability and thus have given it
cultural meaning. But merely noting the treatment, like
attending to the numbers of disabled people, does not fully
address the significance of disability. This treatment, and
the experiences of disability that it gives rise to, need to be
noted so as to interpret them in light of what they reveal
about culture. In noting the treatment of disability, this
book aims to stay with disability as that which can reveal
and illuminate society and so enlarge the understanding
that we already have. Through an analysis of disability
experience, we are provided with the possibility of revealing how societal understandings of disability make disability mean, materialize, and matter in the ways that it currently
does.

Disability is significant because each and every treatment
of it is grounded in and represents societal understandings.

Staying with disability as a significant social phenomenon means, in this framework, being given the chance to recognize and understand these social renderings of how disability must already be understood such that it is experienced in the ways that it is. Treatments of disability occur through action and discourse – in the lives and words of people. This revelation and illumination of social understandings of disability is different from the traditional ethnographic or biographical ways of describing disability, and different from the social scientific process of documenting and explaining disability through quantitative techniques, such as surveys and questionnaires. These methods can provide a sense of how disability is treated and even a sense of how many people or institutions treat disability in this or that fashion. But in many ways, most of us (should) already know that disabled people and disability issues are treated and experienced in a way that marginalizes both the issues and the people. To learn something new about how society treats disability so as to marginalize it does not necessarily require more documentation; but, it does require a different interpretive relation to this fact of social life and to our experiences of marginalization.

Because I want to stay with disability as a space of critical inquiry into the understandings of society, this book employs phenomenological and hermeneutic methods. For example, every chapter begins with my own lived experience of a treatment of disability and moves from there to a consideration of more general societal treatments and cultural renderings of disability. I locate the phenomenon of disability in the goings on of everyday life (interaction), in what is produced from this interaction (knowledge/ images), and in the built environment (setting) within which these interactions and knowledge production occur. Of course, there are at best only porous boundaries separating interaction, knowledge, and setting. Nonetheless, categorizing arenas of inquiry in this fashion does help to keep an analytic focus on disability as a social phenomenon. Making use of narrative accounts of my dyslexia, or of Rod's blindness, or my discipline's (sociology's) treatment of disability, or of other narratives of disability, is not done here so as to simply document that disability is treated poorly. Instead, I begin with these experiences of disability as a way to connect the reader, disabled or not, to her or his own experience of disability and to connect these experiences to the societal understandings within which such experiences can occur in the first place. Disability is typically treated in an oppressive and exclusionary manner leading to the on-going marginalization of disabled people and disability issues. But, if it is true that disability is significant because it is that space of experience within which one can come to reveal the understandings of a society, then a hermeneutics – an interpretation of interpretation – of disability is what is required.

I begin the study of disability and culture by giving some background to my experience with Rod's blindness and my dyslexia. Turning my analytical attention to my personal experiences of disability will allow me to more thoroughly develop the sense in which disability is social and to demonstrate the ways in which we can stay with disability so as to understand it more as a social phenomenon than as an individual one. Thus I will address some everyday, even mundane and ordinary, experiences of disability so as to illuminate the social significance that lies buried in these experiences.

Disability and the Background of the Ordinary

Rod and I moved from Toronto and now live in a small town which has two taxi companies with a total of eighteen taxis. It is not uncommon to have the same taxi driver over the span of a couple of days. A long-time taxi driver, but new to the one taxi company that we use, picked the two of us up on a Sunday, and then picked me up from work on the following Monday. The driver said, 'That man, that man you were with on the weekend, he's blind?'

'Yes,' I said.

'And the dogs that were with you are to help him?'

'Well, one is. The bigger one, Smokie,[1] is his guide dog. The other dog is mine.'

He asked me how long Rod was 'that way' and told me that he began to realize Rod was blind because he took his time finding the door handle and getting into the taxi. The driver then said, 'It's such a shame. How terrible. You know, there's nothing worse than being blind.'

The sense that there is nothing worse than being blind was not delivered to the driver from his seeing that Rod took time to find the car's door handle. The taxi driver's experience of tragedy was nonetheless part of his noticing that Rod took a bit longer to find the door handle and had his guide dog sit with him in the taxi. The driver's direct experience was filtered through the culturally derived conception of who blind people are, namely, victims of the worst imaginable tragedy. Situation comedies, news media, donation appeals, health warnings, and many other arenas of cultural production treat blindness as tragedy. (Indeed, time, energy, and inclination are all required if one is to find blindness materialized as something other than tragedy.) Within such a culture, noticing a blind person taking one's time getting into a car easily becomes just one more piece of the disability puzzle that ends up depicting it as a 'shame,' a real tragedy.

Alone, in the taxi that day, disability, and specifically Rod's blindness, was delivered to me as a tragedy. As someone who travelled with tragedy, I could thus be questioned; for example, when did the tragedy happen? how did it happen? etc. While neither Rod nor I regards blindness as a tragedy and as much as I may resist tragedy as the definition of Rod's situation, it nonetheless remains a social fact that disability is understood as such. This is one of the many ways that disability-as-tragedy enters my experience, and it does so regardless of my personal rejection of such an understanding. Any experience of disability includes others' understandings of it.

I would not want to deny that a sense of tragedy can accompany disability experience and that it does so in many ways. There is something tragic about the collective ability to regard even the tiniest signs of disability, such as locating door handles through touch and not sight, as *ipso facto* tragic. As I listened to the taxi driver, who told me that he had a long history of driving taxis in this small town, beginning in the 1930s, I too was struck by a sense of tragedy. How could it be that he did not know of Rod-the-blind-man-and-guide-dog-Smokie? I was certainly shocked that he did not. It seems as if the whole town knows of this pair. Perhaps the driver was isolated from, or inured to, 'town talk.' Whatever the case, blindness was obviously the worst tragedy that had entered his car in the last couple of days. However such tragedy is located and experienced, it is important to note that the experience of disability gives rise to the opportunity to examine how the meaning of people's lives is built together with other people. Asserting *or* denying that disability is a tragedy is the same, in the limited sense that both refuse to stay with this experience of disability and thus reject the opportunity to reflect upon its cultural organization. In this case, we can come to understand that interaction (opening a door) can be read as symptomatic of a type of person (disabled). Likewise, that opening a door can deliver the experience of tragedy can be read as symptomatic of dominant cultural treatments of disability. Notice, however, that the first form of reading is often privileged over the second, and doing the second type of reading can make us uncomfortable.

Unlike blindness, dyslexia is not readily observable. Moreover, I am a very animated and dynamic speaker, and these qualities usually cover over or remedy the confusion that resides in my scrambled word order, unique phraseology, or misspoken clichés. Blindness can be used to make sense of almost everything Rod says and does, from opening a door to being in a good or bad mood. Almost nothing that I do or say is made sense of through dyslexia, unless I point it out or argue for it. Instead of dyslexic, I am sometimes seen as lazy, forgetful, confusing and confused, even stupid, or I am just a little quirky, original, eccentric, and easily distracted. I do not think that I have ever been regarded as tragedy incarnate. Often, though, I am a bit of a joke.

After three years of living in this small town, with limited freedom of movement because I have been unable to learn to drive, and there is no public transit, I thought it was time to try learning to drive again. On the day that I secured a learner's driving permit, friends came to visit Rod and me. When our friends were leaving, I offered to back their car up to the edge of the driveway and then back it out onto the street. I did this with much concentration and quite a bit of a thrill. Smoothly, I accomplished the task and paused. My satisfaction lasted only a fraction of a moment for one of my friends, Judy, excitedly exclaimed, 'You're on the wrong side of the road. You're on the wrong side of the road.' After fixing this and having not been struck by an oncoming car, we laughed. This was very funny, but it also gave me a lot to think about.

Unless cars are parked on the road or travelling down it, I have yet to figure out how it is that non-dyslexics discern the correct side of the road. Telling the time, distinguishing right from left, using correct word order and sentence structure, giving and receiving directions, and discerning the correct side of the road are things which I can accomplish only with a great deal of focus and repetition, or by following rules. They are never activities that I can take for granted and 'just do.' Sitting in the car, positioned now on the right side of the road, Judy said, 'Well, I see you have a lot to learn!'

My first lesson was already learned – I do not 'automatically' know which side of the road to drive on. It was good to learn this in the company of friends. My next task: how am I to figure out which side of the road is 'my' side of the road even though this will always change depending on the direction I wish to travel?

I began talking to non-dyslexic drivers about how they know which side of the road they should be on without benefit of another car to point the way. These drivers' descriptions were a giant salad of rights and lefts. While it is true that such directions are difficult for me and I might be misunderstanding them, it also occurred to me that all of these drivers do not need to think about the correct side of the road and that they have a hard time articulating their knowledge. It was for them a taken-for-granted aspect of the background order of driving. Before I figured out the 'my' side of the road problem, I learned that most people do not need to do such figuring – they just know.

Recently, I turned to someone who I thought might have to pay more attention to driving, a truck driver. I told him my story, and he quickly responded, 'Always keep your steering wheel as close as you can to the centre of road.' I understood this. It is a rule I can use to mentally position

myself correctly before I set out on any road. (I now prac-
tise this, but not in a car.)

One of the interesting features of disability is that it points
out background expectancies (Garfinkel, 1967) used by people to go about and do the ordinary things of ordinary life.
Background expectancies include rules, procedures, and
norms that guide behaviour, but to which little attention is
paid and thus little thought is ever given. Non-blind people move towards taxis and locate the door handle by using their vision. Non-dyslexic people drive on the side of
the road that they are supposed to. People do such things,
until something happens. Sighted people can get distracted
by other sights and may end up feeling around for door
handles; other people might not pay attention to new or
different roadway signage and end up driving on the wrong
side of road. Thus, not only do background expectancies
organize the flow of ordinary life, but they also organize
the occurrence of ordinary mistakes and what it ordinarily
means to make a mistake.

Notice, however, that it is called a 'mistake,' an 'accident,'
or a 'lack' of attention when non-disabled people fail to
conform to the sets of background expectancies that organize daily life. When non-disabled people do not adhere to
this order, we make sense of it by saying that 'something
has gone wrong' or that the person has 'done something
wrong.' Failure to conform to how things are ordinarily
done is always interpreted, made sense of, and given meaning. Yet, in the face of disability, there is often a slippage
between the meaning of such actions and the meaning of
persons. Seeing Rod as blind, the taxi driver does not see
Rod as visually distracted and making an ordinary mistake
in how door handles are ordinarily located and grasped.
Instead, he sees that something is tragically wrong *with*
Rod.

Seeing Rod as blind is dependent upon somehow seeing Rod himself as a mistake; he *should* have been sighted but for some tragedy. Understanding my self as dyslexic means knowing that I did not make a mistake but, instead, there is something mistaken about the ways in which I make sense of driving and direction. I am mixed up – I did not merely get mixed up, or cause a mix-up. Something has gone wrong, and ordinary life is not being done in its ordinary fashion. But what is wrong is seen to belong to disabled people in a more intimate or personal way than it does to others. Rod is opening the door in an out-of-the-ordinary way because he is an out-of-the-ordinary type of person – he is blind. I am practising driving in an out-of-the-ordinary way (in my imagination) because I am the type of person who has a different relation to the language of everyday life and move-ment – I am dyslexic. Being outside of some ordinary ap-pearances and expectations is typically treated as dis-ability, as an inability to do things as they are ordinarily expected to be done and be seen to be done.

The inability to do things is one of society's primary definitions of disability. Not only taxi drivers but also the governments of most countries and the World Health Or-ganization proceed to treat disability from the understand-ing that it means that one is unable to do what 'normal' people do. Instead of defining disability in relation to the interaction, knowledge/images, and settings within which disability occurs and is noticed, and thereby understanding disability as a social phenomenon tied to experience and its narration, disability is often defined as an asocial, apoliti-cal, biological phenomenon. For example, the International Classification of Impairment, Disabilities and Handicaps (cited in *In Unison*, 1998: 33), developed by the World Health Organization, and employed by many of the world's governments, speaks of disability in the following fashion:

Impairment: 'any loss or abnormality of a psychological, or anatomical structure or function.'

Resulting in

Disability: 'any restriction or inability to perform an activity in the manner or within the range considered normal for a human being.'

Which may lead to:

Handicap: 'any disadvantage for a given individual, resulting from an impairment or disability, that limits or prevents the fulfillment of a role that is normal for that individual.'

Representing disability as something arising from biological abnormality, organic misfunction, or bodily inability, restriction, and limitation consequently leads to, and is based upon, the assumption that disability *is* an individual incapacity – an inability to do things. While it is undoubtedly true that disabled people do not do some things in the ways that non-disabled people do, or may not do some things at all, it is equally true that disability highlights how things are 'normally' done, that is, highlights the background expectancies that order this doing in a culture, and disability is, therefore, much more significant than simply the doing or the non-doing of things. Nonetheless, disability is typically interpreted as, first and foremost, the inability to do things, and thus the whole realm of disability experience is often reconfigured and reduced to the doing and non-doing of things. Moreover, seeing disability as the doing and non-doing of normal things requires that one does not see the interactional, epistemological, and setting expectations which organize and produce a culture's taken-for-granted sense of the 'normal doing of things,' in the first place.

As a member of my culture, I too experience disability in this asocial fashion, and this is how discovering myself driving on the wrong side of the road is, for me, a rediscovery of dyslexia. But notice, that so much more is going on within any cultural experience of disability than simply an expression of some sort of equation between an inability to do and the identification of disability. Consider the fact that I am rarely ever seen as dyslexic. The sets of background expectancies that dyslexia disrupts are not the same ones that blindness does. Dyslexia, more so than blindness, can often appear as *only* an ordinary mistake. The ordinary things that I do not do in an ordinary way are also *not done* by many other 'types' of people. Through the media, for example, and other sources of stereotypes, we are told that driving on the wrong side of the road is done by various 'types' of people: new drivers, drunk drivers, women drivers, dumb blondes, and kids who are fooling around are some of the many ways people can make sense of such an action. 'Dyslexic driver' is not a readily available way to make sense of my driving. Almost everything that I can call dyslexia, others can call something else. Almost nothing which Rod does is ever seen as anything but blindness. This points to the role that 'visibility' plays in constructing our cultural understandings of disability. The primary definition of disability as the inability to do things is connected to the taken-for-granted sense that disability is obviously *in* bodies that have gone wrong. Since disability is rarely conceived of as a relation between a culture and its people, it becomes very easy to assume that disability is simply and obviously a bodily phenomenon. Dyslexia and certain kinds of blindnesses cannot exist outside of highly technologized and literate societies. More to the point, no disability of any kind can appear outside of the social organization which surrounds it and the cultural understandings of it. Disability, simply put, is always done and always experienced with people. Those who find in themselves or in others a 'loss or abnormality of a psychological, or anatomical structure or function' are engaged in social action oriented to and by cultural knowledge, social settings, and unexamined conceptions of normalcy. Understanding this is what allows me, in this book, to treat any experience of disability, be it profound or mundane, as the opportunity to examine culture as well as an opportunity to consider the genesis of a 'disabled identity.'

Boundaries of Disability Experience

Whether visible or invisible to others, the cultural concept of 'disability' holds much efficacy in making up the meaning of people in everyday life. 'Dumb blonde,' 'drunk,' and 'blind guy' can be seen by others through interaction which does not take on an ordinary hue. All of these names refer to types of people and are packed full of meaning. But, there are ordinary ways to lack ordinariness (mistakes) and there are extraordinary ways to do so (disabilities). Disabled people are usually regarded as a transmogrification of mistakes (Low, 1996; Phillips, 1990). In the flow of everyday life, disability usually comes to us as embodied mistakes and, thus, as mistaken bodies. It rarely seems to come to our attention as a unique boundary of experience which requires a rethinking of our typical ways of making sense of our selves, of others, and of our culture (Frank, 1998c: 208). By staying with disability experience, even in matters as ordinary as everyday movement, disability can begin to be grasped as a place from which the culturally constituted boundaries between the expected and the unexpected (Michalko and Titchkosky, 2001: 218), the visible and the invisible, the doing and the non-doing of things, can be considered.

My dyslexia does not mean that I simply lack some of the shared background expectancies of various social situations and environments and thus need to acquire them in a different way. It means also that these background expectancies are never background for me. I teach sociology at St Francis Xavier University in Nova Scotia. While I am teaching, students sometimes say, 'It is quarter after three,' by which they mean that I have five minutes left of lecture time. While this makes perfect sense as I write it down on this page, it makes no sense during a lecture. I grasp that someone is pointing out the time in hopes that I too will pay attention to it. I also realize the imperative behind the 'statement of fact,' but the facticity of 'It's quarter after three' remains obscure. That I started the lecture seventy minutes ago, I understand. What time it was when I started seventy minutes ago, I do not. That there is five minutes left, I understand. What time it will be when I end in five minutes, I cannot say. I cannot quickly make sense of the moving hands of a clock, or the verbal rendering of the time, as they relate to me in the here and now situation of my lecture. I get to class on time either by talking to Rod or other colleagues who work in the same sociology department that I do, or by waiting until the digital clock on my computer almost matches the digitized time written on the class schedule. Telling time always means, for me, measuring it out or seeking consultation.

Yet, I know that people ordinarily tell each other the time and do so in particular ways. I know that the ordinary way to tell time involves never thinking about the ordinary way to tell time. Normally, 'time-telling' is treated as a natural event, not a social one. 'It's a quarter after,' or 'a quarter to,' or 'half past the hour' are expressions depicting time whose meaning I have yet to make familiar and taken-for-granted. The social meaning of time-telling shines forth – but 'the time' does not. Rod says that the same holds true for him in regards to sight (Michalko, 2002a; 1999; 1998). The background expectancies of vision – where to use it, how to use it, how to show others that you are using it – shine forth for him, but the 'seeing of things' does not. Indeed, all experiences of disability as shameful or embarrassing, difficult or infuriating, can be reconfigured into a place where the ordinary order of ordinary life can be thought about in a new way.

Attending to disability experience brings what for many people is part of the background features of life, typically unnoticed and unthought, into the foreground. To stay with disability experience and to make it matter means to treat disability as that place where culture comes to the foreground and is no longer merely the static and taken-for-granted background that goes about unnoticed as it creates meaning. It means to make the familiar practices of daily life that seem normal, and are often treated as if they are 'natural,' shine through in all their sociality. Disability is an occasion to bring culture to the fore, to disrupt it, and even to teach it new ways of creating meaning. For example, I know well and am sensitive to the pleasures of appearing 'competent.' Telling the time, not getting lost on the way to class, spelling a word correctly on the chalkboard are ways to achieve competence. But is there not another kind of competency that lies in knowing that these things are indeed cultural achievements, that competency is a social status made between people (Jenkins, 1998), and that the work of achieving competency can be attended to as such and not merely regarded as a natural-state-of-affairs that a

person either possesses or does not? On the boundary
between competency and incompetency, we are provided
with the possibility of thinking about how matters of competency materialize in our experience and are granted
meaning.

Disability experience can do this not only for disabled
people but also for non-disabled people. As a professor at a
university, I have status as 'someone in the know' and as
someone who has the authority to judge whether others
have become so through the administration of exams and
the grading of papers. Students have no trouble coming to
know me as such. But they also come to know that I do not
drive, cannot often tell the time, ask them strange questions, get them to spell words before I write them on the
chalkboard, and draw diagrams of ideas instead of providing written notes; also, they know that if they follow me to
class they will probably end up in the wrong room. According to my teaching evaluations, I am a good teacher, even a
dynamic one, but I do not do things that most students can
do effectively, efficiently, and without thought. I do not do
things that 'even a child could do,' yet I am their professor.
For some, this experience does not simply bring to mind
that I cannot do what they can. It brings to mind, instead,
their own background expectations that I *should* do all that
they do and more. I can also bring to awareness the set of
social expectations which are generally imagined as belonging to the type of person that culture depicts as possessing the knowledge and the authority to teach. This type
only recently began to include the possibility of young
women, and usually always includes 'suits' and men with
a bit of grey hair. Still, this imaginary 'professor type' is
usually very far removed from any image we hold of disabled people. Status and authority are, says Morris, 'associated with an absence of disability' (1991: 92).

Blindness, too, brings to awareness the unique interrelations between the body and identity as these are organized by culturally produced taken-for-granted expectations. What blindness brings to mind is more powerful or more dramatic than what dyslexia does. The terror and the chaos in Saramago's novel *Blindness* (1997), for example, in which the entire population is struck by an epidemic of 'white sickness,'[2] would probably become a comedy if the epidemic was one of dyslexia. Even though both blindness and dyslexia highlight the background order that organizes print and social space, they do so in different ways.

Shortly after Rod and I both started teaching in the sociology department at the same university, a colleague searched me out. She said, 'So, Rod will be teaching here too this term?'

'Yes,' I replied.

'Hmm, well, ah ... How *will* he teach?'

The hesitancy, the emphasis on the 'will,' as well as the fact that this question was asked of me and not of Rod, indicated to me that this was not a question regarding the techniques Rod employs in order to get the teaching job done. This was a question of whether or not it was possible for blind people to teach, and this question remained despite the fact that the questioner already knew that Rod had a strong teaching record as a 'blind professor.' At a different university, a colleague informed me one day that if it were not for my 'help,' Rod could not teach and thus should not be considered for a long-term contract. That 'accommodation' was a legal right for disabled people was unknown to this colleague. And yet another colleague told me that hiring readers was not an independent way of working: 'Unless Rod gets this computer equipment, he'll never be independent.' (Rod chooses to rely on teaching assistants more than on computers.) The exclusionary prowess of such beliefs is more than obvious here, and it can be of little surprise that the unemployment and labour non-participation rate amongst working-age disabled persons of all educational levels is well over 50 per cent (*In Unison,* 2000: 72–7; 1998: 36; Shapiro, 1993: 27–30). But there is more to learn here than what everyone should already obviously know.

Like my dyslexia, Rod's blindness in the university environment brings to mind the set of background expectations surrounding work (Michalko, 2001). Doing things or not doing things is not the only issue. Instead, doing ordinary things *in* ordinary ways and *with* ordinary conformity within the ordinary order of everyday life is what is at issue, and all this ordinariness is laden with moral value. In the face of disability, the Good of ordinariness comes to the foreground. Ordinarily, professors lecture while making eye contact and grade papers using their own eyeballs, and while there are many exceptions to this, such as using teaching assistants, blindness, according to the first questioner, is not a valid exception. Ordinarily, professors grade, record marks, read printed materials, take minutes at department meetings, all on their own, and while there are countless 'ordinary' exceptions to this, disability is not seen as one of them. Ordinarily, professors use computer equipment, but some do not. Non-disabled professors who do not use a computer mean one thing, while disabled professors who do not use one, or hire others to use one, mean something else. On the boundary between the ordinary and the non-ordinary way of doing things, we are provided with the possibility of examining the matter of normal everyday expectations.

Background expectancies are never just how things are done. Rather, they are part of a normative order ('This is how we normally do things around here'); a moral order ('This is how people ought to do things'); a taken-for-granted order ('This is "just" the way things are'); and a sensible order ('If you are not doing the normal things that normal people do in the normal way, then you may not count as someone who can do anything at all'). It follows that a sense of something wrong arises in the presence of disability, but that something is not usually located within the hegemony of ordinary life. Again, disability provides the occasion for us to understand the hegemonic character of ordinary life, and to disrupt and question the taken-for-granted expectation that ordinary life is merely an ordinary matter. Even though it is usually disabled people who are scrutinized, while the ordinary order of life is not, staying with disability experience allows for the possibility of some reciprocity of attention.

My focus on background expectancies serves as a way to emphasize just how complicated the issues of identity and culture are, especially when their interrelation is brought to light through disability. Disability is never as simple as something gone wrong with the body, what the World Health Organization (WHO) calls 'impairment,' or with how others, or society in general, react to what is wrong, what WHO calls 'handicap' (Ingstad and Whyte, 1995: 5–7; Gadacz, 1994: 27–36). Dividing up the body and identity may have some good political and practical uses, such as pointing out just how oppressive social organization can be. But designing society so as to exclude does not come from nowhere. The often dramatic treatment and exclusion of disabled people is tied to the dynamic interrelations among body, identity, and culture. The matter is far more complicated than any theoretical division between the body and identity can grant.

But some people say, 'We must remember that disabled persons are, after all, people,' or, 'Despite my disability, I am a person first.' The inclination to remind others that disabled people are, indeed, *persons* surely highlights the sorry state of affairs of living in a culture whose conception of people is such that 'disabled people' do not quite fit, and the contrary thus remains something of which others need to be reminded. But such a reminder, found in phrases such as 'persons *with* disabilities,' also recommends that we continue to think of disability as something not quite a part of personhood, and thus not quite part of the self (Titchkosky, 2001a). The reminder serves to put disability, once again, somewhere between 'animal and alien' (Kleege, 1999). Positing the 'ideology of personhood' (Michalko, 1998: 33–4, 129–32; Overboe, 1999: 24; Vaughan, 1998: 12–15; Gleeson, 1999: 20–1) can stop us from thinking about the complex interrelations among one's body, identity, and culture, but it will not remove the phenomenological fact that identity does come to us through our bodies, and does so within a culture that holds various conceptions of both the body and the self. (This is why I use the phraseology 'disabled people' and not 'persons with disabilities' throughout this book.) Disability is, as Frank (1998c: 209) suggests, a call to think about how '... culture inscribes the body, the body projects itself into social space, and [how] the boundary of these reciprocal movements is in flux.' The call to think about, and even define, disability as a form of interrelatedness is a principle guiding this book.

In order to begin to introduce this call, and the worthwhileness of heeding it, I have thus far been making use of examples of interaction between non-disabled and disabled people. Irving Goffman (1963: 13) says that a 'primal scene' for sociologists is just this sort of interaction, what he calls the interaction between the 'normals' and the 'stigmatized.' (In chapter 4, I offer a critique of this sociologically generated dichotomy.) Goffman calls this a primal scene because the genesis of the meaning of social identities can be gleaned from such interaction. But there is also much to be learned about the genesis of identity in the primal scene of the interaction between and among disabled people themselves. There is, for example, an interrelation between my dyslexia and Rod's blindness that has something to say about the formation of our social identities as disabled people, as well as the construction of the meaning of disability in general.

Between Blindness and Dyslexia

While I live with disability through my dyslexia, its significance has been experienced, at least for the last ten years, most intensely in relation to a life with blindness (see chapter 2). As Rod became almost totally blind, our life with blindness and dyslexia has included a constant set of shifts, ruptures, and readjustments. Likewise, over the last ten years, the significance of disability and how one ought to think about it have shifted and moved. What has remained is a life with Rod animated by the desire – if not always the actuality of doing so – to think about the significance of disability as a social phenomenon. The curious intertwining of my dyslexia with blindness finds some unity in the fact that this life in disability with Rod has brought many intense experiences and has thus brought much to think about, and all this is interpenetrated by and intertwined with the activism and scholarship, programs and policies, everyday comments and sophisticated accounts surrounding disability.

A potent experience of dyslexia that I have, in relation to Rod's blindness, is that of 'added danger.' While learning disabilities, of late, have been characterized within the medical and rehabilitative professions as 'risk' factors for dropping out of school or criminal activity (Booth and Booth,

1998: 76–8), the experience of a 'sense of danger' is not a diagnostic criterion. In relation to Rod, however, dyslexia makes me not only experience danger, but also feel like a danger myself. Again, the significance of disability cannot be fully considered outside of those who are in relation with it. Along with confusing left from right, I also do not often know which set of traffic lights I should attend to in order to cross the street. Word and numerical order, object order, logical sequential directions, and spacial order bring confusion and are either arduous tasks that I struggle with or, when I accomplish them, I do so in a non-typical manner. Living and moving with someone who is blind makes these 'mere confusions' into potential hazards. This sense of danger comes to the fore when, together, Rod and I do what should be ordinary things, such as negotiating city streets or moving through public buildings.

While I can see what needs to be seen as Rod and I go about daily life, I often cannot make 'normal sense' of these sights. For example, while standing at an intersection one day, I said to Rod that it was safe to cross because there was a stop sign for intersecting traffic. Rod gave his guide dog, Smokie, the command 'Forward,' and, after one or two steps, Smokie jerked Rod out of the way of an oncoming car. As it turned out, the stop sign was for the traffic that flowed the same way we were walking. Thankfully, Smokie made 'normal sense' of the situation.

The seeable world is not simply constituted through stuff that can be seen; it is constituted through the sense we make of it. There is no way to express what has been seen outside of the sense we make of it. There is no such thing as 'pure, natural' vision. While Rod has spent a lifetime attending to the 'normal order and sense' of the stuff that should be seen, he no longer sees it. I, on the other hand, see all this stuff, yet sometimes I do not make normal sense of it. Like any other companion of any other blind person, I translate what is to be seen into an aural shape and form. While there are difficulties involved in any kind of translation, my difficulties in translating are particularly problematic. In regards to Rod's movement through the environment, my dyslexia is sometimes a hindrance throwing Rod back upon his own way of discernment. In public life, this way of discernment includes attending to what is communicated to him through his guide dog, Smokie, through others, and through his knowledge and memory of the environment, etc.

Notice, though, that the social meanings of vision, knowledge of the visible world, blindness, and dyslexia are constituted in the situations of our relatedness to others. My experience of dyslexia as 'added danger' is neither the final authoritative word on what dyslexia is, nor is it merely a quirk of personal circumstances. It is, instead, if we stay with this experience, a place to consider how the meaning of persons is constituted *in situ*, within social contexts. Given this, is it not an unjust form of myth-making to consider the 'problem' of disability outside the situations within which disability is identified and made problematic?

But there are still other ways that the social significance of disability comes to light in the interaction between Rod's blindness and my dyslexia. My connection to Rod's life as a blind person has meant that I often come to experience my dyslexia as something continually marked with improvement. Reading aloud is a daily part of my life, provided for by blindness. Every word of this book and all my other writing I have read aloud to Rod, and he listens for mistakes and awkward wording and tells me about them. This means that I have to come to see what Rod hears. Because of this, as well as reading all of Rod's work aloud, I continue to become a better reader and a better writer. Despite potential mishaps, Rod does rely on me to translate visual order into an aural one, and if I do 'get it right,' I know, and if I do not, I also know, and more often than not I will have another chance to rearticulate spatial relations. Living with someone who is blind means that I am not allowed to escape from attending to dyslexia and working and moving with it in mind.

In one way, this means that I am experiencing my disability conventionally – as an inability requiring personal work. On the other hand, my dyslexia has also led to an unconventional experience of blindness, which has become both a guide and a teacher. I have experienced blindness as something other than mere inability in need of help: I have experienced blindness as helper, *as* educator. Between blindness and dyslexia, the ordinary authority of 'sight' that structures the flow of experience is disrupted, and this gives rise to the possibility of examining the culture within which our experiences of disability occur in the first place. In this way, Rod and I have made disability matter in ways not usually found in our society. Disability, both my lived experience of it and my experience of how it is represented by others, serves as a kind of teacher revealing the workings and assumptions of the culture within which and through which I live.

This has provoked me to consider why it is that there are so few cultural accounts of disability that regard it as a way of being in the world from which we can learn. The experience of blindness and dyslexia has forced me to pay attention to the social formation of the identity of my self and Rod as disabled people. This attests to the fact that how we talk about, and live with, disability can teach us much about how the body shapes identity, how identity shapes the body, and how both have something to teach us about culture and its values. Disability, *as teacher* (Mairs, 1996;

McDermott and Varene, 1995; Michalko, 1998; Mitchell and Snyder, 2000; 1997; Robillard, 1999; Slatin, 1986), is only possible if we suspend, even momentarily, the need to fix disabled persons or fix up society's treatment of us. Such suspension is necessary if we are to begin to think about cultural ways of speaking of disabled people, of what disability is, and to whom disability experience belongs. Such suspension is also necessary if we are to think about our collective and individual ways of living with these various discursive representations of disability. Suspending the need to remedy disability,[3] and to instead learn from it, is premised upon the possibility that we can locate both the experience and the meaning of disability as that which is made between people within environments not of our own choosing (see chapter 3).

'Fixing' disability experience, either in people or in societal structures, gives only one unified meaning to disability: it is something that needs to be fixed. From things that require remedy, we often learn little beyond the fact that they are broken, and the various ways in which they are so. So long as disability signifies only broken people or a broken society (oppression), we are stuck reasserting that the only thing interesting about disability is that it is a space for intervention (Crawford, 1980: 371). Despite the ever increasing plethora of ways designed to remedy disabled people or social structures and policy, remedy is itself a unified approach that pays little heed to disability experience as a call to think and learn about the 'richness of the flesh' (Hughes and Paterson, 1997: 332). What is rich about the flesh of disability experience is that it illuminates dominant cultural discourses regarding the meaning of persons. I will show throughout this book that disabled people live in-between many different and conflicting discourses of disability and cannot be reduced to any one of them. Living in-between, disabled people, with their bodies and their words, insert into the world the possibility of new meaning and new understandings of disability (see chapter 4).

The Richness of Disability Experience

Given my experience of disability through blindness, I have been provoked to rethink my own conventional relation to dyslexia. Dyslexia is not simply the requirement that I engage in tasks that help me overcome it. It is more than an obstacle in that it, too, is a way of being in the world – both an experience and a way of experiencing. As blindness was and is for Rod (Michalko, 1999), dyslexia is something that I am, while it is also something that I have to become. Identity, of any kind, is a social achievement. As Robert Scott (1969) and Richard Scotch (1994) poignantly remind us, disabled people are not born, they are made. Dyslexia may be understood as something that is being made and through its making can teach us about the culture within which it appears. Dyslexia is not only made in relation to the background expectancies of ordinary life, where, for example, it can function as a not so common sense-making device for common mistakes, such as driving on the wrong side of the road, it also becomes what it is through the making of a life. A story of a life with disability is, at the same time, the making of a life story and the narration of the meaning of disability.

In public school, I was not dyslexic. According to my report cards, I was instead a slow learner, easily distracted, someone who did not apply herself: 'Tanya has been unable to learn how to tell time'; 'Tanya is distracted easily'; 'Tanya talks too much and often disrupts the class.' In grade school, according to my report cards, I was sloppy, and this was the reason why I could not spell. I was lazy and this was the reason why I did not learn multiplication, division, and fractions. At the same time, these report cards also record that I was curious, observant, eager, and reading well beyond my grade level.

Thanks to a grade of 95 per cent in art, my overall average in my final year of high school was just high enough to gain admission into university. I avoided taking any courses that had anything to do with numbers. While I could not write sentences that were structured in a grammatically proper way, I was adept in grasping ideas, themes, arguments, and concepts, and made extensive use of this ability throughout my university career.

I needed, however, a second language to graduate with a BA. This was a problem. In the face of a lifetime spent in a culture strewn with English, which I could not get straight, learning another language did, indeed, seem futile. Concepts such as nouns, verbs, adjectives, etc., were themselves like a foreign language to me even in English, let alone in another language. In high school, I had tried French and German, but failed. At university, I tried these languages again, and even added Norwegian to the list – again failure.

A classroom, I decided, was no place for me to learn another language. I found a program in Mexico that taught Spanish by requiring students to live with a Spanish-speaking family, and began its language instruction on the basis of what students felt they needed to speak about as they were living in a different culture. Through this program, I would not only get intensive language instruction, but I would also receive university credit for it. Because of my difficulties in learning a language, I arrived a month before the program was to begin and attended the language school five days a week while living with a Mexican family.

I was pleased to find a school that operated on the principle that you learn language through living it and where my instruction in Spanish would proceed in relation to the things that interested me in Mexico. I was relieved to hear that only after I had some grasp of speaking Spanish, would I then move on to learning the written word, grammar and all. I was the first Canadian student to enrol in this language school, and I was the first person its instructors had taught who knew nothing of Spanish nor any other language other than English. I was, according to both the school's administrators and teachers, a chance for them to test the efficacy of their methods. Whereas other students might be grouped into classes as large as five people, I always received one-to-one instruction as they wanted nothing to come between me and their methods. In learning to speak Spanish, I exceeded all expectations, including my own, in a short period of time.

But this glorious success came to an abrupt halt when I was confronted with the language in its written form. Nothing remained. No word made the slightest bit of sense. In the face of the written word, I was, literally, speechless. I knew I was supposed to be seeing words that I already knew, but I was not. I could not even read the alphabet aloud.

After many weeks of attempting to get straight the shortest series of letters into something that might have meaning, the director called me into his office. To my surprise, and despite the rule against it, he spoke to me in English. He told me that he thought I had a problem. He thought I was 'dyslexic.' Perhaps it was his accent or the context of the language school, or perhaps it was a combination of both, but at the time I thought that the director was teaching me a new Spanish word meaning lazy, slow, or stubborn. I quickly, in Spanish, assured him that I was none of these things. I was working very hard. I could not be slow, I told him, because I was even learning to speak about Plato and Marx in Spanish. I also emphatically insisted that it was not stubbornness that transformed the written word into gibberish but that it was more akin to agony. He attempted to explain it to me again. I eventually understood that he felt that it was neither the school's methods nor my 'attitude' that kept me from learning. What was holding me back, he said, however, did have something to do with me and thus he was bringing someone in to test me.

In Mexico, at the age of twenty-one, I officially became dyslexic. At the same time, 'lazy, slow, and stubborn' lost their explanatory power.

In the past, I too had diagnosed myself as having a problem. However, I thought that the problem was a kind of mental illness, but a rare kind, as I could not find a description of it. (Unlike the interpretive category 'dyslexia,' 'mental illness' is a common way to make sense of a wide variety of differences and difficulties.) Since about the age of thirteen, I went to garage sales and bought every introductory psychology textbook that I could find, and I spent many weekends in the downtown public library also looking for a definition of my problem. I was searching for a name, which I never found, for my symptoms. What I conceived of as mental illness took shape in strange ways: at times, I would have terrible anxiety, hear a voice that said, 'You can't do that,' and begin to imagine a garbage-dumping ground standing between me and the visible world, especially the world of print. This anxiety was particularly painful when I filled out forms, did mathematics, or when I was sketching. I got through the forms by redoing them many times. Despite my seemingly endless revisions, things which should go one place on the form would end up elsewhere, and even putting my correct birth date in its proper place was frustrated. Sometimes my head would be filled with such mean-spirited voices and ensuing anxiety that I felt as if I was on the verge of a breakdown of some sort. I would literally see only garbage where I knew that I should see print. Mathematics I attempted to avoid. During drills in grade school, such as those which involved repeating multiplication tables, I simply moved my mouth in a way similar to the other students. Drawing, for me, was like therapy. My sketching consisted of attempting to precisely and faithfully render a three-dimensional object into a two-dimensional image. I would literally work through the voices and vision until the last hairy root of a shrub was in its correct position, until every last wrinkle on my hand found its place on the page, until every shadow cast by an object was made into a solid-looking form on the paper.

I told no one of these experiences until a few short years ago. First, I told Rod. Then I began to tell the few university students whose work I read that seemed to manifest the same mis-order as my work did. Today, I begin every new class with an introductory narrative of myself and my interests. In this way, my dyslexia is expressed both in the giving of the account and in its content.[4]

The diagnosis of dyslexia lessened the severity and frequency of my anxiety of 'getting it right' because it changed what 'getting it wrong' meant. It used to signify my never-ending battle against my sense of self as not smart, lazy, or ill, but now it meant something different. Working with a conception of myself as dyslexic meant exactly that – a lot of work – combined with a certain curiosity regarding what dyslexia might mean, and what difference it made to who I was and how I did things. 'Getting it wrong' finally became interesting, and in the cradle of the label 'dyslexia,' what I get wrong in public environments does not seem as humiliating as it once did.

The flux and flow of dyslexia, as it is currently defined,[5] ended up giving me a stable handle by which I could grasp and make sense of my love/hate experience with education. Returning to school in Canada after my experience in Mexico, I came to know that it was not an inability to learn that I had to watch, but instead it was the printed word, including my own, as well as the spatial order that required vigilance. I developed various techniques for doing so. For example, I read my written work aloud, and have often tape recorded it, so that I could 'hear' how it sounded when others read it. I invented this technique, as well as many others, on my own. Despite the diagnosis of dyslexia, I did not turn to any other professionals for help. That I now publicly identify myself as dyslexic to my university classes has provoked me to develop other techniques for living in an educational environment with a learning difficulty; for example, I try to finish writing papers and articles near the end of the school term, so that my senior students can read them and along the way find my mistakes. While these students are helping me, they are also learning something new.

This is my story of becoming dyslexic, and, with Robillard (1999: 33–4), I too can say this story can always be told in different ways. Despite the vast difference between Robillard, who is experiencing a complete shutdown of his body as a result of ALS, and my experiences of difficulty learning, our situations have in common the fact that such phenomena appear through narration by both self and by others. Berger (1963: 55) tells us that it is only from the 'epistemological privilege position of the present' that we can tell the stories of what we are and how we have become so. It is only from my present knowledge of dyslexia, as this interacts with cultural renderings and images of it, that I can speak of myself as dyslexic and, in doing so, become such. The meaning of disability is, at best, partly

captured by medical or rehabilitative definitions of 'conditions' – medicine is but one story among many that help to
constitute what we treat as a disability and how it is brought
to life through narration. Uncovering the social significance
of narratives of disability, whether they are produced by
self or by others, requires that critical attention be paid to
the experience of disability released between such stories
and their readers (see chapters 5 and 6).

Some of my colleagues say that 'learning disabilities' are
just the latest way that students have to excuse themselves
from work, and that 'dyslexia' is just a sophisticated word
for lazy. It is important in the face of the general suspicion
of those with 'invisible disabilities' to make disability visible (Shildrick and Price, 1996; Wendell, 1996), make different ways of learning acceptable, and offer a counterpoint to
cultural renderings of invisible disabilities as simply a syno-
nym for sloth. In the face of such stories, my story changes,
and I have, on occasion, made dyslexia sound like the latest
metaphor for the Protestant work ethic. Some of the students I teach have told me that they have retold my story of
dyslexia to their friends, and I am sure that my story changes
once again in this retelling.

The point is not that stories change, but rather that lives
change in the telling and retelling of stories. For example,
faced with a professor who herself has learning difficulties,
students have told me that they come to consider and evaluate their learning and learning institutions in a new way.
With the story of dyslexia in hand, I was free to pursue an
academic career aware of the necessity to figure out the
techniques and help that I would need in order to do so.
Before acquiring the label, I thought that hope lay in therapy;
now it lies in good proof-readers. But there are other stories
of dyslexia that grant little freedom and much disablement:
for instance, stories of children labelled and separated from
peers at a young age, endlessly tested and measured, with

groups of people making up their educational goals. Such stories are becoming more common (Jenkins, 1998). Proofreaders will not help these children live with the 'professionally sponsored stories' (Mitchell and Snyder, 1997: 1) of lack and inability that surround them.

For quite some time now, the telling of the story of disability has been taken charge of by only a few professions and disciplines. Typically, the authoritative storytellers have not themselves been disabled (Finkelstein, 1998: 28–38). Nor have the official storytellers exercised much personal control over the shape and form of the stories that they tell, as they often simply conform to the bureaucratic requirements which are precisely laid out by their profession or discipline, and which organize the entire process of 'documenting' disability.[6] While such documentation undoubtedly has the power to become 'the' narrative of disabled peoples' lives and provide one or two words (labels) upon which an identity is to be anchored, it remains but *one* story of the relations among the body, identity, and culture. Professionally sponsored stories can be very good for disability professionals' careers and the disability industry (Albrecht, 1992). However, such stories have little if anything to tell us about the socially significant character of the body as it interacts with our experience of self and cultural renderings of a 'disability identity' and other disability matters. According to such professionally sponsored stories, disability is simply the inability to do and a lack of normalcy, which, of course, require professional remedy and thus lead to the self-perpetuation of the status and power of the helping professions.

A Sense of a Problem?

As Rod's blindness continues to deepen, as I begin to move more confidently and critically with the label of dyslexia, and as my sense of disability as a powerful but marginalized educator grows, so too does my interest in analysing the social significance of disability. The significance of disability is constituted in relation to a culture which rarely seems aware of its normative relations to bodily difference. When moments of awareness of the often unjust normative order surrounding the body emerge in academia, they typically do so in relation to gender, race, or sexuality. If disability figures at all in much of this work, it is only as metaphor for the consequences of a normal order structured by the power of the straight, white, male ideal. Our culture, along with its cultural critics, appears unable to imagine that the normal ways of attending to disability might be, not only unjust, but also curiously perplexing and thus thought-provoking.

It is within such a culture, and without much counter-discourse coming from the academic realm, that the identity of disabled people is interpreted as tragedy, strong will, bad attitude, lack, and inability. Disabled people are often conceived of as anything but sociopolitical actors. It is also within this culture, and again without much academic resistance, that disabled people are researched, rehabilitated, treated, operated on, incarcerated, and trained, as if all of these are natural events and not social and political ones. What we do and what we think about disabled people often take shape as asocial and apolitical, and this is itself an interesting social fact and political issue.

It is easy, too easy, to make disability present by making its social significance and political organization absent. The ramifications of not conceiving of disability in socio-political terms can be as serious as life and death (e.g., Kervorkian and Latimer [Enns, 1999]; see also Rifkin, 1998). It seems far too common to interpret bodily conditions as if they do not exist in a complex social web of interaction and

knowledge regarding disability. This is astonishing, perplexing, and even unjust. Our culture is only too ready to
separate its images of disability and disability discourse
from any sense of the social and political organization of
the meaning of disabled people's lives. Disabled people's
lives can be understood as being led side-by-side with an
unexamined cultural temptation to obliterate disability from
social thought. This is all the more striking in the face of the
contemporary claim (Nussbaum, 1997) and complaints
(Emberley, 1996; Fekete, 1994; Bloom, 1987) that politics,
education, and the arts have become 'special interest' matters of identity and difference.

The interpretation of disability as bereft of social and
political meaning is all the more perplexing in relation to
my own life. My lived experience of disability is situated
between many of the typical ways culture gives us to categorize disability: between 'severe' and 'mild,' between
'visible' and 'invisible,' between self and Other. Yet, regarded as full of sociopolitical significance, disability becomes a dynamic thought-provoking and life-sustaining
need to have and to hold onto as teacher *par excellence.*
Disability experience *can* teach us much about our culture
and the social meaning of selfhood as these issues are
brought to us through bodily experience and the interpretations of bodies. 'Disability experience' is much more than
my story of dyslexia or my experiences of Rod's blindness.
Disability experience is constituted by, and can be made to
reveal, the intersecting arenas of interactional expectations,
knowledge claims and cultural representations, and environmental intentions. Still, it is not often the case that
disability is regarded as such.

In *Writing the Social*, Dorothy Smith (1999: 8–9) says: '... I
have not started writing on the basis of research data. Rather,
I have started with a sense of problem, of something going

on, some disquiet, and of something there that could be explicated.' I, too, start with a sense of a problem, or what Hannah Arendt (1994: 310) called 'a preliminary, inarticulate understanding.' There is something disquieting about the powerful way that disability can influence one's experience of self, of others, and of culture, and yet be regarded within both academic realms and everyday life as an apolitical and asocial phenomenon. My sense of a problem: how does this happen and what does it mean? Smith and Arendt insist that inquiry ought not to begin with the production of data (e.g., Dear et al., 1997), nor with hyperformulated research questions (e.g., Blum, 1994). Instead, preliminary questions should be developed and followed as they appear, or can be made to appear, in what life gives us. What has been given to me is diverse experiences in disability, an academic culture that is generally dis-interested in disability, and an everyday life that is oblivious to disability as a social or political phenomenon but very interested in it as an individual problem which produces something to be pitied and/or remedied.

Regarding disability experience as a complex social phenomenon allows this book to pursue an analysis which reveals three *interrelated arenas* within which disability appears: (1) in interaction; (2) in the production of knowledge / cultural images; and (3) in the physicality of both our bodies and social space. Thus, attending to disability is, here, an occasion to think about how interaction, knowledge, the environment, and the body are organized and made to matter. At the same time, the meaning of disability is constituted through particular kinds of discourses that are always related to interactional expectations, knowledge production, and the physicality both of the environment and of our bodies. Regarding disability in relation to these three arenas provides us, first, with the knowledge that we all do indeed live with disability,[7] and, second, with the possibility of glimpsing the significance of societal organization and identity formation that take place through our lives with disability. Even more, it allows for the possibility that disability might influence all this in new and different ways. This book is my occasion to present disability as a life lived in interactional space, arenas of knowledge, and the physical reality of the environment and the body, and these three locales serve here as that space where my preliminary, inarticulate sense of a problem can be pursued and developed. This allows me to present disability as an important *place* for thought, even while this endeavour is impaired by the fact that most disabled people are socially marginalized and treated in medical ways. Disability can make us think, *if* we resist the thought that it is some kind of object of lack and limitation requiring only diagnosis, rehabilitation, and care.

My interest in the social significance of disability has been further nurtured by the new and rapidly emerging interdisciplinary field of disability studies.[8] A common principle organizing this work is that the body and its vicissitudes need to be regarded as existing in relation to a complex web of interpretations, knowledge and images, interactional expectations, and environmental intentions. While disability studies is a new and still marginal field of inquiry, it is, nonetheless, another way in which we can now have a life with disability. Disability studies calls upon researchers to treat any discursive representation of disability as potentially teaching us something about the organization of culture and what this kind of culture means for disabled people.

I lead a life of disability personally, politically, and academically, and I do so in the midst of a culture that also lives with disability, in its ways. The need to think about the ways in which we live with and give meaning to disability lies behind the writing of this book. While many readers will not share in the particular complexity of my life in dyslexia and with blindness, some of the ways that I live with disability are common to us all. Each of us lives with images of disability, and all of us have something to say *about* and, sometimes, to disabled people. These experiences undergird the writing of this book and lead to my general lack of concern for methodologically generating data while tenaciously pursuing an analysis of even the most mundane experiences of disability. Despite the plethora of disability experiences there is something that remains common. The experience of disability, any experience, can teach us much about the organization of culture and the formation of our self-understanding.

There are two main concerns that course through the pages of this book: first, I show that regarding disability as a place for thought is a powerfully rich formulation; and, second, that such a choice is a difficult one in that our culture is almost unable to imagine such an enterprise. Through recounting my experience of living with someone who is blind, my own struggle with dyslexia, academic and governmental renderings of disability, and the work of the newly emerging field of disability studies, I show the socio-political work that is necessary to regard disability as the place where people can grapple with the meaning of disability as well as with the ways that culture influences the social formation of the identity of disabled people and other disability matters. I also show some of the many ways that language and culture resist this enterprise.

Reading Disability Studies

Discussing books about disability that are read both by people in disability studies and by more mainstream audiences, Irving Zola said in 1988 something that is still applicable today:

> While I welcome the attention, I am uncomfortable with what I see as two extremes of reaction – an uncritical acceptance (often by people who seem to have no consciousness about disability) and a lesser but still evident controversy within the disability movement over which, if any, of the current writings speak with an authentic voice. (1988:8)

To speak with an authentic voice, in a disability book, would mean to speak with the voice of disability. It would mean not letting mainstream culture 'voice over' disability with its stereotypes and not letting it whitewash disability by transforming the whole of it into an individual's quest for normalcy. It would also mean not letting any one organization of disabled people determine what *the* voice of disability sounds like before disabled people have a chance to speak it. This book attempts to speak with authenticity about disability as a process of identity formation and meaning-making within a culture which has done much to obliterate the complexity of disability experience. My voicing of disability is directed, however, to many different people, those in the know and those who are not, those who are disabled and those who are not yet.

In regards to those readers who are a part of the disability movement and/or disability studies, there is one final issue raised by Zola that I wish to discuss. It might be claimed that 'personal narrative' on the part of disabled people, their allies, or their significant others is, at best, dangerous and, at worst, complicit with the mainstream culture's stereotypes and oppression of disabled people. It could be argued that attention to narrative only serves to augment the attachment of 'normals' to being ordinary and the sense that disability is indeed deviant. It is, after all, very 'normal' to be curious about embodied difference, and to come to know many things about 'it,' while never risking any kind of thoughtful engagement with the meaning of disability. Still, throughout this book, I have pursued my preliminary questions, first, through the use of personal narrative and, second, through more general narrative accounts of the experience of disability. It is entirely possible, and perhaps even probable, that this book will be for some readers nothing other than yet one more curiosity tale distancing them from the really Real work of interpreting disability and developing an ability to think critically about these interpretations. This possibility is no less probable within accounts that describe instead the oppressive structures of society, and the material reality of oppression in the lives of disabled people. Documenting oppression, too, can become nothing but a curiosity tale. The attempt to eliminate subjective experience by making disability into simply the effect of oppressive societal structure is proposed by some as a solution to the problem of the power of mainstream normalcy to dictate our relation to disability. This solution proposes, once again as if for the first time, to split up the issue of the body and identity, albeit with emancipatory aims guiding the objectification of disability in society.

However disability is spoken of, the hegemonic hold of normalcy dictates that 'normals' should only learn *about* disability, and that they should not learn that disability is a place to think about the human condition, or that disability is a teacher in this place. I have made the informed decision that the hegemonic hold of normalcy both on my life and on the lives of those who read this book can only be loosened by narrating how our lived experience with and through disability can, in fact, be a teacher. What follows is my narration of this decision.

Through phenomenology this book aims to provide rich accounts of rather mundane and ordinary treatments of disability as they are experienced in everyday life and within other spheres, such as medicine and sociology, that make claims to know disability in more sophisticated ways. Through a hermeneutical orientation towards treatments of disability, this book aims to comprehend these experiences in relation to larger social contexts and thus to allow disability to serve as a teacher *par excellence* of collective understandings of disability. Finally, through the principle that disability can and ought to 'stay' – that it matters – this book aims to exemplify the ways in which we can make ourselves be taught by such experience.

CHAPTER TWO

Situating Disability: Mapping the Outer Limits

For the past five years, I have lived in a small university town, Antigonish, Nova Scotia. During the summer, most students leave to look for work and many tourists come to visit the town. Both new students and tourists receive verbal and pictorial maps of the town. Despite the town's small size, I have seen at least a dozen professionally produced maps of it and many more hand-drawn ones. Some maps are so sparse in their detail that they could be used only to arrive at the event they are intended to advertise – the Highland Games at Columbus Field or the Ceilidh at Pipers' Pub. Other maps, especially the ones oriented to students as consumers, contain so many details that the path of travel is obscured by the indication of stores and sights along the way. Maps come in many different shapes and sizes, and communicate many different intentions. Even maps of the same locale can appear radically different from each other and have different interests and aims. Maps do not simply correspond to the geography of a place. Instead, different maps draw out different meanings that a place holds. All maps try to impart a sense of the significance of place as this relates to the map producers' interpretive relation towards the readers of the maps.

Culture, too, gives us many different maps of various

things, including disability (Gleeson, 1999). One such map represents buildings and events which are accessible to disabled people; Braille maps with embossed configurations are constructed for use by blind persons. But there are other types of maps that are not so conventional, maps that point out disability itself. Sometimes disability is regarded as a place requiring some delineation of its appearance and its significance. The criteria necessary to qualify for a disability pension, for example, are one such map; government officials use this map to locate disability and to manage disabled people. There are others, such as demographic counts that map out disability rates in a population. They aim to show what part of a population is made up of disabled persons, as well as what part of a person is made up by disability by locating it in the body – 'mobility impairment,' 'vision impairment.' These maps point out the severity of the disability landscape by using such terms as 'mild,' 'moderate,' and 'severe.' These maps are also used as a way to predict one's chances of arriving in the place of disability. According to Zola (1982: 242–3), such statistical mapping shows that disability is the *norm* and that 'anyone reading the words on this page is at best momentarily able-bodied.' Still, most cultural maps refer to disabled people as a 'them' and not as an 'us.' This separation performs the function, says Bauman (1990: 40, 42), of dividing people into categories, and calling for different attitudes and different behaviours; this, in turn, lends cohesiveness, inner solidarity, and emotional security to any 'us' who has something to say about 'those' disabled people.

All maps of disability reflect a conception of its place and space within culture (Pile and Thrift, 1995). The mapping of disability is an imparting of some version of what disability is and, thus, contains implicit directions as to how to move around, through, or with it. Disability is mapped

differently by various societal institutions and cultural practices, and these representations influence one's relation to
disability.

In this chapter, I begin to show some of the ways in
which disability is mapped, and I show how each topography supports a different conception of disability. I do not
follow, however, any single path provided by these maps.
Instead, I interrogate the representations of disability found
within them. I argue that this critical relation to maps and
their use serves as an alternative topography that points
out the socio-political character of body anomaly and identity. This alternative depicts disability as a social space
(Grosz, 1995: 83–101), constituted from the inter-subjective
relations to the disabled body, disability identity, and interpretive relations that are developed to both. As a way to
develop a full sense of the social topography of disability, I
make extensive use of my own experience as a dyslexic
woman living with a blind person, as well as the postmodern
principle that reality is a discursive accomplishment (Corker,
1999, 1998b; Corker and Shakespeare, 2002). My social mapping of the inter-subjectively constituted place of disability
supports the idea that disability is not merely an individual
matter but a sociopolitical one (Oliver, 1996, 1990; Shakespeare, 1998). My aim is to demonstrate that disability is
social and political, not only in regards to what culture
'makes' out of impaired bodies, but also because the body
in all of its vicissitudes already comes to us through cultural maps and is, thus, *always-already constituted from social
and political discursive action.*

Mapping Disability: Opposition and Ambiguity

Recall that more than ten years ago I began sharing my life
with fellow sociologist Rod Michalko, who is blind. Shar-

ing life with Rod has meant experiencing a life of blindness in varied and often dramatic ways. Rod has spent most of his life on the outermost edge of the legal blindness continuum – '10 per cent of normal acuity.' Measuring a person's percentage of visual acuity is a medical way to map blindness. This map says little about blindness itself, but says much about how far a person is from 'normal' sight.

When I first met Rod, I did not experience '10 per cent of normal acuity.' I met Rod as a blind man, but one who could see. He could see … but not quite; what I could understand, count on, or see as seeing was never all that clear when I was with Rod. It was a confusing state of affairs which threw into question for me what seeing and blindness were supposed to mean. Back in the beginning of our relationship, Rod pointed down and said, 'Your shoelace is undone.' I thanked him, and picked up my pencil … and wondered. Perhaps Rod had regained his sight. Yet, if he had, why did he see my pencil as a shoelace? Still, if he is blind, how did he see my pencil? Rod certainly could see, but I could not understand what or how.

This confusion flowed from my conception of blindness and sightedness as radically opposite. Either Rod was sighted or he was blind. 'Fixed oppositions,' according to Joan Scott (1998: 33), 'conceal the extent to which things presented as oppositional are, in fact, interdependent.' Not only did my oppositional conception of blindness and sightedness conceal their interdependence in Rod, it also concealed from me the need to think about this interdependence – thus, their interdependence in me was also concealed. I was working with a 'cultural map' that pointed out the land of blindness and that of sightedness with a clearly defined border between the two. What's more, my map did not indicate any border crossings; either you were in the land of the blind or in the land of the sighted. Rod seemed to be on the border. But, instead of thinking about how sight and blindness rely on each other for their meaning, I tried only to decipher whether I was seeing a blind person, or not. As obvious as it is now, it was not so obvious then; blindness, be it 10 per cent, total, or what lies between, or notions such as going blind and being blind, are not clear-cut matters. Clearly, my cultural map was oversimplified. Between all the different ways that sight and blindness appear lies something much more meaningful and much more complex than sheer opposition.

Living with Rod meant living with the experience of uncertainty in the face of things of which I was so certain that never before did I question them – things like 'being blind' and 'having sight.' Notice that our language frames the concepts of 'blind' and 'sight' in different ways: a person can *be* blind or a person can *have* sight, and it sounds as if these are two very separate things. Outside of the disability movement, people are not usually referred to as being able-bodied; nor is 'non-disabled' a common way to categorize people. Instead, the common expression is that people *have* normal acuity, normal hearing, normal mobility, or normal use of their appendages. We grow up with a language that allows us to speak of our bodies while, at the same time, giving us ways of conceiving of them. We conceive of our bodily faculties, for example, as a possession, and we conceive of disabilities as neither a faculty nor a possession but, instead, as a lack of both.

The words 'disability,' 'handicap,' and 'impairment' have a complicated history (Barnes, 1998: 65–78; Davis, 1995: 1–22; Gleeson, 1999: 18–19; Oliver, 1990; Shogan, 1998; Susman, 1994: 15), and diverse social and political meanings. Despite the nuanced meaning of these words and various attempts to pin down or simplify them, all these words are regularly made use of in everyday life to refer to bodies for which something has gone wrong or is missing, or to bodies that lack. This way of speaking gives people a map of disability through a series of negations – something in the body is *not* there, *not* right, *not* working, *not* able. Blindness, for example, is regularly conceived of as simply *not* seeing, and during Rod's 10 per cent days, I wondered and I was asked by others what it was that Rod *could and could not* see. I was not asked about blindness as an 'in itself.' By speaking about disability in the way that people typically do, disabled people are brought to life as if the entire meaning of being disabled can be grasped simply as *not being* able-bodied. So common is it to map disability through a series of negations that it might be easy to miss the strangeness of such a process. This strangeness is revealed if we try to map other types of people in a similar fashion; for example, a man is a person lacking a vagina. It would seem ridiculous today to conceive of gender in terms of negation. The feminist movement has shown us that gender is not a matter of simple negation. Woman is not woman because she is not man, and man is not man because he is not woman. The language of everyday life does not provide for such expressions as 'There goes not-a-man.' But it does provide for expressions such as 'There goes someone who can't see' or 'There is that woman without arms.'

Language suggests that we regard the disabled body as a life constituted out of the negation of able-bodiedness and, thus, as nothing in and of itself. If, as Smith (1999: 133) insists, discourse *is* social organization, the everyday ways that the body is spoken about organize being disabled and having able bodies *as if* they are radically opposed phenomena. Our language tempts us to think that the 'normally working body' has nothing to do with the ways in which we organize our world, go about our daily affairs, or speak about disability. Our language recommends that we conceive the non-disabled body as something that just comes along as we go about daily existence. People *just* jump into the shower, run to the store, see what others mean while keeping an eye on the kids or skipping from office to office, and, having run through the day while managing to keep their noses clean, finally hop into bed – all of this glosses the body that comes along, while, at the same time, brings it along metaphorically.[1] However, if we have a bad day, we must stumble through, limping along while blind to the ramifications of not standing up to the boss and letting the kids run all over us. Through this way of speaking, 'normal bodies' escape from being understood as something which could be mapped, insofar as such a body is regarded simply as movement and metaphor.

Like other sighted people who follow the recommendations given by culture and its language (maps), I thought that blindness and sightedness were polar opposites. Such opposition was dependent upon my being secure in the illusion that Rod did not have sight and, thus, was blind, whereas others, including myself, simply have sight. Adhering to these categorical oppositions meant that I possessed sight, really good sight – I saw that my pencil was not a shoelace – and in seeing this I also saw Rod as blind.

Mapping Sightedness

While opposition was one way that I initially tried to map the significance of blindness, there were other ways. Rod and I would often walk together. Initially, no hand-holding, cane, or elbow guidance was part of these walks. I began to pay attention to how I watched out for bumps and obstacles and to how Rod must be doing the same. Rod, however, was not doing the same. He was watching me.

Before I met Rod, I had moved through the world with

the implicit assumption that my sight would see whatever needed to be seen. Walking with Rod, I paid attention to how my sight worked, and I assumed that Rod's partial sight would work the same way, albeit with more effort and more time. 'Less of the same' did not, however, capture my experience of Rod's way of seeing. What Rod did was observe me as a sighted person, and it was his stance (Harding, 1996: 146) between blindness and sight which provoked him to do so. My belief in the illusion that sight is *the* means to observe the world but is not itself observable began to disintegrate – sight too could be mapped.

Experiencing and attending to the outer edges of legal blindness can bring to consciousness the ambiguity that lies between sight and blindness and can show that some of the security that sighted people possess is indeed illusory. Wittgenstein (1980, 14e–15e: 75) puts the matter this way:

> I can observe ... I can also say, 'You see, this child is not blind. It can see. Notice how it follows the flame of the candle.' But can I satisfy myself, so to speak, *that men see?*
>
> 'Men see.' – As Opposed to *what*? Maybe that they are all blind?

Of all the things that sight can see, it often does not observe the intimate relation between sight and blindness as ways of being in the world. As Wittgenstein indicates, attending to sight usually only occurs in relation to blindness and what we have to say about blindness.

Blindness made me take notice of myself as sighted and helped me understand that being sighted was more complex than ownership of yet another, albeit highly valued, possession. Sight need not be regarded as simply one more possession, since it influenced who I was, how I acted, and my engagement with the world around me. My body and my life are the terrain upon which sight can be understood as inscribing itself (Bordo, 1993: 142; Foucault, 1979). Rod became expert in deciphering these inscriptions. While walking or sitting in a pub, for example, Rod could see that I had just seen something worthy of note. Sighting a server or an unnerving glance of a stranger was observable to Rod in the position of my head, my posture, my movement. Rod's blindness began to teach me that sighted people look as though they have seen something. Living with Rod included living with disability and non-disability (sight) as an ambiguous experience. This ambiguity grows out of the assumption that blindness and sightedness are not opposites but do express an interrelatedness observable on the level of interaction.

Ten per cent of normal vision is not simply the outer limit of blindness; it is also the outer limit of sightedness, and it is both at the same time. The first five years, or so, of our life together were spent in this mix of sight and blindness. It was for me a curious mixture. I wanted to see blindness, or see what it saw, perhaps influenced by the illusion that seeing *is* understanding.

One day, in yet another of my attempts to see his blindness, Rod and I mapped out what ophthalmologists would refer to as his visual field. Rod focused on the centre of a tabletop, and I moved objects from his point of focus towards the edge of the table until Rod indicated that the object had appeared in his peripheral vision. I left the objects in the places where Rod began to see them. Soon, using fork, spoon, knife, salt and pepper shakers, the table top displayed a circle of sorts – his field of vision.

There it was – Rod's visual field and his blind spot, concretely represented for me to see. Rod, too, took a look. He took many looks, moving his gaze around his visual field and blind spot, both the one on the table and the one of his vision. This reminded him of some of his ophthalmological

examinations: the same sort of mapping of his vision occurred when he was asked to look at eye charts, or when
photographs of his retinas were taken. Despite this some-
what painful reminder of past mapping, Rod worked to
give me a representation of his vision, and he worked to
see this representation for himself.

Mapping, measuring, or providing a kind of topography
of blind spots and fields of vision is one way to conceive of
blindness, as well as sight. It is, literally, a static way: Rod
could not move if his vision was to be charted; and once
charted, the representation itself was immobile, objectified.
As static, such an image is already distanced dramatically
from the lived experience of blindness and sight. No matter
how precisely produced and minute in its detail, such a
map could not tell me how Rod moved, used, and lived
with this blind spot and this peripheral vision. Although
forks and knives are not part of the ophthalmologist's tools
of examination, the procedure of objectively mapping is
tied to the common-sense desire to come to know disability. But such a map told me little. It could not tell me much
about how I could or should travel or move with a blind
person. This mapping procedure did serve to announce
that Rod was different, which, of course, we already knew,
for why else would we be involved in such an activity.

Measures, such as inability to see the big E on the eye
chart, ability to see hand movements at three feet, field of
vision charts, photographs of bodily damage including retinas, or surveys of activity limitations resulting from bodily
differences (Gadacz, 1994: 31–4; Harrison and Crow, 1993),
help to make blindness, and other disabilities, into a concrete *individual* issue, abstracted from *interpersonal* interaction and interpretation. The social practice of measurement
always needs to measure some *thing*; in this case, we were
making and measuring what Taussig (1980: 3) refers to as a

'biological and physical thinghood.' Through measurement, disability can be made into a thing, a reality in and of a person's body (Murphy et al., 1988; Scott, 1981).

These measures objectify blindness, making it concrete and easier to deal with, and 'to see,' than do the complex self-reflective practices of noticing and reading the work of blind persons as they interact with sighted others in situations, environments, and histories not of their own making. 'The thingification of the world, persons and experience,' says Taussig (1980: 3), produces a 'phantom objectivity,' and 'denies' and 'mystifies' the body's fundamental nature as a 'relation between people.'

The great quantity of statistical data that is produced and disseminated by governmental, medico-rehabilitative, and even political organizations is testimony to Western culture's proclivity to regard disability as thing-like. For example, the statistical rendering of disability can be found, in one form or another, repeated over and over again, in various governmental department publications, at disability-related web sites, in textbooks and policy statements, in fundraising material of various helping organizations, and in disability community coalition documents. Many of these sources, which have something to say or to do for disabled people, begin with quantification and thus the objectification of disability. Even among those who recognize that the definition of disability has much to do with how disability gets measured, there is still the unquestioned assumption that disabled people are best understood as measurable objects of limit and lack.[2]

The measurement, the counting, and the policies that follow are dependent upon the illusion that disability is objectively given (Goode, 1996: 1–5). This conceptual map of disability begins with the assumption that disability is readily observable, easily quantifiable, impervious to interpretation, set in stone. As the plethora of disability statistics indicate, being counted as disabled means being given a probable fate of unemployment and poverty. As with disability and the need to measure it, so too can unemployment, poverty, etc., now be spoken of *as if* they are dictated by, or caused by, the disabled person's body. For example, learning that only 2.3 per cent of disabled Canadians (530,000 persons) make use of the disability tax credit, and that many more disabled persons are unemployed, do not participate in the labour force, or are poor, has led to multiple nationwide governmental task forces, all of which recommend changes to the disability tax credit and to employment, training, and rehabilitative programs for disabled people (Fawcett, 1996). Report after report – *Obstacles, The Will to Act, In Unison* (Canada, 1981; 1996; 2000) – recommends, on the basis of these statistics, that something ought to be done, and what ought to be done often includes the reproduction of these statistics. The objectification of disability reaches its highest sophistication in the current development of foetal tests oriented to eliminating disabled persons before they enter the population (Hubbard, 1997: 187–201; Langer 1997: 47–66). And, such objectification processes have even supported sterilization and extermination programs (Russell, 1998: 13–55). The unquestioned map of disability as a thing leads to the unexamined presupposition that programs oriented to ameliorating disability or managing disabled people are just as objectively given as are impaired bodies themselves.

The problem with the measurement and management of disability is not simply that it begins and ends with an unexamined conception of disability as objectively given. Nor is the problem only that such measurement and control practices must take for granted the current social milieu that says that it is right and good to measure, count, track, and manage disabled persons. The problem is that this thing-like conception of disability requires, as did Rod's and my measurement of it on the table top, a bracketing off of the Really real work involved in being disabled. Disability as objective lack and inability understood as located within a person's body means ignoring disability in relation to the social character of our bodies. The problem, too, is that ideology and assumptions of non-disability often remain unmapped and unexamined, even though it is from a non-disability perspective that disability is most often objectified.

The body's significance *is* social in the sense that bodies are only found within locales of interaction, within interpretive milieus and ideological structures such as health and beauty, and the specific language or genre (Bakhtin, 1986) through which all this is expressed. This sociality lies behind every conceptual map of disability, even at the level of 'mere bodies' and 'impairment.' The work involved in being disabled is always accomplished in the midst of the social character of bodies and their political arrangements. Mapping disability as if it is an object and developing policy on the basis of such a map is a little bit like giving people a map of the city of Toronto which only indicates its hills, rivers, and valleys, and telling them to find Paupers' Pub. Adhering to the belief that disability is concretely given in some people's bodies requires that we do not get close to the lived actuality of disability. Yet, such mapping is often accompanied by the illusion that all sorts of things about disability can be mapped.

Life with Maps

There is, however, a more life-filled reality to disability to which we can attend. This reality appears within the objectifying practices of measuring and managing disabled people, and it even appears within the objectification of blindness accomplished around the table that day with Rod and me. Consider, for example, what might be learned if we shift our attention away from the objective representation of Rod's vision which was laid out on the table top and 'focus' instead on all that went on *around* the table top. This is a shift in attention to the making of the map and away from the map itself.

Around the table top, Rod produced a different image of blindness, one that was more difficult to attend to, but more dynamic, filled with effort, interest, and work. Rod had to work to see. He had to take an interest in seeing forks and knives. He had to use his knowledge of a context to figure out what there was to see – what should be seen and what not. Big blind spot or not, charting its existence could not answer routine questions such as should I tell Rod that something is in his way or leave well enough alone. The image of blindness produced *around* the table top that day told me that whatever is in Rod's way could only be deciphered by reading his use of vision in relation to the people and the environment around him.

To gain even a slight understanding of the production of Rod's vision would require that I attend to something much more dynamic than the facticity of his blind spot, much more complex than the concrete stuff of the physical environment. In Rod's terms, seeing is a project insofar as we always see through a life (Michalko, 1999: 15–17; 1998: 39–40; on the body as project, see Shilling, 1997: 69). The project of seeing for a legally blind person on the outer edges of both blindness and sight is one filled with conscious effort, will, and desire. For sighted people, the project of vision is usually something to which no attention is paid.

But Rod paid attention. Not only did he focus on the

table top, but he also focused on that which surrounded the table top and on that which brought it into view. He saw that he was in a bar and that he was surrounded by other table tops around which people sat. Music, sounds of drinking and eating, laughter – all of these sounds Rod 'saw' as his 'being in a bar.' The forks and salt and pepper shakers I used to map his visual field were seen by Rod not only by his peripheral vision but also through the lens of his being in a bar. Rod never saw these things when an ophthalmologist mapped out his visual field. The map we drew was drawn with the material of our life. And as objective as this map was, it was constructed from Rod's 'subjective seeing' of his world. We were engaged in a project of vision, transforming Rod's 'seeing' into the objective fact of vision. Ophthalmologists were engaged in the same project with Rod, but this project is not 'seeable' through the ophthalmological lens.

Any project of vision is accomplished not only in relation to the things and events of the physical world, but also in relation to the habits and customs of a culture – Rod expected to see forks and knives on a table top in a bar, and so did I. Vision is accomplished in relation to other people, with conflicting interpretations of what there is to see and with shifting meanings of blindness in different and changing circumstances. What did people see as Rod and I walked into the bar, his hand on my elbow? Did they see a blind person and sighted guide? Did they see an ordinary intimate couple? Did they see both or neither? Did they see a sighted person mapping out the visual field of a blind person on a table? Did they see two people engaged in animated conversation, perhaps about staging a play or the moves of football players?

Like the people in the bar, Rod's seeing is embedded in the particularity of his body, his interests, his attention, his energy, and his effort. Around the table top, Rod worked to give me a representation of his vision. Moreover, he worked to see this representation for himself. In both the making and the observation of his representation of blindness, Rod showed me that his way of being in the world meant living with a conscious awareness of vision as an accomplishment. To help or hinder, to experience or ignore, Rod in this accomplishment would be dependent upon the kind of attention that I paid to it. Blindness began to teach me that seeing is culturally organized. Blindness and sight conceived of as an accomplishment, as *work*, more clearly represents that which I actually was experiencing with Rod.

The Map of Interactional Work

Insofar as seeing is cultural, sight is a social accomplishment, and blindness is a kind of forced consciousness of the work necessary to achieve it. This is a key lesson which accompanies my shift away from attempts to reduce disability to a concrete reality and towards mapping disability as a complex set of social and discursive interactions. This lesson did not simplify my understandings of 'being blind' and 'having sight.' It showed me that there is no way to concretize what will be seen and what will not. There is no rule book or chart which will tell me what being blind or sighted means. For example, doors left ajar, which are normally closed, are hazards for anyone who lives on the outer edges of sight. Using objective measures, such as Rod's ability to see hand movements at three feet but no further, I could invoke a rule that I will now announce to Rod all such doors within a four-foot radius. The rule that Rod would also need to invoke is that such announcements will be made. Our movement through the world would now involve a series of announcements. But announcing open doors opens up the necessity for announcing a plethora of other features – curbs, stairs, posts, pedestrians. The list never ends. The world would no longer be experienced by Rod; it would be announced. This rule would mean that the world would now come to me in an interpretation of what is announceable and to Rod as announcements. This rule would mean that I would rule what Rod experiences.

Together with the production of the hegemony of sight, such a rule is also impractical and, indeed, works against gaining any sense of the social topography within which we live. The knowledge of blindness that comes with rules and charts excludes any experience of my sight or Rod's blindness as an accomplishment. Mapping the accomplishment of vision requires that I pay attention to context; for example, what events surround the door that has become ajar? To address this question, I need to take into account Rod's bodily position in relation to the door, the people around the door, my judgment of their ability or inability to imagine the standpoint of blindness, whether or not Rod is orienting to the particular environment as familiar and routine or as uncertain and hazardous. All of these interactional factors need to be read in the process of making a decision regarding my role in Rod's way of being in the world.

The interaction between blind and sighted people, disabled and non-disabled people, and everything in between, always involves such decisions. One of the most important decisions a sighted person needs to make is *not* 'What should I do or not do?' Nor is it 'Should I tell the blind person this or should I not?' The crucial decision is whether or not the sighted person, in the face of blindness, will be oriented to her or his decisiveness. To be oriented to such decisiveness requires that the sighted person begin to do what the blind person is almost always doing – engage in the conscious work of seeing as a social accomplishment, and do so in relation to the reality of blindness. Reading the topography of the social environment permits the understanding that the significance of sight and blindness cannot simply be found in their objectified physicality and must, instead, be sought in the lived actuality of self and others. Only by attending to the ways in which disability is conceptualized (mapped) can we gain any social understanding of disability. 'In fashioning some kind of theoretical approach to disability,' Lennard Davis says (1995: 11), 'one must consider the fact that the disabled body is not a discrete object but rather a set of social relations.' I move now to a consideration of this set of social relations, particularly as it is grounded in the relations between disability and non-disability.

CHAPTER THREE

Mapping Normalcy: A Social Topography of Passing

If blindness is a social accomplishment within a set of social relations, and if blindness and sightedness are not opposites but instead dialectically connected, then sighted-ness, too, must be involved in its share of work in order to accomplish itself. But there seems to be something extremely unequal between the work of being blind and that of having sight. I only became conscious of such work in the face of blindness. I became aware of the social topography of all kinds of vision only as I began sharing a life with a blind person. This cannot mean, however, that outside of blind-ness, sight is natural, and alongside blindness, sight is cultural. Whether sighted people are conscious of it or not, habits, customs, values, illusions, knowledge, etc., forever organize seeing. Medical practitioners and rehabilitators, for example, receive much formal and informal training in order to see in medical, rehabilitative, and bureaucratic ways (Canguilhem, 1991; Foucault, 1973; Smith, 1990, 1987). One must, for example, be trained to see all the interaction that occurs *around* the measurement of blindness as having nothing to say about the interaction of disability and non-disability. Thus the complexity of such interaction can be bracketed through conceptions such as efficient bedside manner, and friendly or cold rehabilitative practices.

The social workings of sight include the ever present possibility, or danger, depending on one's point of view, of opting out of attending to sight itself as an accomplishment. A sighted person sees *as if* seeing involves no effort, no decisiveness. The 'ability' to be unaware of choice becomes part of the inequality between disabled and non-disabled people even as both engage in the projects of seeing and embodiment. It is, after all, a choice I make when I pay attention to the fork, spoon, and salt and pepper shakers which make a circle on a table top. I must choose to see this circle as a representation of Rod's blind spot. It is also a choice to watch Rod's effort to represent his vision and to watch Rod as he works to see this representation. I could even choose to attend to myself watching both of these representations of blindness and begin to evaluate how I decided to see blindness. But, only this last choice requires me to suspend the illusion that I see without work and decisiveness. Sighted people can choose to orient – or not – to the choices involved in coming to see what they do.

That sighted persons do not often regard their vision as employing decisiveness attests to the fact that sight is taken for granted. This does not mean that sighted people do not appreciate *what* they see; we display such appreciation regularly by making comments about the world around us: 'Did you see that!?' 'Oh, what a sight!' Nor does it mean that we do not appreciate *that* we see – often I have heard people say, 'I'd die if I went blind.' Instead, sight *is* taken for granted in the sense that it is not socially necessary to be conscious of it as a production. Sighted people see *as if* it is natural and thus do not attend to the sort of life that animates their vision. Nonetheless, sight remains cultural in that it is culture which tells people what to look at or not to look at, and sight remains linguistic in that we say that seeing is believing or that knowledge is sight. I have often said, 'Oh, I didn't see that!' not because of 'momentary blindness,' but because decisiveness and will are part of vision, and yet I do not have to attend to my will to see and my seeing what I will. For blind people, this work is obligatory.

Passing as a Map of Normalcy

During his 10 per cent days, Rod says (Michalko, 1998, 1999) that he learned a great deal about the everyday life of seeing. Learning about sight and its topography allowed Rod to imitate it. He imitated the ways in which sight makes an appearance in culture. Thus, Rod spent time and energy making his outer edge of legal blindness function in a sighted way, and thereby he often passed as a sighted person. At this time, we lived in Toronto. Rod travelled, met with friends, and worked while using his vision, his memory, and his familiarity with places to do so. His appearance as sighted was also achieved by using his member's knowledge of the routine organization of the physical environment – bars, offices, and homes each have there own form of organization that he attended to and thus expected to see. Rod read the cultural expectations informing what, in general, sighted people look like, do, and say, and in so doing, he passed. He did not move through the world with any obvious indicator that he was blind – no white cane, no guide dog, no one's elbow as a guide. Legal blindness was more or less Rod's private affair, which he aimed to manage by pushing the limits of his outer edge of visual acuity to work towards his goal of appearing sighted.

People on the outer edges of any mainstream identity category are often faced with the possibility of engaging in this kind of imitation. Such a possibility arises from the fact that marginalization from some 'normal' identity category always involves at least two kinds of obligatory work. First, there is knowledge-work. Marginalized people come to know the culture of the mainstream-ordinary-other as they begin to experience their self as somehow distanced from normalcy and ordinariness (Harding, 1996; Hartsock, 1997; Ferguson et al., 1990). The marginalized person thus develops some kind of map of ordinariness.

Then, there is the question of what to do with such a map. Thus, the second kind of work: the work of judgment (Arendt, 1994, 1951). What ought one do with this knowledge? Should sameness or difference be emphasized? Should this marginality be treated in political ways or remedial ways? How does one secure his or her competent participant status among various people in changing social situations? Knowing and emulating an identity from which a person has been marginalized is one possible relation to the obligations that come with a disability. Passing was one relation Rod developed to being marginal, and he did this with great artfulness and skill.

So skilled was Rod at passing that within the anonymity of public city life, few people 'on the street' knew that he was blind. I watched people, and none of them looked as though they were seeing a blind person. Friends and acquaintances have told me and Rod that not only did they not know Rod was blind, but they did not believe it once they were told (recall that even I did not believe him when he initially told me).

During his adolescence, knowledge of his blindness was hidden from everyone but his own family members (Michalko, 1998: 102–27). But during his adult life, and during our life together, friends, family, co-workers, and the people he taught did, indeed, know that Rod was legally blind. What even the people in these more intimate and/or adult relations did not know, or did not orient to, or did not seem to want to know, was the incredible amount of work involved in passing. I had some sense of this work; or, at least, I was learning about this work directly from Rod and from my attempt to understand the meaning of the experience of blindness.

In this learning, I became part of Rod's project of passing. I could guide or bridge the path back and forth between the edges of sight and blindness, and I could do so without marking Rod as a blind person. I wanted to be part of his passing. I wanted to use my newly acquired 'insider's knowledge,' and to experience the constraints and creativity that come with living on the outer edges of both blindness and sight. My role in this liminal endeavour took shape quietly and unobtrusively; in private or hidden ways, I helped Rod do what sighted people do and what sighted people expect others to do.

While walking on a busy city street, I would tell Rod that someone we knew was just up ahead, and unobtrusively I would indicate when the person was within greeting distance. Rod would greet the person and do so by name. Greetings were exchanged in a completely sighted fashion, and rarely did anyone 'blink an eye.' I would also keep my eyes peeled for the more dangerous habits of sighted persons. If something was put out of place while friends were visiting us, I would nonchalantly move it or, failing this, lean against it. Privately, I would tell Rod that our friend had got a haircut or was wearing a new blue shirt. Rod would then bring this 'observable' into conversation, and, again, usually no one would blink an eye. That a sense of normalcy can be achieved by a *known* blind person commenting on the details of a friend's appearance attests to the very strange politics involved in the production of the normal.

So taken for granted is the work of seeing in the production of a cultural sense of normalcy, that anyone appearing normal, competent, average, or ordinary is often seen as sighted despite knowledge to the contrary. Through this experience, I soon learned that appearing sighted has much to do with appearing 'normal.' Still, 'doing sight,' and thus appearing normal, was accomplished from the standpoint of the lived actuality of blindness.

To be marginal and to pass as ordinary is to find one's self positioned somewhere between a set of expectations about what any 'normal' self ought to be and the actual work involved in these 'doings of ordinariness.' The experience of being on the edge, of liminality (Murphy et al., 1988; Turner, 1985), or of between-ness (Titchkosky, 1998, 1997) involves, at least at some level, the development of an awareness of normal social organization. Marginality always involves making some types of people distant from their culture and outsiders to the taken-for-granted status of the practices which are treated as 'normal' or typical aspects of everyday life.

Sociologists have a long history of studying passing and have produced a large body of knowledge regarding deaf people who pass as hearing, stutterers who pass as 'normal' speakers, gay persons who pass as straight, ex-convicts who pass as non-convicts, and women who pass as men or men who pass as women. In the latter case, the mainstream-ordinary-other is constituted through the expectation that any 'normal' gendered identity is *either* male *or* female, but not both, and that 'normal' gender does not explicitly involve a choice (Garfinkel, 1967; Grosz, 1996: 58–61; Kessler and McKenna, 1978). Almost all analyses of passing are dependent upon the assumption that the passer's marginal identity is best understood as an instance of deviance. Passers are regarded as deviant people trying to achieve, or even eke their way back to, normalcy. Studies of passing focus on the concrete interactional techniques employed by the passer in order to manage what Goffman (1963) refers to as a 'spoiled identity.' Most sociological studies of passing use detailed ethnographic descriptions of passing techniques in order to produce a map of what is ordinarily done in normal everyday life by normal ordinary people. For example, a blind person arrives early to a meeting with sighted others; this means that these others must now announce themselves in one way or another, thus letting the blind person know that he or she is at the right place with the right people. A deaf person smiles and laughs, not necessarily at the content of a joke, but with the event of joking, signified by the smiles and laughter of his or her hearing associates. In these ways, and many others, identity can be secured, and the sociological documentation of passing produces a map of normal order. The study of passing, then, is usually a charting of a *deviant individual's* techniques which he or she employs in order to negotiate a stance in the land of normalcy.

Still, passing as sighted does not mean simply doing what sighted people do. It is not copying. Rod cannot simply look and see, and do what sighted people do. Instead, passing means knowing: it means knowing the minutest details of how everyday existence is oriented to the expectation that sight is an ever present feature of that existence; it means knowing the customs, habits, and signs of seeing people. Passing means knowing how to do things with eyes, and knowing what to do that looks sighted when one is unsure of what to do because one cannot see. It means knowing one's limits and advantages within the particularities of a culture and its expectations. Passing as sighted means orienting to, and knowing how to manipulate, the cultural expectation that all people are sighted 'until further notice' (Garfinkel, 1967; Schutz, 1973). Passing is a way to work with cultural knowledge while achieving normalcy or competency. (How all this social knowledge is reified into 'deviance' is a question I address in chapter 4.)

My role in Rod's passing project began to teach me that there is something more significant involved in it than a multitude of individualistic techniques based on the passer's knowledge of the socially constructed character of ordinary life. Something more than the disabled individual's techniques needs to be depicted if a fully social topography of passing is to be developed, and this is despite the fact that traditional sociological representations of passing do much to expose the social construction of ordinary life.

Something More

This sense of 'something more' initially arose as I began to pay attention to my role in Rod's passing project. I took great pride and pleasure as I moved with Rod in his travels on the outer limits of blindness and sight. Through the passing project, I came to possess a secret sense of private privilege because I was not excluded from the actual effort and artfulness that are required in order for a blind man to appear as a fully sighted one. I also experienced anxiety. It was never an anxiety of being 'found out' – after all, many people 'knew' Rod was blind. I was anxious because I thought that it was dangerous to keep one's blindness a private affair. (Later, however, I was to learn of the many dangers that come when a blind person bears an observable public mark of blindness.) At that time, however, I was concerned that Rod's hidden difference would suddenly appear in the shape of an accident or in the stress of 'going it alone.' Given my dyslexia, I was never that helpful in more practical matters such as the placement of objects in relation to each other (chairs to tables, tables to windows, ashtrays to people), and I am always nothing short of a hindrance in verbal renditions of directing the way to go. I was embarrassed when I did not smoothly bridge the path between blindness and sight. I was concerned that my inability to clearly communicate spatial arrangements and directions would hurt Rod physically or hurt him at the level of identity. My pride, anxiety, and sense of my own limits combined and reflected the fact that I experienced passing as a highly charged emotional endeavour. Something much more complicated than the achievement of ordinary life was going on within the practice of passing.

Moreover, ordinary normal life was not the whole of what Rod and I shared through this passing project. My role meant that I would need to focus on seeing what Rod would need to see in order for him to pass as sighted. In this, we shared in a kind of sighted-blindness, yet did so from very different perspectives. Through this sighted-blindness, we produced a sense of normalcy for others, but it did not give either of us an ordinary experience. The sighted-blindness, existing between Rod and me, became a place to *think* about the ordinary organization of culture but did not give rise to ordinary experience.

Eventually, there was also frustration. Passing required an envelope of privacy around the actual workings of blindness and sight. It is this interactional work that can teach anyone, anyone who attends, a great deal about societal expectations regarding sighted interaction, and ordinary daily life. While passing *is* working with cultural know-how, and *does* give rise to a corpus of intense and inspiring cultural knowledge, all this knowledge must remain 'out of sight' if passers are to secure their normalcy and pass. I was frustrated with the fact that some kind of injustice had relegated blindness-as-teacher to serve only as a private tutor. I began to realize that the phenomenon of passing shows more than the routine construction of normalcy and ordinariness. It had something to say about the complicated character of just and unjust relations to social difference. I have begun, only recently, to locate this injustice by thinking about the strange phenomenon of a *known* blind person easily, readily, and with so few questions being treated as sighted. Stranger still, and perhaps equally as unjust, is my sense of Rod's and my participation in this treatment.

Mapping Inequality

Rod *was* known as blind. Rarely, however, did this knowledge come from people's direct experience of themselves as sighted people interacting, watching, and dealing with a blind person. Rod was known as blind because he *told* others that he was – his blindness was known to others mostly through statements, stories, descriptions, or the answering of questions. More often than not, blindness was experienced by Rod's significant others as a strictly aural phenomenon.

While Rod is an extremely artful passer, it is not true that others never came face-to-face with the observable and direct influence of blindness upon their here-and-now interaction with him: the missed call of a waitress's eye; a lost package of cigarettes placed elsewhere on a table top; a chair, a person, or a glass known to be one place suddenly forcefully confronting his body and senses as elsewhere. In these ways, blindness could make a direct appearance, put a wrinkle into the smooth flow of interaction, and appear in its most conventional way as inability and lack. Yet, even this conventional view of blindness was given little space, as the wrinkle was rapidly ironed out by all involved. At a pub with a group of friends, Rod bumped someone's glass, which had been put into what would normally be regarded as his space at the table. The contents of the glass did not spill, but it did cause an interactional mess. Comments and jokes began to abound. 'Clumsy today?' 'Sleepy?' 'Hey butter fingers, pass me the ashtray.' More often than not, such signs of blindness were simply regarded as 'mistake,' 'accident,' *'faux pas,'* and others quickly helped to put things right.

As it turns out, and perhaps without any reflective aware-ness, *everyone*, not just me, was helping Rod to pass. Even the most minimal sign of blindness in face-to-face interac-tion was taken as excessive and was further minimized by treating it as a 'normal' accident that could happen to any-one. Under the interpretive rubric that 'everyone makes mistakes,' blindness could be made to disappear, while its appearance could be seen as making a mistake.

Still, in the midst of group efforts to produce the passing situation, and shared expectations that passing is both nor-mal and desirable, blindness would be talked about. In the process of obliterating a here-and-now experience of blind-ness, people, including myself, would say they wanted to know about Rod's blindness or learn about the state and fate of disabled people generally. Much enjoyment would be had through the story of the store clerk who, upon hearing that Rod couldn't see and would like to buy some milk, points to its location. Pleasure and laughter flowed as Rod told of teaching public servants about human rights and accommodation policy – such as how people would insist on raising their hands to speak right after Rod had told them that he is blind and that a raised hand will only make for a sore arm. 'What's it like Rod?' was not a ques-tion that was to be addressed to our interaction with Rod. Instead, it was a question for Rod alone, either alone with the particularity of his way of seeing or alone in his interaction with distant others. Nonetheless, disability once removed is always up for discussion. It is this strange state of affairs which led to my experience of passing as a project filled with an overwhelming sense of inequality, a kind of double bind that seemed ubiquitously enforced by those who have sight, including myself, upon those who are blind.

The double bind can be expressed as follows: act as a normal sighted person while you tell us all about the abnormalcy of blindness. Give us blindness as an object for conversation, but do not give us blindness as a subjective state of affairs which reorganizes and influences our normal means of engagement. The double bind is grounded in an implicit imperative: say what you will, but do as we do. When I pay attention, this double bind appears to me to be a guiding principle behind much blind/sighted interaction. The imperative represents another way to make disability thing-like in that it involves offering blindness up as an object for discussion while obliterating any subjective interactional consciousness of blindness. Blindness as an interactional event, out there, can be charted. But it is like looking at a map of a foreign land which no one has any intention of visiting. This map can be interesting but remains inconsequential for those who gaze upon it. It is not, of course, inconsequential for the life of the person so mapped.

Speaking in relation to representations of disabled people in literature and the arts, David Mitchell and Sharon Snyder (1997: 15) put the matter this way:

Physical and cognitive differences mark lives as inscrutable and mysterious, and thus we approach these artistically embellished differences with a distanced curiosity that simulates intimacy while staving off the risk of an encounter. We experience disability through an anticipation of our desire to 'know' the secret labyrinths of difference, without significantly challenging our investment in the construction of difference.

Artistically rendered or not, the differences that are used to make up the mark of disability provoke curiosity. But as soon as these differences make any requirement on the 'normal's' normal rules of engagement, curiosity falls away and disruption follows. Mitchell and Snyder suggest that talking *about* disability is best understood, not as 'knowledge,' but rather as a way of constructing difference (Scott, 1995). Asking Rod, 'What's it like?' while refusing the touch of blindness upon our own lives, constructed the difference of blindness as something that belonged to Rod alone. Minimally, the familiar situations within which Rod's blindness was discussed constructed disability as 'out there,' while constructing normal as that position which can take interest, even pleasure, in all sorts of human variation and differences so long as they remain 'out there.'

This is part of the body-politics of normalcy. Regarding signs of blindness as 'normal accidents' manages to control a disrupted sense of normalcy by putting everything back into a sensible (ordinary) space. Moreover, all this interactional work, oriented to achieving normalcy, conforms to the normal sense that disability is simply the negation of ability and is a position defined by lack.

Getting as close as possible to 'normal' standards of bodily engagement, as when blind persons pass as sighted, is a cultural expectation of disabled persons and assures that normalcy maintains its status as a dominant but taken-for-granted phenomenon. This expectation requires that people should simultaneously be and not be disabled, and also leads to normalcy-as-able-bodiedness remaining an unexamined societal ideal. In these ways, the influence of blindness on the face-to-face interaction can be treated as accident, mistake, *faux pas*, but not treated as possessing any particular substance distinctive in itself. Such a map ensures that blindness will not be regarded as a legitimate and unique place in the world. My role in Rod's passing project meant that I could learn much about culture as it relates to sight, while I remained complicitly resistant to any societal representation of blindness as a place for experience, for politics, and for thought.

On Rod's part, it has never appeared to me that he has suffered observable signs of blindness as 'normal accidents,' but he has suffered. A psychological interpretation might locate this suffering in Rod's failure to maintain the passing position in perfection and purity. A sociopolitical interpretation, in contrast, would understand this suffering as an act of resistance (Kleinman, 1995: 120–46; Kleinman and Kleinman, 1997; Bordo, 1993: 154–64). By suffering signs of his blindness *as* disability and not accident, Rod resists the hegemonic control of the standpoint of normalcy. However, 'Hey, Rod, lighten up – it's just an accident' serves to once again isolate and de-politicize disability experience.

The phenomenon of passing certainly has taught sociologists and others about the routine expectations that help to order daily life. Charting the techniques used by people who pass can make everyday societal expectations readily observable. There is benefit in the mapping of the routine organization of everyday life. I have tried to indicate that there is, however, more to passing. More is available if curiosity and wonder are not solely generated from some unacknowledged site of normalcy and if, instead, a disability perspective is employed. In the face of blindness, we can learn that seeing is a cultural achievement surrounded by a set of culturally specific valued practices; for example, sighted ways of greeting, gazing during conversation

(Robillard, 1999), or supplying a ready list of things to be talked about (Goffman, 1963; Scott, 1981). Acquiring such knowledge means that I have used blindness to learn about myself as a normal/sighted person. Thus, in the face of blindness or any other disability, everyone can learn how normalcy is socially constructed and not naturally given. I suspect, however, that most people know this already.[1]

At the level of the question of justice, what becomes perplexing is that it is possible to know all sorts of things about disability and yet remain somehow impervious towards the difference disability makes. It is possible to map disability medically, statistically, and interactionally, and yet disallow these maps from showing us anything about the meaning of disability beyond the observation of its details. It is possible, indeed probable, that in gaining knowledge of disabled others, nothing is transformed, let alone understood. Herein lies a painful injustice which is difficult to articulate because it is difficult to understand.

Developing a fuller social topography of disability requires attention to the issues of justice and inequality. While knowledge regarding the routine ordinary order of normal life can be gained by charting disabled people's interaction with non-disabled others, this knowledge can perpetuate injustice if we do not consider the kinds of relations that people develop in regards to such knowledge. Attention needs to be paid to the ways in which people relate to and make use of culturally specific maps of disability, and this requires an ability to interpret interpretive relations, a hermeneutics, a mapping of cultural maps.

However, there is little new about the ways in which we go about mapping disability. Western culture has a long history, especially since the Enlightenment, of being very curious about human difference as abnormalcy and pathology, often treating bodily differences as an object of curiosity, conversation, and examination (Canguilhem, 1991). Non-disabled people have spent time and energy mapping human difference through such means as freak shows, medical rounds, pathology taxonomies and texts, popular novels and books, demographics, the generation of statistical probabilities, and talking to disabled persons about disability or observing passing and other forms of interaction. What theoretically oriented disability research is bringing to light today is that normalcy often remains the unobserved position from which disability is defined, documented, and examined. Thus, disability is mapped as if it is a foreign land, and a distanced curiosity remains one of the most repetitive, debilitating, yet 'normal' ways of regarding the life and work of disabled people.

Beyond Passing: The Need for a Better Map

My sense of the oppressive double bind surrounding interaction with disabled people has, as of late, only increased – there is a strange politics of normalcy surrounding those who bear the mark of difference. However, my awareness of this has not grown simply because I am ever vigilant in attending to unequal expectations or because I am forever angered by the failure of sighted people, including myself, to imagine the standpoint of living between sight and blindness. My sense of the double bind increased in relation to the fact that Rod's vision began to change. Rod's orientation to his position between sight and blindness was more and more being experienced from the side of blindness. Rod was a blind man, but he was also a man going blind.

The necessary adjustment time between bright light to dim, or dim light to bright, began to take longer and longer for Rod. The noticing of shoelaces or pencils or anything else on the ground began to disappear. At some point, I too became invisible. I now needed to make my exit or entry into a room aural. As visual cues and markers began to disappear, my dyslexia became more obvious to both Rod and me. Saying, 'Turn left' when I meant 'Turn right' could now lead to a collision with unseen objects. I became more anxious about giving correct directions, and this led to more misdirections. (Now, when I say turn left or right, Rod points to the direction that I have said, and I confirm if this is the direction that I meant. But there is no such easy way to fix the difficulty that I have giving more complicated directions.) Word order within a direction-sentence is often askew, especially if I am rushed: 'There is a chair, at our table, facing the same direction as we did as we walked through the door that we just did.' Or: 'There is a post, past the fence, near the gate, which has been removed.' Rod was losing those visual aids (a missing post? fence? gate?) which had in the past helped him to put straight what I was saying. And, as Rod was going blind, I was once again mapping disability as simply inability and lack.

Almost every time Rod arrived home, he had a story regarding the disappearing visual world he was now living in (Michalko, 1999: 11–15). Almost weekly, one landmark after another would disappear, and his vision began to move towards seeing shadows and light. But seeing shadows is confusing – is the shadow a post or is the post a mere shadow? Learning to translate the appropriate shadows into solids became an abiding feature of the type of work involved in this form of vision – the artfulness of passing now included the arduousness of deciphering, memorizing, listening, not only to the ways of sighted people (in this Rod was expert) but to the physicality of culture. In this world of multiplying shadows and disappearing people, I said to Rod, 'It is like you are going blind, over and over again.'

Blind people who are going blind are in an awkward

state of affairs. All the shifts in Rod's blindness meant a shift in his way of orienting to the world. Every change in vision requires a reorganization of the type of work that is necessary to move through everyday life (Howes, 1991). Yet, the everyday world remains that place that usually expects nothing other than sighted persons or their opposites. The blind person who is going blind is living testimony to the radical inadequacy of simple dichotomies. The richness of the flesh of disability includes 'illegitimate fusions' (Thomson, 1997a: 114) between what is assumed to be binary opposites. Given the culture's dominant inclination to frame sight and blindness as opposites there is no readily available language to express the phenomenon of going blind, when one already is. Once a person is identified as blind the loss of the valued ability is supposed to be obvious and final. Within this oppositional framework, it is not as if one is going blind over and over again. Instead, it is as though the blind person is not handling the blindness that she or he already has or is. (It is just such an understanding that supports many rehabilitative and therapeutic practices and, even, sociological accounts of such practices, for example, most disability-as-deviance research.)

As Rod's vision began to change, I began to develop very mixed opinions towards both his blindness and his sightedness. My interaction with Rod would sometimes give rise to a sense that his sight was 'getting in the way.' It was as though his remaining vision was playing tricks on him by making objects appear where there were none. He was never sure which landmark would disappear, nor when. I also had experiences that gave rise to an opposite opinion, an intense anxiety regarding what would happen if Rod went completely blind. Strangely enough, this anxiety was mostly wrapped up in a concern for whether or not I would be able to discern that blindness had 'really' arrived: would I mistake total blindness for just another day filled with bad lighting; would I know what to say if it did arrive? I would say to friends that 'Rod is going really blind.' My friends would say, 'You said that already,' or, 'You said that last month.' One possible response to approaching blindness is to simply focus on how it is already present. However, this did not address how afraid I was that I was going to miss the event of Rod's going blind and, even if I noticed it, I would not know what to say. Despite all my attempts to map blindness, I was beginning to face the fact that I did not know what it would look like. Thus, I worried that blindness would finally arrive, or we would arrive in blindness as some kind of crisis, and, ironically, I was also worried that I would not know it.

These worries were not resolved before 'complete blindness' arrived. When complete blindness did come, it came first in the shape of a new identity for Rod.[2] Rod acquired a guide dog, Smokie.

I was very excited when Rod went to a guide-dog school for a month of training. I read all I could about dogs and about guide dogs. I was working with a map that told me that getting a guide dog meant the acquisition of an object (dog) and a tool (guide). I had not anticipated that acquiring a guide dog would also mean acquiring a new identity. Rod arrived home with a beautiful new dog and an expert guide. But there was more. With Smokie, Rod was seen as blind. Staring, grabbing, helping, offers of prayers or medical advice, groping for words or even a voice are some of the many ways that sighted people show that they are seeing a blind person. Through these interactions, Rod was given the identity – blind person.

Mapping Sighted Spectacles

I thought that bearing a mark of blindness would, at least, lessen my anxiety regarding Rod's safety. In this, I was only partially correct. In the past, Rod would cross a busy street with no marker that he was blind. He also crossed with every sense and every bit of his cultural knowledge tuned to the crossing. This has not changed. But now Rod has a guide who also looks out and will disobey the command 'Forward' if it is not safe to cross. Moreover, sighted people now have a marker of blindness, which they use to orient to Rod as blind. These signs of blindness have not necessarily made sighted people less dangerous; in fact, quite the opposite.

Some people in cars or on bikes see a blind person and guide dog and interpret this as 'slow pedestrian,' speeding up and ignoring Rod's right of way. Yet, Rod and Smokie are not slow; they are usually the quickest pedestrians on any given city street. If it were not for Rod's and Smokie's strength and competence, many near misses might have been otherwise. Other people see a blind person and guide dog and interpret this as 'spectacle,' and in a way similar to a roadside accident, they slow down to stare. When a car slows down, especially on a busy street, it is difficult for anyone not to interpret this as a stopping car whose driver is giving the right of way to the pedestrian. The slow-to-stare-but-sail-on-by sighted person manoeuvre has put Rod and Smokie at risk of being hit numerous times. Another sighted person ritual often occurs at crosswalks. A driver abruptly stops for Rod and Smokie and then waves them on. If I am close by, I can interpret the wave as directed at me as a non-blind onlooker who ought to say something to the blind person. But I have witnessed this sighted behaviour from a distance and when no other sighted person was available to verbally communicate the driver's wave. When I have been close enough to be in the communicator role, I have noticed that the waving driver does not look at me, which means that the driver has not indicated that her or his wave is intended for me. In this abrupt stop-and-wave behaviour, I can only assume that in seeing a blind person, the driver sees a potential hazard – but a sighted one. Some drivers even appear frustrated that the 'hazard' does not respond to their wave and in a fluster drive through the crosswalk. Making blindness obvious does not necessarily change the cultural inclination to treat disabled people *as if* they are not. The binding imperative 'Say what you will, but do as we do' seems to increase alongside the increased intensity of disability experience.

That a blind person and guide dog on a busy street rarely elicit a reasonable response from sighted people, such as non-visual forms of communication, is socially significant. On occasion, I have thought that it signifies sighted people's rudeness or ignorance. But these bizarre responses are so common that I would have to believe that the majority of sighted people are rude or ignorant, and this cannot be true. Friends and students have said that waving at blind people, usurping their right of way, slowing to stare, or silently opening a door that a blind person is trying to open are all signs of the hegemonic hold of sight. By this they mean that it is impossible to drop a sighted point of view. I sometimes share this belief, especially if I have just pointed as a way to indicate which way Rod should go, or have pointed to indicate where an object is located.

But notice that all these bizarre sighted behaviours occur in relation to *seeing* a blind person. There is an interpretive chain of reasoning whereupon noticing signs of blindness, the sighted person does something she or he was not doing moments before. It is not the case that sight is so powerful that it restricts its possessor from ever imagining anything other than itself – after all, we do *see* a blind person and we do *do* something. Claiming that the standpoint of vision does not allow sighted people to imagine the viewpoint of blindness is a form of justification reflecting the taken-for-granted cultural map of vision as 'natural.' The claim that sighted people stand in sight and can do no other, con-structs exclusionary structures and interactional doubled binds *as if* they are products of nature.

In seeing a blind person, the 'normal' expectation of the ubiquitous presence of sight is disrupted, a wrinkle is put into the normal state of affairs, and something must be done – speed up, wave, rush to open the door, point. What-ever is done, it is achieved in relation to the conceptions of blindness that circulate within culture. These doings are testimony to the powerful symbolic efficacy of blindness – even the minutest signs of difference seem to give way to an excess of interpretive possibilities. Blindness is thus made to overflow with meaning, well beyond any practical rea-soning that the situation, such as street crossings, would require.

Perhaps, these bizarre sighted behaviours are not so much signs of the power of vision but are instead signs of the power of culture. This is not to imply that vision is not a cultural phenomenon, but, rather, it is a way to high-light just how radically powerful the cultural organiza-tion of vision and the idea of sight are. There are many different conceptual maps of disability that circulate in culture. Disabled persons do not simply move through a physical environment, but also move through an environ-ment within which a plethora of differing conceptions of disability abound (Michalko and Titchkosky, 2001). Each conception of disability maps disability differently and offers different answers to the question 'Who are you?'

I have described two different social situations that seem to have radically contradictory conceptions of and conse-quences for blind people. The first social situation was passing among friends, and the second was public street crossings. In the first, even the most minimal sign of blind-ness is regarded as excessive, and remedial action to secure the hegemonic hold of 'normal' standards of interaction follows. If blindness is to make an appearance, it is only in its minimized shape as something to talk about. In the second, nothing normal or reasonable seems to hold. In the street-crossing situation, the sighting of a blind person confidently and competently crossing a street overflows with an excess of meaning. This excess of meaning has consequences for disabled people that range from silly annoyances to putting disabled people in threatening and dangerous situations. Between the minimized and excessive interpretation of the lived actuality of disability lies the constant possibility of obliteration.

Disabled people exist in a culture in which little space is given for the experience or articulation of disability from the standpoint of being disabled and moving through the world. The inaccessibility of the physical environment is matched, even superseded, by the exclusionary prowess of the symbolic environment. Mapping disability as a physical entity of difference and debility, mapping it as a statistical quantity or probability, or mapping it as a series of interactional procedures used to secure a place in the land of the normal are all practices which produce knowledge about disability without having to pay attention to the powerful symbolic environment within which disabled persons move, live, and interact. Usual and ordinary maps of disability usually and ordinarily exclude any mapping of culture's powerful role in making up the meaning of disabled persons. Still, the last two chapters represent a beginning to the work of mapping the ways in which we typically conceptualize and map disability.

The Destiny of Cultural Maps

As Rod became more and more blind, and as I began to experience my dyslexia more dramatically, we began to pay more attention to the ways in which culture inscribes meaning onto the lives of disabled people. This included attending to the meaning ascribed to disabled people's significant others. The power of culture to make up the meaning (Liggett, 1988) of blindness, or any other disability, is not only diverse but also far-reaching. I am not blind, yet my identity too is often constituted in relation to blindness (Gowman, 1956). Soon after Rod came home from the guide-dog training school with Smokie, a store clerk in our Toronto neighbourhood said to me, 'Is that blind man with the dog your husband?' I said, 'Yes,' as I put change on the counter for a chocolate bar. 'You are very good. It is good that he has you. You are a good woman,' responded the clerk. In a big city neighbourhood, or now in a small town where we currently reside, I am often identified as the woman who lives with that blind guy and his guide dog. Usually, this identity means that I am, *ipso facto*, a 'good woman' – even if I have just forgotten that Rod, too, wanted a chocolate bar.

So far-reaching is the symbolic power of blindness, so overwhelming is its assumed abnormal nature, that even my own achievements and social roles are marked by blindness. Even though many people know that I am dyslexic, I am spoken to as if disability can only be located in Rod or in some distant 'they,' as in 'How do they teach?' One academic informed me that I could not claim authorship for this book – after all, the accounts of blindness belong to Rod alone, and even my own experience of blindness 'belongs' to Rod.

These opposing interpretations of my relationship with Rod are also reliant on conceptual maps of the significance of social difference (Rajchman, 1995). There is, however, no way to escape from using some kind of conceptual map as people move and live with disabled persons. *What is unjust about this situation is that these maps are made and remade, used and reused, and yet there is no cultural imperative to pay attention to such making and such use.* Maps of social space are often oriented to reducing the complexity of a situation and simplifying one's movement through the environment. But there are few people who, when looking at a map of a foreign country, make the claim that they are at the same time visiting it. While it is impossible to escape from the power of a culture's maps to make up the meaning of its people, it is not impossible to begin to consider what these maps are constructing and how.

Just as my colleagues and students, as well as people on the street and in public establishments, have a plethora of interpretations through which they see blindness – so too do I. Living with Rod has also meant finding myself in different relations to blindness: I fear it, fret about it, suggest ways to get around it, take advantage of it, and, of course, I help. While I easily fall into these sorts of relations with blindness, I have also searched for others. Mostly, I search for ways to have some part in blindness that transforms or transcends my relation to Rod as his 'helpmate.' That this is a primary interest for me is directly related to the fact that I can, Rod can, and everyone else can, quickly and easily, reify all the things that I do with Rod into instances of 'helping.' Surely a life with blindness playing, working, and fighting, with all that Rod and these experiences have taught me, with our ongoing work on conceptions of the body and society, normalcy and abnormalcy, surely in all this there is something much more significant going on than 'helping.'

Still, I know that I help. I take pride in doing so. I also know that most others see me as a helper. But, I also know that my identity as helper is the easiest way not to think about what a life with blindness means. That women are traditionally conceived of as caregivers, and that blind people are conceived of as being in need of care, contributes to the ease with which my identity can be typecast as helper, and it is a role my culture holds out for me to clarify whatever questions I have in the face of blindness. Despite the uncertain meaning of being blind and having sight, and despite my struggle with the question of going blind when one already is, my culture says that I can always and forever help. It always strikes me as a little strange that there can be so much 'help' in a milieu of so little understanding, and that I can be regarded as 'helper *par excellence*' when the meaning of the interrelations among disability, self, and society remains for me so obscure. This strangeness is resolved when I conceive of the helper identity as one way culture 'helps' me resist the need to think about disability.

When Rod acquired a guide dog, my secure role as helper became unstable. Wherever Rod went, he now did so smoothly and quickly with Smokie. To work a guide dog correctly, all attention must be paid to the dog – holding my hand or talking with me while walking down the street was now out of the question for Rod. If Rod was going to an unfamiliar location, we would sit together in the calmness of our home and consult a map in order to count city blocks and chart the direction. In such a situation, I rarely got mixed up, and Rod could double-check the direction he was to turn against the map's north arrow. As Rod has said (Michalko, 1999), he and Smokie represent the 'alone-together,' and alone the two of them moved together through and to whatever events Rod chooses. Both the impact of my dyslexia and my role as helper were being disrupted.

Ironically, this disruption to my role as primary helper spawned one of the more creative ways that I have attempted to resist the cultural assumption that in relation to Rod I am nothing more nor less than a good-woman-helper.

With Smokie, Rod was showing me that there was something adventurous about blindness, and instead of falling
into a distant relation to Rod as a disabled person, I felt
excluded. Here was a situation within which my role as
helper would not help me, and, moreover, 'help' can be an
inappropriate and insulting way to engage a guide-dog
team. At the same time, there is something very exciting,
even enchanting, about such a team, and I did not want to
lose my share in this experience of blindness. Six months
after Rod came home with his guide dog and a new identity, I, too, acquired a dog, whom I named Cassis.

Passing as Blind

I got Cassis with the intention of learning to do guide-dog
training. I thought that this would be challenging, fun, give
me some share in Rod's new experience, and, perhaps, help
me better conceptualize 'left' and 'right' because of having
to teach these commands to a dog, through repetition. I
trained her. Cassis learned to act like a guide dog. Eventually, I learned to act like a blind person. And, my accuracy
with left and right has improved dramatically – Cassis
however, is still better than I.[3]

With Cassis, Rod has helped me to pass as a blind person.
Together, with guide dogs in hand, we share in a kind of
blind-sightedness. In the small university town in which
we now live, people know I am not blind even while I am
working a dog who is wearing a guide-dog harness. In
town, I put a sign on Cassis's harness that reads 'In Training.' In town, I never pass as blind.

In big cities, however, Cassis does not wear a sign on her
harness. In cities, I pass as blind. Rod and I have travelled
this way together. Rod manages most of the more detailed
aspects of blind/sighted interaction, such as signing credit

slips, asking for directions, and checking in and out of
hotels. In these ways, we minimize sighted people's engagement with me as a 'fake' blind person. Under the cover
of blindness, my role as the helping 'go-between' disap-
pears, and I can share differently in the interactions between blind and sighted persons. Together, our travels with
this sighted-blindness have allowed us to conduct ethnographic research and consider how the lived actuality of
blindness interacts with other people's treatments and
images of it.

Passing as blind with Rod has led to experiencing blindness as other people imagine it, which is observable in
people's treatment of persons whom they interpret as blind.
For example, we returned to Toronto for ten days of research and to visit friends. During this trip, we decided to
go to a major office supply store that had in the past sold
Rod a high quality dictaphone. Dictation is the method
Rod uses to write, and as he was beginning a new book, he
wanted a back-up dictaphone should anything go wrong
with the first, older one. Guide dogs in the lead, we entered
the store, passed the check-out counters, and gave the command 'Forward, find the counter.' There was a counter at
the back of the store where the more expensive technology
was displayed behind glass. Here, we waited ... and waited.
Store clerks were milling about the store – but none would
approach us at the counter. Rod called out, 'Excuse me,
could someone serve me at this counter.' Not one, but two
clerks responded to his call. By model name and number,
Rod asked for the device. Mostly silence and inactivity
followed his request, and then, as if from nowhere, a box
was put in front of Rod on the counter. I whispered this fact
to Rod, as well as the fact that the clerks were beginning to
slink away. He found the box and asked loudly for the
price. One clerk remained and gave Rod the price, which

was higher than we had expected as it was an old model in a dusty old box. Rod began to express this to the clerk. The clerk silently moved away – never to return.

To one another, we expressed our astonishment that silence and slinking away were the clerks' preferred methods to deal with blind people. Our astonishment was not grounded in the rarity of such events. They are not rare. Blatant avoidance is always-already astonishing. Slinking silence does not come naturally and surely runs contrary to any training a person might receive in general sales work. While slinking silence does not fit the typical practice of sales work, this practice does fit various cultural maps of blindness: blindness as lack of knowledge leading to 'Oh, they won't know'; blindness as excessive disruption leading to the clerks' return to 'normal work'; blindness as inability and/or poverty leading to 'They couldn't possibly have any real interest in expensive technology, and thus we don't have any real interest in them as customers.' Whatever the precise details of the map of blindness that these clerks possessed, it was such that it allowed for avoidance through silently moving away.

Sharing in this blind-sightedness has become a place for Rod and me to think about the images of blindness which are inscribed upon blind people's movement and interaction with sighted others. Of course, Rod never escapes from such inscription and certainly does not need a sighted-blind person to tell him about it. But in finding some part in the sport-like adventure of guide-dog work, and in attempting to resist my role as good-woman-helper, I have also been granted further access to the cultural maps of disability which surround disabled people. Thus, together, we can observe sighted others, and we can do so in both blind and sighted ways.

While surely more concrete than is necessary, the experience of passing as blind bespeaks the efficacy of taking a disability perspective for conducting an analysis of the abilism of everyday life. However, the law has a different way of mapping this sighted-blindness. It is illegal to pass as a blind person when one has sight. The illegality of passing as blind is tied to taking advantage of a traditionally disadvantaged social identity for one's own profit. More subtly, the law is also tied to basic interactional requirements necessary for the order of public life, what Goffman (1959) has charted as the ubiquitous societal expectation that *one is as one appears*. Still, as suggested earlier, the 'one is as one appears' rule becomes very complicated when one's identity is structured through a noticeable social difference – when one is what they should not be. Being someone who everyone else thinks no one would normally want to be, typically means being expected to act as much as is possible as one isn't. Disabled persons are, in general, surrounded by an obligation to pass as 'normal.' This is not illegal. The tough work of mirroring the life of advantaged identity categories and reproducing the sense and power of normate (Thomson, 1997a: 8) culture is both legal and expected.

One of the most poignant lessons that has come from this shared sighted-blindness has come through my reflection upon my own reaction to the often asked question 'Are you training Cassis to be Rod's next guide dog?' I know that this is a valid question. But where does its validity reside? Again, it resides in the dominant interpretive scheme of 'help.' I am not training Cassis as Rod's next guide dog, but I often say that I am.

In the face of this question, I experience an overwhelming sense of inability. I do not know how to explain that I am training Cassis because it is fun. I cannot bring myself to utter that I do this because it is a way to share some part

in the experience of blindness, or because it aids my research in disability and, more important, it helps me with
my dyslexia. I feel I will be misunderstood if I say that I did
not want to be left out as Rod found a new way of moving
through and negotiating the social environment. And saying that it is a unique and interesting experience seems out
of the question.

I trained and I work with Cassis because I want to be a
part of blindness and grow in understanding. This I do not
say. I sense a rush of embarrassment and fraudulence when
I am with Cassis in harness and I am asked the question. I
remedy all this by saying, 'Yes, I am training Cassis for
Rod.' Once again, life with disability is simplified through
my use of the map of myself as a good-woman-helper. This
has taught me just how difficult it is to resist the meaning
given to us by our culture. And this lesson comes in the
midst of consciously attempting to resist my role as helper.

Mapping of Maps

As I have shown, culture gives people many ways to map
disability. There are ways to map how far from or close to
able-bodied standards our bodies come. There are statistical maps to indicate the chances and probabilities of acquiring a disability. There are sociological maps which depict
the socially constructed character of normal life and normal selves. What all these maps share in common is that
they reflect, enter, and influence culture without requiring
anyone to pay attention to their production and their use.
Moreover, these maps share the fact that they influence
the destiny of disabled and non-disabled people. These
maps delineate 'normal' paths upon which we are to move
and live with our bodies and their interpretations. Like all
tools, maps are cultural products, and thus they are the

stuff of culture, which provides for the possibility of critical reflection.

Whatever the meaning of the lived actuality of disability may be, it is constructed in relation to the maps of disability that culture provides. Some people may take only short and sporadic trips with disabled people or with the experience of disability, yet all of us, in some way or another, travel with disability. And all of us do so under the guidance of one cultural map or another. *Nonetheless, there are few cultural maps that show us how to pay attention to the phenomenon of mapping itself.* By making use of my experience of dyslexia and Rod's blindness, I have attempted in this chapter to do a mapping of some of the common maps of disability. This mapping of maps serves as an alternative topography. I have not just provided yet one more topography of disability. I have also provided a topography of a few of the ways in which culture maps disability. This mapping of maps is essential if we are to develop a self-reflective relation to culture and our bodies.

Such an alternative depiction of culture's re-presentations of disability holds out the promise of doing and learning something more than merely how to move through a culture in the ways that it has predetermined for us. Mapping cultural maps gives rise to the awareness that disability can be interpreted in a multiplicity of ways, each of which holds symbolic social significance. This is the significance which makes up the meaning of the bodies and lives of disabled people, and the meaning of the relations between disability and non-disability identities.

In this chapter, I pursued a mapping of cultural maps by paying attention to my own lived experience with disability, but I paid little attention to the physical and social environment in which disability moves and lives. I now turn to an examination of this environment.

CHAPTER FOUR

The Expected and the Unexpected

Whatever else it might be, the meaning of disability comes to us through an environment. Our environment sometimes bears signage indicating where a disabled person might enter, might move, might go to the washroom. But, disability is often a powerful absence whose presence can be felt in the obvious exclusionary character of environments oriented to idealized 'normal' bodies. Sometimes disability appears in the transformative suffering of self-understanding; at other times, the environment reminds us of the lack and limit of socially vulnerable bodies,[1] and at still other times, disability is simply someone to stare at while walking down the street. That all of us share in these experiences means that it is impossible not to have a life with disability as we move through the social and physical environment. The significance of disability is always a part of the environment, even if only as a noticeable absence. As I showed in the last chapter, how we come to experience disability in daily life is tied to how we interpret disability, and this is informed by the ways in which culture has already mapped the significance of disability for us.

Culture does map the significance of disability, but it does not do so only through its dominant conceptions and stereotypes of disabled persons. The significance of disability is also 'declared' in the constitution and maintenance of the environment. The ways we live with our disabilities or with those of others, the culturally defined maps of disability, and the physical structure of the environment are, of course, decisively intertwined. I will interrogate the declarations of the environment, and I will use this chapter to show how they are grounded upon favoured interpretations of both disability and disabled people. Attending to the everyday-concrete-actual ways in which we speak of the inaccessibility of the environment gives us access to the dominant societal recommendations for mapping out a life with people identified as disabled. How we decide to live with the interrelation between the environment and cultural maps of the significance of disability influences the type of life we have as, and with, disabled persons. This chapter will show that these decisions are reinscribed in the concrete reality of the environment, and these inscriptions are declared on every occasion when the inaccessibility of the environment is explained or rationalized.

Encountering Inaccessibility

Most people know that the physical and social environment is exclusionary. When non-disabled persons take a flight of stairs together and find themselves breathing a little harder at the end of them, they will say, 'I thought that I was in shape' or 'I must be out of shape.' Regardless of the empirical validity of the speakers' evaluation of their physical fitness, these comments declare that the environment puts them in mind of the shape and limits of their bodies. On my university campus, it has become almost ritualistic to groan while opening the heavy doors of the building that houses the sociology department. Groaning through one's brief struggle with a door is a public announcement that this environment requires a great deal of bodily agility, effort, and strength if one is to secure access to it. We tell each other in subtle everyday ways that we know that the physical and social environment is in many ways an exclusionary one. Yet, the question remains: what do we do with this knowledge?

I notice a flight of stairs. Really, it is only two stairs which lead up to the old library. I use these stairs, and so too do others. Mostly, I use these stairs and don't even notice that I am doing so. But today I notice. Today I am forced to pay attention. A disabled person is approaching the stairs. She stops. She and her wheelchair are at the bottom of the stairs. She is studying a map of the campus, staring up at it as it hangs there affixed between two large posts. The wheels of her chair and the stark angles of the stairs fall into juxtaposition. I notice now the handrails – pure decoration, not functional. I notice the steps – uneven, slippery when wet, and requiring their users to go up before they go down and down before they go up. Nonetheless, they frame the door nicely – they are aesthetically pleasing ... until I see the woman in her wheelchair.

Should I tell her that there is a ramp in the back, an elevator by the delivery door? Should I offer the assistance of my able body – perhaps I could lift her, lift the wheelchair? Maybe, I'll need help. I may just stare, wonder at her ingenuity, marvel at her pluck, lament her lack of courage, let my imagination posit her state, her fate, her past, and her future. These stairs, I decide, were intended to please the eye, but not the rest of the body. I decide to do nothing. I have decided too much.

Knowledge of the inaccessible character of the environment is awfully easy to come by. What is more difficult to apprehend is what is made of this knowledge. Is mobility within the environment a question of having the right know-how for movement in it? Is the environment a chance for help to be given to some and a stage for others to display their agility and strength? Is physical mobility much the same as the dominant conceptions of economic mobility, namely, a matter of right attitude and correct work ethic, tinged with the influence of one's personal resources? Perhaps one's place in the environment is not so much related to individual know-how or spirit or resources, as it is to the accident of fate of being born into a culture that privileges aesthetic pleasures over and against the value of access, a culture that, moreover, regards these two values as somehow unrelated yet antagonistic.

The local newspaper reported the comments of a politician during our town's disability awareness week. She said, 'I am shocked by how inaccessible the town businesses and establishments are.' I was shocked when I read that she was shocked. Maybe the councillor really meant that she shocked herself in that she had not noticed this inaccessibility prior to the town's disability coalition's discussions with her. Her statement may mean that she had not realized what an extensive impact inaccessible structures have on disabled people's lives. Whatever she meant, she did declare that 'shock' is a reasonable response, reasonable enough to have been reported by the local newspaper.

Since 1975 the National Building Code of Canada has required that any public building, constructed after 1974, be accessible to disabled persons, and that renovated buildings must also include at least some partial provision for accessibility. The Code also says that accessible washrooms and doors are to be marked with the international disability sign. Before 1974, public environments depicted disability as an exception, and its inclusion was, at best, framed as a 'suggestion.'[2] Since 1975, disability has been depicted, at least partially, as a feature of public life.

But the good news of legislated inclusion contains more than just 'good news.' The practices legislated by the Building Code declare that being disabled means being the type of person whose presence is partially expected; that is, some disabled people, some of the time, and in some places are expected. There is no requirement to post signage indicating that a building or its washrooms are *not* accessible. The Building Code notwithstanding, environments are at best only partially accessible to some disabled people. For example, the Canadian Building Code sets minimum public doorway widths at 29.5 inches, whereas the Americans with Disabilities Act enforces a minimum 36-inch doorway width. These minimums, among other things, declare and enforce who can and cannot enter public buildings. Whatever reasons are given for this partiality (economic, pragmatic, unintentional thoughtlessness), the environment remains largely inaccessible to disabled people. After all, the average non-motorized wheelchair is 30 inches wide.

What should be asked is not how much it will cost to make a society completely accessible to all with physical difficulty, but rather why a society has been created and perpetuated which has excluded so many of its members. (Zola, 1982: 244)

Unlike the local politician, Zola is not shocked by the inaccessibility of his environment. He is shocked, however, by a society that is actively involved in excluding the very thing it requires, namely, members. What version of membership must a society have in order to exclude its disabled members? As a way to explore these issues, I turn now to an analysis of a shocking encounter between me and my partner, Rod, and a senior tenured professor, whom I will call Harry, at a university that I will call Cape University. With the exception of our names, all other names have been changed, including the name of a second university, which I call St Elsewhere.

Shocking Encounters[3]

Outside of a bank on the main street of a university community, Rod and I 'ran into' a senior ranking professor from the university. Rod was accompanied by his guide dog, Smokie, and I with my dog, Cassis, who was also in her harness. Immediately after this encounter, I went to a café and made detailed notes. Here is a representation of this encounter:

Professor (P): Oh, Hello.

Rod (R): Hi.

Tanya (T): Hi, this is my partner, Rod.

P: Oh, your partner [Tanya] has been telling me about you. I've been wanting to meet you. I have a special interest in the handicapped.

T: I'm sorry, I can't remember your name.

P: It's Harry ____. So, Rod, I hear you will be teaching here in the winter term?

R: Yes, I'm looking forward to that.

T (to a passerby): No, please don't touch the dogs. She's in training.

P: Yes, I guess you need to be pretty firm with seeing eye dogs. I ran into Heidi [student] and her guide dog, ah ... Spruce, on the elevator yesterday. I asked her if it was difficult to find the right button on the elevator. You know, there's no Braille on the elevator. Do you think it's difficult?

R: For some blind people it is. But, it seems to me, that Braille on elevator buttons is the least of the problems this university has with accessibility.

P: Oh? Heidi said she could make out the floor because she could feel the embossed numbers on the buttons. Anyway, you know, we *don't* encourage the handicapped to come here. St Elsewhere University is all set up for them.
R/T: Laughter.

Rod and I soon realized, however, that discouraging some students from attending Cape University was not a joke for Harry. He took his position on this matter quite seriously, telling us that it was the only 'reasonable and pragmatic' way to approach the issue of disability. Despite this, Harry said that he was doing many things 'to help the handicapped' on campus and around the community. (Later we were to discover that Harry, in fact, has received awards in public recognition for this help.)

From our standpoint, Harry's comment regarding the discouraging of disabled students from attending Cape University could only be a joke. From his, it was not. This was certainly a meeting of what Paul Ricoeur (1974: 10) calls rival interpretations. Rod, Harry, and I are meeting rival interpretations *of* the environment with regard to disability.

Ricoeur (ibid.: 19) suggests that '... it is only within the movement of interpretation that we apperceive the being we interpret.' As Rod and I move about at Cape University, conducting the affairs of everyday life, we meet up with others' interpretations of the environment. These interpretations sometimes conflict with our own, and sometimes the interpretations Rod and I hold conflict with each other. Ricoeur is not suggesting that somehow all these conflicts can be settled, so that interpretations match some version of a given environmental reality. Instead, he is suggesting that what is really Real about the environment is that it is made up of rivalries and conflicts. This is why we can read the environment for its 'movement of interpretation' – for the social significance that lies between interpretations of an environment's exclusionary character as a joke for some and as a practical matter for others.

These interpretive conflicts are not just declared by us, but are also declared by the environment itself. The conversation between Harry and Rod and me took place outside a bank that bore the universal sign of accessibility, and the bank was situated next to a building that bore no such sign, sporting many stairs and narrow doorways. Examining the conflict of rival interpretations encountered in everyday life requires that attention be paid to how the interpretation 'joke' and the interpretation 'serious practical matter' are both provided for by the social significance of the environment as it relates to disabled people.

But in the midst of this conversation on the street, the conflict was not being examined – it was being declared. Throughout the rest of the encounter, Harry, Rod, and I attempted to declare and clarify our positions. While there was much to disagree about, there was some agreement. For example, Harry told Rod and me that many of the buildings on campus were built many years ago and that 'retro-fitting them' would be an exorbitant expense. With this, Rod and I expressed our agreement. Rod told Harry that this university was particularly inaccessible to disabled people and that it must be hard on non-disabled people as well. With this, Harry agreed. I said that there were, however, many 'little things'[4] that could be done; for example, the gaps in the handrails along the stairs could be fixed, ramps installed, the sidewalks fixed, etc. Harry told us that he always wants to hear about the 'little things' that can be done, and he told us that he can get such things done. But sometimes 'big things' are to be done to the environment, and this, according to Harry, is not pragmatic: he said that he had heard about a university in the United States that was asked to make the books in its library accessible to persons in wheelchairs by placing the books on shelves no higher than four feet. 'You know,' said Harry, 'that's the height people can reach from a wheelchair.' 'Strange,' I uttered, captivated by the idea that such an act of inclusion might be pursued. 'That is quite out of the ordinary,' said Rod. Harry noted, 'Every handicap is different,' and Rod agreed. There was apparent agreement regarding the fact that the great variety of disabilities makes the issue of accommodation a complicated one (Bickenbach, 1993; Butler and Parr, 1999; Gleeson, 1999; Imrie, 1996).

Nonetheless the conflict remained:

P: It's ridiculous to fix this and that, and spend all that money, for just a few students. We have to be pragmatic. You know, a deaf student came here once. But she left after only a year. Now we're stuck with all the thousands of dollars of equipment that we put in for her. There is a university all set up for the handicapped. St Elsewhere gets all the funding.

Rod said, 'You can't blame her for not staying.' I added, 'More than a *few* people are disabled. What about as professors age? Anyone here could become disabled.' Rod continued his response: 'Any able-bodied professor wouldn't like to be told there is only one university they can apply to for a job.' And Harry argued back: 'Oh, but it happens all the time. One university for Celtic studies. Another one for Engineering ...'

R: Isn't that a different issue? Would you like to be told there is only one university you can teach at and that it's simply a matter of pragmatics? It's not pragmatics – it's a justification.

This encounter on the street ended in the following fashion:

> P: Well, anyone who has just got their PhD, and they put out their three hundred applications, they would find that they probably couldn't find a job anywhere.
> R: But isn't that a different issue?
> P: Of course. I'm trying to do all I can.
> R: Well, Braille on the elevators would be a nice gesture.
> P: Yes, a gesture. I'm not part of the handicapped committee. You know, once you're part of a committee, you have to work as a committee and nothing ever gets done. But I have enough seniority. I can go into anyone's office and make a request. So, if you see anything that needs to be done – let me know. I have to run though – I have a doctor's appointment. Good to meet you –
> R: See you again.
> P: So to speak. Yes, I'm sure you'll recognize my voice next time we meet.

Rod and Harry shook hands. Harry went on his way and we on ours. As we began to walk down the main street of this town, Rod said to me, 'I thought he was joking.' I said to Rod, 'So did I. I can't believe he wasn't.'

To Laugh or Not to Laugh

While the points of view in this encounter were clarified, no epistemological transformation occurred – no one changed their mind. That all disabled students should go to St Elsewhere University remained a pragmatic issue for Harry and a joke – a bad one for Rod and me. This is an encounter between rival interpretations of the environment which gives shape and meaning to the lives of disabled people. What can be learned from these conflicting interpretations? From what understanding of the environment and of its people is this conflict derived? What permits laughter to be a response to such a statement of exclusion? What is the meaning of disability produced through this interaction and reflected in this environment?

The posing of these questions is not done in service of establishing whether it is truly pragmatic or truly a joke to discourage disabled students from attending this university. Rather, the 'truth' to be found in this encounter is the meaning derived from the conflict of rival interpretations regarding disability. This kind of questioning situates us in the midst of these conflicting interpretations and provides for an examination of the conceptions of the environment and its people that would allow for the conflict in the first place. How 'in the world' could I possibly hear Harry's statement as a joke?

Recall some of the obvious features of this interaction. It is obvious that Rod is a disabled person since he uses a guide dog. Anyone who meets Rod is met by a clear sign of blindness. My connection to Rod was also obvious. Harry knew that Rod was my partner. I bore a further sign of my connection to disability in that I, too, was accompanied by a dog in a harness. Recall that Cassis wears a harness which has a sign on it that reads 'In Training.' Training a guide dog also contributes to making disability a feature of my life and of this environment. While Harry has no knowledge of my dyslexia, it is obvious that I am attached to blindness insofar as I am known to live with a blind man and there is a dog guide, of sorts, by my side. All these signs of disability were obvious on the street that day.

Another obvious feature of this encounter is that disabled students, despite St Elsewhere University, *do* attend Cape University. After all, Harry told us of his encounters with a blind student and a deaf student. He also said, 'I have a special interest in the handicapped,' adding still another sign of disability to this encounter. Most obvious of all, Rod is a blind professor about to begin working at this university.

Harry's comment regarding disabled students and where they should go, took place within the obvious context of the presence of disability in the environment. Stating the obvious, or obviously ignoring it, often serves as a resource for the accomplishment of humour. I heard Harry's comment that disabled students are discouraged from attending this university as 'joking around.' But Harry was not joking. Did I merely misinterpret him?

'Misinterpretation' would lead me, however, to conclude that I simply held a faulty sense of what Harry and I held in common. I would only discover, for example, that we did not share an interpretation of disability as an occasion for joking. Instead of rival interpretations, I would be faced with supplanting one interpretation (disability can be joked about) with another (disability is not a joking matter). If I were to treat this interaction as simply an instance of mis-interpretation, the conflict of rival interpretations would begin to disappear.

What I heard, however, was a joke that Harry did not tell. When Harry walked away, Rod said, 'I thought he was joking.' I responded, 'So did I. I can't believe he wasn't.' I felt that Harry's comment *should* have been a joke. My sense of what should have been, yet was not, points to conflict, not to misinterpretation. In the midst of an envi-ronment filled with signs of the *possible* inclusion of disabil-ity and in the face of actual disabled persons, the act of justifying current exclusion and attempting to perpetuate more, moves me not only to outrage but also to wonder. How 'in the world' could I possibly conceive of Harry as joking around, especially as he is very certain that disabil-ity is no joking matter?

Unexpected Encounters

An initial meeting between a non-disabled person and a disabled one is often experienced as a first encounter of a special kind. However, 'first encounter' does not necessarily mean that this is the first time that someone has met a disabled person (even though this may be empirically true). All of us possess some idea of disability provided to us by how our society collectively maps it out (Davis, 1997c; Fries, 1997; Higgins, 1996; Ingstad and Whyte, 1995; Michalko, 1999; Scott, 1969; Goffman, 1963). Whether we have met a disabled person or not, we have met disability through our common-sense understandings, through the social conceptions of disability we already possess.

'First encounter,' therefore, occurs on every occasion that we meet a *particular* person with a *particular* disability. We bring our general understandings (common stock of knowledge) regarding disability to these particular meetings. For example, meeting Rod, Harry said, 'Oh, your partner has been telling me about you. I've been wanting to meet you. I have a special interest in the handicapped.' Harry is greeting Rod with his understanding of disability, a 'special interest in the handicapped,' *in general*. His general interest in the 'handicapped' is expressed in his *specific* interest *in* meeting Rod, in *particular*; Harry is particularly interested in meeting Rod insofar as he (Harry) is generally interested in the 'handicapped.'

My conception of the social representation of disability as the 'right' to accessibility and as a morality of belonging in the world led me to see Harry's comment as 'nothing but a joke.' By saying that disabled students are discouraged from attending the university, Harry is suggesting that 'their type' and, therefore, disabled people themselves do not belong. Without conceiving of disabled people as belonging 'anywhere in the world' and without assuming Harry held the same conception, I would have interpreted his comment as an act of discrimination and exclusion and, therefore, not funny at all. Remember, Harry has a special interest in the 'handicapped.' Unless I assumed that Harry has a special interest in telling disabled people that they are unwelcome, I could hear his subsequent comment only as a joke. In a world in which I assume disability to be an essential feature, even though that world builds barriers to disability and often treats it as inessential, I must understand Harry as joking. Interpreting the comment as a joke is premised upon Harry and I living in the same world and sharing similar conceptions of disability. *This* is how in the world I could hear Harry as joking.

This assumption also generated my experience of shock – I was shocked that Harry was not joking. There are, of course, many ways in which the meeting between nondisability and disability can be shocking. For example, one day Rod and I were working our dogs along a street that bordered Cape University campus. As is often the case, Cassis and I had fallen far behind Smokie and Rod. I was, however, still within range to witness the following. A car was leaving campus. It came down a side road which intersected the sidewalk we were walking on. Its driver, looking only for oncoming traffic from the left, did not attend to Rod and Smokie on the right, who were in the process of crossing the street. As the driver pulled out and turned right, she caught sight of Rod and Smokie, who, by this time, had abruptly stopped to avoid the collision. The driver then greeted them with a wave.

When Cassis and I caught up to Rod and Smokie, I told Rod that it was Professor Helen who had pulled out in front of him without looking. Rod said, 'You'd think that since I have met Helen many times, and she knows about me and other blind people on campus, she would be a little more careful.' Indeed, earlier that same month, Helen had been present at a university-wide public talk that Rod gave. There were blind people in attendance and blindness was discussed. Rod assumed that this professor would be awake to the fact that she lived in an environment that included blind people as one of its features. I said to Rod, 'That's not all. Helen waved at you.' We both laughed. Whatever the professor's conception of the environment, it was such that even in the face of blindness, and even after almost hitting a blind person and his guide dog, blindness was not an imaginable part of it. Thus, the wave.

This shock is on a par with that elicited by a non-disabled person's opening a door for a blind person in absolute silence, and then watching while the blind person gropes for the door. The non-disabled person orients to the environment as setting up certain difficulties for some people. Yet, the sighted person who silently opens a door for a blind person is somehow unable to address a person *as* a disabled person, or is addressing that person with an *unworkable* conception of disability. Silently opening doors for blind people does display the collective representation (map) of blindness as a sign of a 'need for help.' But this 'need' remains alienated from *who* may need help. In silently opening the door for a blind person, the 'helpful' one is only open to his or her ironic understanding of blindness as a 'helpless sighted person.' A blind person approaches a door. A sighted person, 'knowing' that the blind person will have 'trouble' opening the door, opens it. The sighted person does not indicate that the door is open. The blind person 'should see' that the door is open. But not seeing this, the blind person tries to open it. The sighted person is surprised at the blind person's trying to open an already opened door. Both stand groping. The door to the building remains open, but the door to any interactional development of what it means to be blind remains closed tighter than ever.

These apparent closures to disability are shocking. It is shocking that Harry would advocate the discouraging of disabled students from attending his university, especially when he does so 'in front' of a disabled person who *is* at his university. It is shocking that Helen waves at Rod. It is shocking that doors are silently held open for blind people. Shocking as these interactions are, they are also humorous in their irony, and they point to the complex set of social relations that exist between the environment and people.

Given the unique character of human interaction and interpretation, Hannah Arendt (1958: 178) correctly asserts that the only thing that humans can assuredly expect from each other is the 'unexpected.' What I did not expect was that Harry could say, 'We don't encourage the handicapped to come here,' and to say this in a serious way. Harry did not expect to face laughter, for he was, as he explained, acting reasonably and pragmatically. We can assuredly expect that these unexpected responses to the phenomenon of disability point to unique interpretations of the meaning of disability within the environment. The three of us are engaged in an encounter with the environment as it speaks to the issue of who disabled people are and where they belong. Rod and I, and hopefully Harry as well, came face to face with rival interpretations of, and conflicting relations with, disability. This raises an epistemological question: what conceptions of the environment, disability, and their interrelation are being employed throughout this encounter?

Disability as a Depiction of Environment

Harry framed his first meeting with Rod with a special interest in Rod's experience of the university environment.

Initially, this interest was represented in the discussion re-garding blind people's use of elevators. Harry went on to tell us about many other disabled persons he has met. He depicted each disabled person in relation to the university environment and the difficulties this environment imposes on them. For example, midway through this encounter, Harry told us of a student, new to Cape University, who uses a wheelchair. Harry told us of the difficulty he and other professors were having 'figuring out' how this stu-dent could participate in the chapel program. 'Right now,' said Harry, 'some bigger guys are hoisting him up the stairs to the chapel and down the stairs once inside the chapel.'[5] All of Harry's encounters with disabled persons were framed by his sense of the difficulties disabled stu-dents will meet within the university environment. *Who disabled persons are* is constructed in relation to the fact that they are moving and living in an environment that in vari-ous ways is not 'set up' for 'them.'

Harry addresses the relation between disabled people and the environment from a position which holds that en-vironment brings out *who* disabled people *are* and disabili-ties bring out *what* an environment *is*. For example, meeting Heidi on the elevator is framed by Harry's special interest in evaluating the university environment. Addressing Heidi as a disabled person means, for Harry, addressing the struc-ture and function of elevators as an environment constructed to accommodate certain types of people (non-disabled), while making movement potentially difficult for other types (disabled). Harry mentioned how cheaply and easily Braille could be added to the elevator. He recited the price of Braille pad additions and the name of the company that could do it. He rejected Rod's suggestion of speaking ele-vators or the installation of chimes to announce floors as too expensive and difficult to accomplish. Doing things to the environment for disabled people (accommodation) is a part of Harry's interest in 'the handicapped,' provided these accommodations are inexpensive and can be accomplished with ease. Whoever disabled people are, they are people whose inclusion in an environment can be addressed in a partial way, since addressing them also means addressing expense and ease. Thus, disabled people are those who require accommodation, while the environment is an entity willing to do so if it is not too expensive or difficult.

This suggests the 'intentionality' of an environment. Harry implies that his university environment is intended to accommodate non-disabled people. Any environment intended for an imagined population will certainly show its intentions when the 'unintended' (disabled people) show up. Except for inexpensive and easy accommodations, the university environment need not alter its intention for disabled students. After all, disabled students can attend that other university – an environment *intended* for them. Harry's university was not constructed with the *intention* of the possibility of disabled students.

Hannah Arendt notwithstanding, environments do not expect the unexpected. Harry's 'special interest' is a special interest in how each disability, and each disabled person, draws out the intentions of an environment. This environment never intended disabled students to be part of the student body. Harry encounters disability as a *living depiction of the intentions of an environment*. Within the context of this encounter on the street, wanting to meet Rod *as* a 'handicapped person' and asking him about inexpensive elevator accommodations serves Harry as a way to reaffirm the intentions of the environment. A disabled person could be having a little bit of trouble moving through the environment, and another person could be having a lot. Nonetheless, both serve as reminders of whom the environment intends to include insofar as their bodies are read as texts or monuments of environmental intentionality.

The Body as Text

Social theorists such as Susan Bordo (1993), Helen Liggett (1988), and Michel Foucault (1979) understand the environment as inscribing itself on individuals and their bodies. The work of these theorists can be used to suggest that these inscriptions present particular meanings and serious limits to disabled people. Harry understands the seriousness of these limits. But, what is particular to Harry is his conception of what constitutes a serious relation to the intentional character of an environment as shown by the limits it inscribes on the lives and bodies of disabled people.

A serious relation towards disability is, for Harry, a *pragmatic* one. The presence of disability represents an opportunity to change the environment, but only in easy and inexpensive ways while, at the same time, reconfirming the intention of that environment. Disabled people represent the collective's need to regard an environment's intentions pragmatically – to show that slight changes to an environment can pragmatically preserve its intention.

A pragmatic understanding of the relation between disability and environment can result in a community treating the interests, aims, and goals of disabled people as self-evident: thus, a library with books shelved no higher than four feet. While pragmatics cannot explain why exclusions or inclusions occur, it does allow for action oriented to making the environment accessible to disabled people. Harry's pragmatism, however, does not result in the 'self-evident character' of the interests of disabled people nor in the subsequent need for accommodation. Instead, his pragmatic relation is oriented to the intentions and interests established by his institution. Intended as it is for 'able-bodied' students, Harry's university did not expect disabled students to show up. For Harry this 'unexpected minority' (Gliedman and Roth, 1980) is even more unexpected given that some other university is imagined as 'all set up for them.'

This pragmatism is held together by the following assumptions. First, the intentions of the institution's physical organization should be recognized as given and primary; they should be seen as both obvious and reasonable. This intention is reaffirmed by discouraging the participation of disabled students. Second, the pragmatist must assume that it is obvious, even natural, that an institution was 'never intended' to be 'set up' for disabled persons in the first place. This intention is reaffirmed on every occasion of noticing a disabled person in the university environment. Finally, this obvious organizational feature of the environment should be treated as *reasonable* given the bureaucratic reasonableness ascribed to the institution. This form of pragmatism is grounded in the assumption that institutional organization is obviously rational and undoubtedly reasonable within the context of its intentionality. This helps to constitute what Zygmunt Bauman (1990: 79–84, 131–7) calls the 'collective fiction' of any bureaucracy. Just as a bureaucracy establishes the fiction that any task or office can be reduced to a singularly clear aim, so too can the people within a bureaucracy be regarded as a singular type with a singular goal.

But disability serves to remind us all that people cannot easily be framed within the bureaucratic fiction of a 'singular type' or, for that matter, singular goal. There are a variety of types of disabilities as well as a variety of types within a specific disability. The reality of such differences cannot be taken into account when disability is an unintended and thus unexpected feature of an organization. The construction and preservation of a bureaucracy's collective fiction of a 'singular type' depend upon disability being 'seen' as an unintended participant. 'Unintended participant' is a bureaucratic method for establishing a singular, manageable conception of who disabled people are.

The standpoint of pragmatism constructs the reasonable and rational character of its intended exclusions in equally reasonable and rational ways. Exclusion is made a reasonable feature of the university, in part, by establishing the belief that there is some other institution that is pragmatically 'all set up for' disabled people.[6] Exclusion is also rationalized on the basis of the bureaucratic logic that insists that critiquing an institution for something it never intended to include in the first place is not a pragmatically oriented evaluation and, thus, should only be regarded as a spurious and unreasonable 'complaint.' A pragmatic position *cannot* understand environmental intentions, inscribed upon the lives of disabled people in the form of limits, as a reflection of 'historical over-sights' derived from cultural conceptions of the 'normal (non-disabled) type.' Exclusion is not an 'over-sight' since the university did not have disabled people 'in-sight' in the first place. Thus, '... we don't encourage the handicapped to come here.' Exclusion is also made reasonable on the basis of the pragmatist's ability to quantify human experience: 'It's ridiculous to fix this and that, and spend all that money, for just a few students.'

The strength and weakness of pragmatism begins and ends in its ability to engage its people as quantifiable things. These 'things' are measured in relation to the costs and benefits they present to an institution, which is conditioned by its finite resources and is governed by pre-established and rationalized intentions.

Nonetheless, it is pragmatically necessary for the people within any environment to deal with unintended and unexpected participants, if they happen to show up. The physical organization of institutions does not expect the unexpected, but the intended participants of an institution cannot escape from noticing and dealing with unexpected participants who happen to come along. There are no moral or even legal grounds for preventing the unexpected from showing up or for asking them to leave when they do so. What the pragmatist faces when he or she meets a disabled person is a challenge – the challenge of what to do in the presence of the unexpected.

Disability as a Challenge to Pragmatism

The presence of disabled people in a university environment represents, for some, the requirement of additional expense[7] and reorganization. There is the expense of accommodations such as wheelchair ramps, elevators, Braille signage, interpreters for those who speak sign language, and so on. Faculty are often required to reorganize their teaching methods to accommodate disabled students. Traditional methods of administering examinations, for example, may not work with dyslexic students. These types of reorganization and additional expense, as well as many others like them, are understood, by some, as a drain upon university resources. Across North America there is a yearly increase in the number of learning-disabled university students and a growing debate and battle over their administration and funding.[8]

The challenge that disability presents to the pragmatist is the need to develop a justification for such additional expenditures. This is not to say that Cape University is not challenged by those expenditures required by their intended (non-disabled) students. Fund-raising is, today, an integral part of any university's life. But the raising of funds in order to construct a new building, upgrade computer systems, and the like, is a justifiable activity for the pragmatist insofar as these expenditures are required in order to serve an intended student body. However, the raising of funds for wheelchair ramps, elevators, etc., in order to serve students who are not conceived of as part of the intended student body, is understood as an additional expense and as a drain on university resources.

Harry insists that his university was neither constructed nor organized with the intention of serving disabled students. Thus any reconstruction or reorganization is as unexpected and unintended as is the presence of disabled students themselves. Of course, any unexpected expense is always met with the need for justification and rationalization. This is part of the challenge Harry faces when he meets disabled students. He frames this challenge within a cost/benefit paradigm. What possible benefit could disabled people present that can be tallied against their cost to the university? Harry's challenge is to 'balance the books' on disability.

Harry has found, however, a way to develop such accounting procedures by transforming the lives of disabled people into 'living depictions of environmental intentions.' This is the benefit of having disabled people around. Harry sees a benefit in disability since it brings to the fore and clarifies the intentions of his university. This is the *only* pragmatic justification for the presence of disability, even though this justification does not entirely rationalize the additional expenditures.

In order to balance the books on disabled students, it is necessary to make assumptions regarding what is valuable and what is not. Pragmatism cannot establish the value of anything since it assumes its value. For example, the value of a university education must first be assumed before any pragmatic action as to its organization and implementation can take place. The value of a student body which the university intends to serve must first be assumed before a university can measure the benefits and costs of serving them. If such value is not assumed, the pragmatist would fall into the never-ending question 'Well, what's the benefit of doing that?' Charles Taylor (1989: 31–2) puts the issue this way: 'The utilitarian lives within a moral horizon which cannot be explicated by his own moral theory. This is one of the great weaknesses of utilitarianism.' The pragmatist bases his/her decisions on their eventual utility and thus never addresses the 'moral theory' which generates these decisions.

The doing of 'little things' for disabled people reflects their assumed value – their value is so minimal that 'little things' are all that is required to be done. This 'minimalist' version of disability ensures that there is minimal expense as well as minimal reorganization of the university, especially of the sense of its intentionality. At best, disabled people *raise* the issue of the intentions of an environment. But the environment responds to the raising of the question of its intention by pointing to the intention itself as a justification for minimal acts of minimal inclusion, for the doing of little things. Disabled students are costly participants *only* insofar as disability represents what is not intended by an environment. This version of pragmatism produces disabled people as an unintended minority. This production of the unintended lies at the heart of the social significance of disability and severely restricts the horizon of interpretive possibilities in relation to disability as a form of life.

The Societal Production of Unintended Persons

The structure of the environment, together with conceptions of and interaction with disabled people, construct disabled persons as unintended. The interpretation of disabled people as 'unintended' does not belong to Harry alone. What is idiosyncratic about Harry is that he precisely repeats that which the environment seems to be declaring. At every turn, at every stair, at every missing handrail, and within every fixed-seat classroom organized only for the intended student body, so that even the presence of left-handed people is not imagined, the environment declares, 'Disabled students, we weren't expecting you to show up.' What is not idiosyncratic is the belief, reflected in the environment, in help, in special budgets, in widespread myths about 'that other university,' that disabled people are *ipso facto* unintended participants.

The wording of the Cape University 'accommodation policy' is grounded in this understanding. Individual disabled students are expected to file a request with the Senate Committee contact person,[9] who will 'communicate with students with disabilities' and who 'will make arrangements with the appropriate administrative office,' which 'might respond to their [disabled students'] special needs.' The students are expected to inform the contact person of their 'personal' accommodation needs. The university environment, for example, is not accessible, to persons who use wheelchairs. These individuals must make a request that space be organized to accommodate their wheelchairs in the *particular* classrooms, and only those classrooms, in which they will be attending classes. There are only a few classrooms which are wheelchair accessible which attests once again to the environmental 'fact' that disabled students are not expected. *An assumption guiding the functionality of this system of personal requests is that disabled students will conceive of themselves as unintended participants and request only those types of accommodation that will not radically influence the environment's intentions to conceive of them as such.* Despite this piecemeal accommodation policy, it too is not idiosyncratic. This policy represents the dominant ideology which articulates disabled students as unintended. Harry represents this ideology, indeed mirrors it by functioning as its unofficial mouthpiece, but he did not invent it on his own.

The environment reaffirms its intention by continually raising the unintended character of disability and thus is committed to the doing of 'little things,' since any 'big thing' would mean a radical change to its intention. Even though disabled people exist 'in the environment' there are few signs of full integration of disabled people *with* the environment. Rarely have I witnessed interaction that regards disabled people as an expected feature of an environment, even within environments that are being accessed by a disabled person.

Disabled people remain the unintended and unexpected minority, even though this minority may not be so minor. Anyone at anytime and anywhere may become disabled. Disability is, as René Gadacz (1994: xi) says, 'a social category whose membership is always open.' Given the age of tenured professors and staying within the language of 'probability,' professors like Harry and Helen, as well as administrators involved with the university accommodation policy, all have a good chance of joining the ranks of 'the disabled' (ibid.: 28–35).[10]

Between People and the Environment

Between culturally derived maps of disability and environmental depictions of the place of disabled people there exists people. People are not cultural maps, although they can use them, and people are not the environment, although they must always move within one. Even if we conform completely to the dominant cultural maps and environmental intentions, conformity is still one relation among many that can be developed with respect to cultural maps and the environment's organization. As I have shown, 'being pragmatic' is one such relation, and it is a very active form of conformity. Even though a pragmatic point of view has much to say about disability, it does not typically understand *itself* as a relationship between disability and the environment, helping to constitute the meaning of both. The pragmatic position holds that it is *not establishing* a relation between disability and the environment. Instead, it is only measuring, evaluating, or working within the confines of what already exists between an environment and its people. What is obvious to the pragmatist is that disabled people have trouble within environments which have no intention of including them. Intentions, for the pragmatist, belong to the environment. From a pragmatic point of view, the intention of real live disabled people to be educated and work in environments that are 'not set up for them' becomes a surprise. The pragmatist is surprised by anything or anyone who represents a gap between what the environment intends and what is being done, said, or desired. Acknowledging this gap, let alone widening it, is simply not pragmatic.

There is no doubt that a pragmatic point of view 'sees' a difference between persons who are disabled and those who are not, and even sees that the two hold different environmental requirements. The pragmatist frames these differences as a 'natural gap,' not between environments and people, but rather between that which is intended and that which is not. The gap between the intended and the unintended is to be filled with practical action or justifications for inaction. This understanding can lead ironically to both the segregation of disabled people ('That other university is all set up for them') and the beginnings of integration (the doing of 'little things'). However, until pragmatism is understood *as* a relationship between disabled persons and the environment, segregation and integration will be orientations which have equal justification.

Disability, like non-disability, is never *only* a pragmatic matter. It is always lived within an environment, and the relation between the two is always a matter of development. The relatively new, but rapidly growing, field of disability studies (see chapter 5) often turns its analytic gaze to the environment within which disabled persons move and live. For example, René Gadacz (1994: 5) says that 'disability can be viewed as a relationship between a person with a physical or mental impairment and the social and physical environment around him or her ...' This version of disability, however, does not draw out the difference between a person who is disabled and one who is not since both find themselves in the midst of a social and physical environment. The difference between disability and non-disability springs from the imputed intention of an environment. For whom is the environment intended? For whom is it constructed? It is only when the answer to these questions is 'able-bodiedness' that the difference between persons who are disabled and those who are not emerges. The relation between disability and the environment is, therefore, framed by the problem of living a life in an environment which neither intends nor expects disability.

The practical relation between a person and the social and physical environment is not only *one* way disability 'can be viewed'; it is often the *only* way. Disability often comes into view as a confrontation with a social and physical environment. Pragmatism frames relations with disability within the intended/unintended dichotomy understood as confrontation requiring remedy, but not requiring reflection on, or the transformation of, these intentions. Pragmatism as ideology, as what 'groups take to be natural and self-evident' (Spivak, 1982: 259), organizes both theoretic and practical approaches to disability.[11]

Pragmatism encourages us to read the interaction between people and their environment as if it is only a text of institutionalized intentionality. This intentionality appears remarkably clear when I observe a person in a wheelchair confronted by a flight of stairs. Regardless of the standpoint from which disability is viewed – whether from rehabilitation (e.g., Harrison and Crow, 1993), from university administration, from consumerism (e.g., Gadacz, 1994; Shapiro,1993), or from disability itself (e.g., Barnes, 1996; Corker, 1998b; Kuusisto, 1998; Oliver, 1999) – the text of the intention of the physical and social environment is inscribed, to borrow from Foucault, upon the lives of disabled persons as they move through it.

But what is inscribed is always more than what an environment intends. Even if it is accepted as fact that the environment intends to treat disabled people as unintended and unexpected, and even if disabled people are simply used to confirm these environmental intentions, disabled people are nonetheless now part of the environment. A retelling:

There she is. She and her wheelchair are at the bottom of the stairs. She is studying a map of the campus, staring up at it as it hangs there affixed between two large posts. The wheels of her chair and the stark angles of the stairs fall into juxtaposition. I notice now the handrails – pure decoration, not functional. I notice the steps – uneven, wobbly in places, slippery when wet, and requiring their users to go up before they go down and down before they go up. Nonetheless, they frame the door nicely – they are aesthetically pleasing ... until I see the woman in her wheelchair. My experience of this environment is different now – although it is not clear how.

Should I file a complaint with the equity officer? Should I remind the library of the university's accommodation policy? Should I organize a sticker campaign so that inaccessible structures are marked for all to see? Should I ask the woman what she thinks about these various ideas? Perhaps I should tell her about a university in the states that was required to shelve its books no higher than four feet. I should not, I decide, do any of these things unless I am also willing to reflect upon the complex interrelation between the environment and people. I have decided neither too little nor too much.

As soon as disabled people become a feature of public life, the gap between an environment and its people is made observable. This gap makes pragmatism stand out as one, *and only one*, possible relation that can be developed between people and their environments. Put bluntly, it is often not pragmatic for a disabled person to move, live, and work in some environments, but it is valuable. The disabled person *is* there. Disability is a part of the environment, and the reasonableness of this cannot be made sense of through pragmatism. Disability, as an observable feature of environments that do not intend to include disabled people, represents the radical possibility that other non-pragmatic readings exist between people and the environment. This possibility, too, is part of what is inscribed upon some bodies as they move through some environments.

Discursive Power

Theorizing forms of exclusion, Dorothy Smith (1993: 347) reminds us that 'texts are the primary medium (though not the substance) of power ...' The text of an environment's intentions is mediated through the interaction between the physical and social environment and the lives of disabled and non-disabled people. But this mediation, says Smith, is not the substance of power. The substance of power lies elsewhere; it lies in the discursive practices of people who have chosen to read the interaction between disabled people and the environment in a pragmatic way. *The power of pragmatism lies in its exclusion of any imaginative relation to disability other than that of practicality.*

Theorizing the relation between reading and power can assist in developing the relation between disability and the environment. Despite the fact that the discipline of cultural studies generally omits the identity category of disability, it has spent much energy theorizing the relation between reading and power. Karen Atkinson and Rob Middlehurst (1995: 113), for example, say:

> Questions regarding the manufacture and institutional legitima-
> tion of social inequality, together with how counter-power chal-
> lenges these forces, are axiomatic as prioritized concerns in the
> critical theorization of culture ... however, even here scant regard
> has been given to the fact that texts are multiply read and their
> meanings negotiated, even resisted.

Interactions between rival interpretations (e.g., institution-alized inequality and counter-power challenges) are 'axiomatic' for the critical theorization of cultural organization and the possibility of 'resistance.' It is not sufficient to only note or describe the texts of oppression and exclusion writ large on the bodies of disabled people within modern environments. What is needed is a concrete analysis of the actual ways that these texts are read by actual people who assuredly, but in unexpected ways, interpret them differently. I have tried to do exactly that in this chapter. Attending to the crossroads of rival interpretations makes present and explicit the possibility of alternative readings or, at least, readings which can attend to the values and assumptions which ground them. Perhaps, this is why Ricoeur says that it is only through addressing the conflict of rival interpretations that we can understand the meaning of anything, or why Goffman (1963: 13) claims that the interaction between the 'normals' and the 'stigmatized' is a 'primal scene' requiring inquiry.

That there are multiple ways to read the way in which the environment inscribes its intentions onto the lives of disabled people is thus highly significant. Focusing our reading on the interactional accomplishment of an environment's supposed intentionality allows for a reading that goes beyond pragmatic interests such as assessing the cost of accommodation or measuring the extent to which disabled people have been excluded. If the text of disability is understood to reveal the interpretive axes of able-bodiedness/disability and social constraint / social agency, then not only will rival interpretations come into focus but readers can also begin to ask, along with Zola (1982: 244), 'why a society has been created and perpetuated which has excluded so many of its members.'

This chapter suggests that one answer to Zola's question is that the assumption of environmental intentionality, grasped through the ideology of pragmatism, does not require us to attend to ourselves as readers of the environment. Instead, we see only that the environment gives us 'roles' as its makers, or its managers, or its unintended Other.

The confrontation between disability and an environment often seduces members of a community (non-disabled and disabled people alike) into conceiving of pragmatism as the *only* way of reading the interactions that occur between an environment and its people. This is not to say that pragmatically oriented readings of the environment, which serve to endow the environment with intentionality, are not decisive acts, for they certainly are. However, it is, after all, people who produce such intentionality and reproduce it through pragmatic justifications and practices.

The sensibility of pragmatically justified exclusion does not lie in the cost disabled people are said to represent. Moreover, the radical exclusion of the pragmatically organized environment does not only exist in an abundance of stairs, poor lighting, missing handrails, doors that can only be opened by a 'strong man,' or elevators without Braille markings. It exists, too, through the reading of disability and the environment which maintains the rational and reasonable character of exclusion itself.

This chapter has attempted to exemplify the fruitfulness of opening conflicts between rival interpretations. This is an interest shared among many people who work within the rapidly emerging field of disability studies. Proposing alternative readings of the phenomenon of disability is an ongoing aim within such studies, but such an aim is often glossed by the ubiquitous use of the qualifying phrase 'new disability studies' by researchers in the field. In the next chapter, I pursue my interest in opening the conflicts between rival interpretations surrounding disability by addressing the difference between mainstream social scientific readings of disability and those of the 'new' disability studies, which is grounded in both the humanities and the social sciences.

CHAPTER FIVE

Disability Studies: The Old and the New

'Psst, do you have notes from last class?'

       'Where's John?'

'Yah, I got notes. Are you go'n to the game?'

              'He's sick – It was too much last night.'

'Where were you last night?'

                'We're go'n to Pipers at about ten. Why don't you come?'

'I couldn't go, too much work.'

                            'Hey, I love that shirt.'

                'It sure was.'

Anyone who has ever been anywhere near a large lecture hall of undergraduate students will recognize comments such as these as part of the routine life that surrounds a professor who is beginning her lecture. My classroom is no different. These comments, and many more like them, rumble through the classroom as I begin. Professors deal with them in many ways; some glare at students who do not stop talking; some shout as a way to ask for silence. Whatever the method, professors do attempt to bring their large classes to order, and some students persist in their comments even when the classroom takes on a relative quiet. These comments, often in staged whispers, sometimes erupt here and there throughout the lecture, and professors again stare or embarrass these students into silence.

I would stare if I could get it right. Of course, this would require me to locate the student who is doing the talking, something which is nearly impossible for me to do. At such times, the classroom voices seem to come from everywhere in a nowhere kind of way. These comments distract other professors, but they confuse me. My dyslexia turns these distractions into a hubbub of undifferentiated noise. I try to locate the comments, but I cannot.

What's more, my classroom is often filled with dyslexia and other learning difficulties. The Disability Office at my university, having found out that I am dyslexic, counsels and encourages students with learning difficulties to take my classes. Now a bunch of us are confused by the noise. Some of the students cannot take notes, some cannot focus on my words, some join in, and I, of course, am still attempting to get through my lecture while losing track of class discussions when the stage whispers erupt.

I could shout, but this somehow never occurs to me until after the lecture. And, as I said, staring is out. I have a problem. Not only is my dyslexia a problem in this situation, but so are the learning difficulties of many other students. We have a problem.

This 'problem' exists everywhere in my university. The Disability Office organizes programs for disabled students, including those who are learning disabled. It assists students in writing exams, provides them with self-advocacy training, conducts courses on note-taking, and provides one-to-one counselling. But the 'problem' is more ubiquitous than this. Some professors are very suspicious of 'special' treatment, and they often speak about these 'invisible' disabilities as institutionalized 'excuses' for students to receive special treatment, such as more time to write an exam. Students speak about the 'unfair' privileges that these 'problem' students receive. My university, like many others, has applied programs, such as nursing and special education, in which learning disabilities are discussed as 'problems' to be remedied. These programs make use of research data which identify the etiology of learning disabilities as biological or psychological, and even more data are invoked to demonstrate remedies for such 'problems.' These programs typically identify the 'problem' in the individual and suggest that, without remedial action, students with learning disabilities will drop out, experience psychological trauma and social isolation, and perhaps even end up in jail (Kantowitz and Kalb, 1998; Farrington, 1993).

The Problem of Disability

There is nothing new about this. Our culture represents disability almost exclusively as an individual problem requiring remedy. Identification of learning disabilities and research regarding their etiology and appropriate treatment is always presented as offering neutral and objective facts about the 'problem.' But so too are the more lay comments: 'It's just an excuse' or 'They're getting special privileges' are also presented as objective and neutral facts about the 'problem.' All of this 'hangs together' *in* the cultural representation that disability is a 'problem' embodied in a person in need of remedial techniques and technology.

'Problem' is the definition of the situation of disability (Thomas, 1971: 276). While excluded from the making of the cultural, political, and intellectual world, disabled people are, as Paul Abberley (1998: 93) points out, often 'only relevant as problems.' Such an understanding does not arise simply because our bodies, minds, or senses give us problems; the problem is brought to people through interaction, the environment, and through the production of knowledge.

The overly deterministic sense in which our culture gives us disability *as* a problem is still not the final word on the social significance of being disabled, since other representations of it also arise within everyday life. In the university environment, I, like others, do not exactly 'fit' the typical shape and form of the *problem* of dyslexia. I do not receive the assistance that the Disability Office usually provides. Instead, I receive students who have learning difficulties. Together with these students, I give shape and form to learning disabilities in the classroom. I use my dyslexia, as well as my status as a young female professor, as a teaching aid to disrupt traditional forms of professorial authority. After all, professors are usually male and noticeably older than their students; they certainly drive cars, know left from right, and, of course, have excellent memories. Not only am I a young woman, but I, *their professor*, possess very few of these professorial abilities. Even though I cannot stare, nor do I yell at students who talk and whisper in class, I do speak about the significance of these disruptions for me and others who have learning difficulties. I show how such distractions cause confusion and thus exclude dyslexic students from learning and me from teaching. I describe how I and many others experience the hubbub, and thus I transform 'disruption' into 'unnecessary exclusion.' My classroom uses dyslexia as an occasion to address, not just what is learned, but how we learn, and what counts as learning.

Dyslexia is more than 'my problem.' Indeed, learning disabilities in general are more than a 'problem' in my classroom. In a 'learning environment,' especially mainstream mass education environments, 'learning disabilities' are an opportunity to think about learning, knowledge, and education. This representation of disability, too, can be found at my university. The only thing 'special' about education in my classroom is that I try to pay sociological attention to differences that already make up the educational environment.

A Gap

There is a gap between the dominant stance, which takes disability as a problem, and mine, which understands disability, and any of its social representations, as an opportunity to think about learning and as a tool to highlight the social construction of education and knowledge. That I notice such a gap does not mean that I have rejected mass versions of knowing and learning, nor does it mean that I have perfected techniques for the education of students who learn in different ways. Rather, I seek out gaps between how things are said to be and how they are lived because, like Murray Simpson (1996: 94–5), I follow the claim that 'pluralism is important in countering domination ...' Noticing that there are various ways to understand the social significance of disability is the first 'step' in facing how culture continues to give us a map of disability as a problem, and noticing this plurality is also testimony to the fact that things could be otherwise.

Such pluralism, interestingly enough, is rarely encouraged. For example, professionals who work with learning-disabled students are acutely aware of the general suspicion towards, and de-legitimation of, 'invisible disabilities.' If learning-disabled students are regarded as simply lazy students with a medical misnomer, those who work with such students are not much better. The directness of describing a plurality of ways of learning, as against the singular mystified way proposed by mass education, is often not considered to be a viable method to address the suspicion surrounding some forms of learning difficulties. The current solution being proposed by professionals in the United States, the United Kingdom, and Canada is that better (more precise and standardized) definitions of the *problem* of learning disabilities be developed, that self-advocacy be promoted (training students to precisely articulate the *problem* in sophisticated ways), and that professionally documented assessments of the student's *problem* be made available to those who are deemed in need of convincing (Hicks-Coolick and Kurtz, 1997). This process may or may not end up allowing students to pursue an education. Regardless of what ends up happening, what *is* happening is that this solution takes up the dominant representation of disability as a problem and enhances it, sophisticates it, and fortifies it. Disability is represented, yet again, as a problem.

Alternative Representations of the Problem of Disability

Discussing the issue of social representation, Richard Dyer (1993: 3) says that a culture's representation of its people is *not* a mirror reflection of reality in that '... reality is always more extensive and complicated than any system of representation can comprehend ...' Still, Dyer insists that there is something very real about a culture's representation of its people, especially its 'problem' people. The reality which is of concern lies in this: '... representations here and now have real consequences for real people, not just in the way they are treated ... but in terms of the way representations delimit and enable what people can be in any given society' (ibid.). The fundamental social character of representations of people lies in their ability not to 'get' reality but, instead, to 'give' one. Representations have real consequences for real people, but these consequences go beyond the people whom are being represented since there are consequences for those who make these representations as well. Thus, 'how we are seen determines in part how we are treated; how we treat others is based on how we see them; such seeing comes from representation' (Dyer, 1993: 1). The most authoritative representations of disabled people arise from medical and/or therapeutic disciplines, and the social sciences. Anyone who is to be regarded as 'in the know' about disability must show that they know that *it is a problem*, and the more details they possess of the problem thing, the better. This is the 'official textbook'of disability represented in our culture.

What Dorothy Smith (1999: 73–95) calls the 'official text producers' of a society always rely upon and enhance the ideological constructs of people and things that already circulate within a culture. These producers, who claim to have the most important word on their subject matter, have more resources, authority, and institutional support to 'put the word out' than do those who use, repeat, or are simply the subjects of, their texts. Such official definers of disability have usually come from medical jurisdictions: medical and rehabilitative practitioners, pathologists, psychologists, occupational therapists, and, most recently, genetic researchers.

But the social sciences, too, have a long history of producing textual knowledge on and about disabled people (Davis, 1961; Shur, 1979; Jones et al., 1984; Higgins, 1996). My discipline of sociology has prided itself in opening some gap between its way of producing knowledge about disability and the medical way of producing it. What counts as sociological knowledge is organized through a complex arrangement of social practices, such as theoretical and methodological training and accreditation, peer review journals, net-working, and connection to publishing houses and their editors. Sociology produces knowledge about disability within this framework and distinguishes it from the knowledge produced by medical disciplines. Even though traditional sociology often confirms disability as a medical issue, it has suggested that there is a social aspect to it as well. The gist of traditional sociological research is that the 'problem' of disability is often exacerbated by social structures, stereotyping, and processes of interaction. The body (the realm of medicine) obtrudes in the social world, making it a sociological problem. Thus, while there is a difference between medical definitions and treatments of the problem of disability and sociological ones, the fact remains that disability has a long and complex history of being regarded as a problem by both medical and social scientists.

But there is a 'new' disability studies. According to Simi Linton and others (1995: 8), disability studies argues that traditional social scientific research, and the curriculum which is developed from it, 'strengthens the control that the rehabilitation/medical industry and the special education system have over disabled people.' This traditional approach has served to keep disability research 'isolated in the applied fields' (ibid.). The rapidly growing body of 'new' research highlights the oppressive character of much of the traditional research in the area of disability. Still, according to some, there is nothing new.

The Problem of Meaning

'Disability Studies should *not* be considered as a newly emerging field': this was one of the reasons a mainstream American 'social problems' journal gave for rejecting the paper that I had submitted to it. The reviewers claimed that disability studies was at least thirty years old, citing the work of Goffman as proof. Of course, the reviewers could have gone as far back as Durkheim (1915) for an example of 'the disabled' conceived of as an object for sociological inquiry. Or, back even farther, they could have turned to the Enlightenment, during which 'the disabled' first became an interpretive category, bureaucratically tracked, counted, managed, and subsequently evocative of a peculiar fascination for thinkers of the time (Davis, 1997c: 9–28; 1995). The Industrial Revolution, wars, and medical advancements have also coincided with an ongoing concern for disability as a social problem (Jones, 1994; Liachowitz, 1988; Longmore and Umansky, 2001; Shapiro, 1993; Stone, 1984).

From the perspective of some in the social sciences there is nothing new: disability *is* a problem and it is one of the many problems sociologists have studied. I agree – there *is* nothing new about treating disability as a problem. Manifestations of the problem of disability and even institutional processes of its amelioration and control are things that sociologists have studied for many years. Nonetheless, I had assumed that it had become common knowledge that much of the social scientific research *on* disability supported the oppression of disabled people, and supported as well the ideological tyranny of the bio-medical model (Barnes and Oliver 1995; Linton, 1998; Oliver 1996, 1990; Shakespeare and Watson, 1997; Zola 1988, 1982). I assumed that the academy's participation in this oppression was obvious but did require critical understanding.

Many others who publish within the field of disability studies also claim that they are engaged in a new area of inquiry. Simi Linton and others (1995), in their discussion of disability studies' curriculum, claim that it began 'some fifteen years ago.' In his *Disability Studies Reader*, for example, Lennard Davis (1997b: 1) claims that

this reader is one of the first devoted to disability studies. But it
will not be the last. Disability studies is a field of study whose time

has come ... People with disabilities have been isolated, incarcerated, observed, written about, operated on, instructed, implanted, regulated, treated, institutionalized, and controlled to a degree probably unequal to that experienced by any other minority group. As fifteen percent of the population, people with disabilities make up the largest physical minority within the United States. One would never know this to be the case by looking at the literature on minorities and discrimination.[1]

Since 1997, there have been a number of readers and individual studies of disability, almost all of which make claims similar to those of Davis (e.g., Butler and Parr, 1999; Corker and Shakespeare, 2002; Holzer et al., 1999; Rogers and Swadener, 2001; Shakespeare, 1998; Wilson and Lewiecki-Wilson, 2001).

There are very few academic conferences in the area of disability studies. Unlike women's studies, race relations, or minority studies, disability studies is not (yet?) regarded as a hiring, research, or curriculum interest within sociology – at best there is deviance, health and illness, or aging. If disability studies has been around for over thirty years, it appears to have exercised very little influence upon the day-to-day decision-making processes of sociology departments, conference organizers, and journal editorial boards. (The same cannot be said of women's studies or race studies.) I had assumed that the exclusion, oppression, and devaluation of disabled persons had, in the last ten years or so, become obvious to most wide awake sociologists.

However, sociologists *have* studied 'the disabled,' have done so for many years, and have not made any claim of participating in a new field of inquiry. Many current mainstream deviance textbooks (Clinard and Meier, 1998; Delos, 1996; Goode, 1996; Heitzeg, 1996; Pontell, 1996; Rubington and Weinberg, 1999) include such phenomena as deafness, blindness, wheelchair use, stuttering, and physical 'deformities' as topic areas for the sociological analysis of deviance. Disability is also likely to be included as a research area in considerations of health and illness. Yet, it is rare that mainstream introductory sociology textbooks include disability as a distinct topic area, often only dedicating a page or two to 'disability rights.'

Conflicting Claims

Thus, there are two different claims: first, disability has been an object of sociological study for a very long time; second, disability has just recently become a site of critical inquiry. 'How can the conflict of rival interpretations be arbitrated?' (Ricoeur, 1974: 10). One way to arbitrate these conflicting interpretations of disability, within the academy, is to 'settle accounts.' Settling accounts means to prove one side as mostly true and the other as mostly false. It is true, for example, that the discipline of sociology, since its inception, has treated disabled persons as an object of inquiry. Perhaps, or so the argument could go, people working within the field of disability studies are unaware of this fact. Thus, the conflict could be settled if one side is proven correct and the other wrong, misguided, or ignorant.

Regardless of falsehood or truth, the question of meaning remains: what meaning can we glean from the truth claims which surround disability? What meaning can be gleaned from analysing both the constitution and deconstruction of conflicting interpretations? If we do not rely on the true/false dichotomy, and its necessary assumption that one side is mystified by its own ignorance, what other possible ways come to the fore in order to arbitrate these conflicting interpretations of disability? By sidestepping the 'settling of accounts,' the language through which disability is represented, and the resulting conflicting representations, can themselves become an object of inquiry. Instead of arbitration, we could ask, 'What meaning do these conflicting interpretations of disability point to?'

Such questioning allows us to treat the conflicting arguments as documents (Schutz, 1973: 208–34; Garfinkel, 1967: 9–34; Smith, 1990: 61ff) of the way our culture and its 'learned people' interpret, and thereby represent, disability. As Paul Ricoeur (1974: 11) says, 'Is it not once again *within language* itself that we must seek the indication that understanding is a mode of being?' Disability studies' 'mode of being,' its particular interpretation of disability and how it ought to be studied, can come to light through an examination of the field's claim of newness in relation to mainstream sociological discourse on disability. In this way, it becomes possible to think about the 'actual' (Smith, 1999: 6) language used to articulate disability as a field of inquiry. Focusing on the academic language surrounding disability allows us to develop an understanding of how disability has been made an object for research. Such a focus requires that I regard my preliminary assumptions (Arendt, 1994: 310), and how they are rejected by others, as food for thought and not simply as an occasion to argue about truth or falsehood.

Disability: Nothing's New

Concerning the position of those who reject the notion of a new disability studies, I turn now to Goffman's work. Within more traditional sociological examinations of disability, Goffman's work is cited, used, critiqued, revisited, and revised extensively (G. Frank, 1988; Herman and Miall, 1990; Jones et al., 1984; Manning, 1992; Marks, 1999; Nijhof, 1998; Norwich, 1997; Shilling, 1997; Susman, 1994). Following a brief explication of his conceptualization of disability, I will analyse a sociology deviance text on disability that is typical of the kind of sociological research that has flowed from Goffman's insights. I am concerned here with drawing out the concrete ways that disability has been conceived, worked on, and represented within social scientific research.

Goffman's *Stigma* (1963: 4) makes disability a sociological topic in that he speaks of societal reactions to 'abominations of the body.' In this work, he speaks of stigma as a 'special kind of relationship between attribute and stereotype' (ibid.). 'Stigma' is a social phenomenon for Goffman in that the meaning of a mark of difference (attribute) is generated *between* people. The mark *becomes* a stigma through interaction, but marks of difference are not treated by Goffman as *ipso facto* leading to stigma. Depending on the context and its interactants, a mark of difference is regarded by others as a stigma, which eventually can lead to the social construction of stigmatized people.

A stigmatized person is a blemished, not quite human person. 'By definition, of course, we believe the person with a stigma is not quite human' (5). A stigma is used by others to define a blemished person as different from other humans, thus making the blemished person not quite human. Stigma itself comes in three basic types or forms: (1) abominations of the body or 'various physical deformities'; (2) blemishes of character or 'weak will, domineering or unnatural' beliefs, values, and attitudes; and (3) tribal stigma or 'race, nation and religion' (4). Thus many different aspects of human practices and appearances fit under the umbrella concept of 'stigma.' This means that many different humans are regarded by others as not quite human. For example, stigma can be attached to visible and non-visible disabilities, physical abnormalities, unusual body shape or marks, interactional quirks, mental illness, body shape or marks, interactional quirks, mental illness, and, depending on the context, aspects of gender, sexuality, race, and class.

Regardless of such a multitude of specific differences, Goffman says that any stigmatized person

> ... possesses a trait that can obtrude itself upon attention and turn those of us whom he meets away from him, breaking the claim that his other attributes have on us. He possesses a stigma, an undesired differentness from what we had anticipated. We and those who do not depart negatively from particular expectations at issue I shall call the *normals*. (5; italics in the original)

Potentially stigmatized people interact with others who can potentially stigmatize them. The others who possess the potential to stigmatize people are referred to as the 'normals.' Normals are those who have many different attributes, but who do not, in the interactional situation in question, have an attribute of difference. Normals are those who, at least in the face of some individuals and within some interactional situations, do not represent 'undesired differentness.' Thus, the many different attributes that make up the appearance and the behaviour of any normal person are regarded as desired differences. Normals, at the same time, do not possess an obtrusive difference from humanity – thus they are normal. Moreover, it is normal for normals to notice those who are endowed with undesired differences.

In Goffman's delineation of the social construction of stigma, 'normalcy' is the standpoint which does not obtrude but, rather, *allows* for the recognition of who or what is stigmatized. Normalcy is the unmarked site from which people view the stigma of disability. Goffman anticipates that both reader and researcher are 'normals.' Normals are a 'we' that includes Goffman, his imagined readers, and all others who do not depart negatively from normalcy.

Normals never depart from their sense of being connected to normalcy. *They* do not depart, according to Goffman, because they do not possess the condition of bearing a mark of difference. The normals do not possess a stigmatized or stigmatizing attribute which will obtrude upon others and force them into an interactional relation with an undesired differentness. Insofar as Goffman conceives of some human attributes as conditions of differentness and conceives of the stereotypes which surround such attributes as a social phenomenon produced through interaction, he can regard encounters between normals and stigmatized as 'one of the primal scenes of sociology' (13).

'Primal scene' is a term that Goffman has borrowed from Freud (1973 [1917]), which refers to formative traumatic encounters, such as a child witnessing his or her parents having sex. When we encounter such traumas, according to Freud, we come to recognize our difference from others (I am not dad), and we make something of that difference (I am inadequate). Such scenes give us an initial or primal sense of self. Just as Freud aimed to return his patients to such primal scenes in order to unwrap the mystery of their psychological problems, Goffman suggests that sociologists need to return to the primal scene of interactions between the normals and the stigmatized in order to unwrap the mystery of the genesis of social identity and difference.

Interactions with disabled others are, for Goffman, one such primal scene. Through his theory of the processes of stigmatization, Goffman unwraps the disturbing character of those disabled persons who are found in the midst of the normals. At the same time, interactions with people whose bodies are an abomination to the normals' sense of the normal body serve Goffman as a way to highlight the concrete interactional processes of stigmatization. Thus, in both theory and content, Goffman studies disability. 'Abominations of the body' are, after all, one of Goffman's key types of stigma, and a major source of data throughout his work. It is easy to understand that disability certainly can be conceived of as an interaction between attribute and stereotype, resulting in a discredited, discreditable, failed, or not quite human person. Disability can be regarded as a powerful and obtrusive trait, a master status, marking all of the other attributes a person possesses. All of this helps to explicate the *problem* of disability.

Goffman's research consequently represents disability as both a 'thing,' a problematic attribute, and also as an 'occasion.' Disabled people occasion a trauma of recognition which obtrudes upon a normal's sense of normalcy as an expected feature of daily life. Thus, disability is highlighted in Goffman's work as an occasion that has led to a consolidation of the 'we-the-normals' experience, as well as to the possibility of unpacking the normal/disabled interactional scene.

Disability Knowledge

Today, many stigmatized types of persons have secured their status as 'human' in law. Disability was, for example, categorically included in the Canadian Charter of Rights and Freedoms in 1985, and in 1981 'handicap' was excluded as a valid ground of discrimination in the Human Rights Code of Canada (the Code itself was introduced in 1962) (Jones, 1994: 91–2). In 1992 the Americans with Disabilities Act (ADA), signed into law in 1990, took effect and began to offer legal protections against discrimination, just as minorities and women had secured them with the 1964 Civil Rights Act (Shapiro, 1993: 105–41).

While legally 'persons,' disabled people are still treated as deviating from normal representations of normal people, and disabled persons have thus been studied as such. This is how disability comes to represent the social problem of deviance. The primal scene, which includes interactions with disabled *others*, has served as a source of data for the study of the social construction of deviance, especially what some sociologists call 'involuntary deviance' (Sagarin, 1975: 210–13). What knowledge have sociologists typically gleaned from this primal scene?

In order to consider this question, I turn to an exemplary textual representation of knowledge about disability that flows from a traditional way of conceptualizing disability within the social sciences. The text is from the tenth edition of Marshall Clinard and Robert Meier's *Sociology of Deviant Behavior* (1998). I chose this text for the following reasons: it is published by a major mainstream publishing company (Harcourt Brace College Publishers); it has been deemed to be reprintable at least nine times; it cites and makes use of a vast quantity of mainstream sociological work on disability published from 1960 to 1995; and the website advertisement for this text claims that its chapter on disability is 'new and updated.' (However, this text is not an anomaly.) Written initially in 1957, and revised and updated numerous times, here is what this deviance textbook has to say about disabled persons in its 1998 edition:

> The central difference between a physical disability and another form of deviance is its identity as a condition rather than a behaviour; a disabled person exerts no control over this condition ... Society considers both visible disabilities, like those caused by physical disfigurements, and less evident ones, like mental retardation, as deviance because they depart from normative conceptions of 'normal' conditions, and affected people experience sanctioning processes that lead to social stigmas. (482)

Disability is treated as a 'condition' interpreted as a given. Disability is the condition of having a body that is a problem. Thus, disability is stripped of any social location or social significance. It simply is. As 'objectively given' (Goode, 1996), it becomes the material made use of in 'sanctioning processes' leading to the eventual production of social stigmas. It would appear that the primal scene is truly a traumatic one (Freud, 1973 [1917]: 308) for the normals: in the last thirty-odd years, some normal sociologists have lost any sense of a physical disability as a 'stigma*tized* attribute.'

In the face of the asocial condition of disability taken as a given, 'society considers' ... The first thing society considers is that it has nothing to do with noticing disability-as-a-condition and is unrelated to making *it* meaningful as such. The next thing society considers is that disabled persons are just like able-bodied persons in the (mystified) sense that both 'exert no control over this condition.' Beyond the common and shared conception of disability as a problem condition, other similarities between non-disabled and disabled people disintegrate or disappear in the primal scene of interactional engagement with disabled persons.

Following the lead of society's consideration of disabled persons, the work of sociologists begins. Society considers disabled persons as deviant, and sociologists study disability as 'deviance because they [disabled persons] depart from normative conceptions of "normal" conditions.' The conditions that Clinard and Meier's text highlights include blindness (487–9), mental retardation (489–90), physical handicaps, referred to throughout as 'crippled people' (490–2), and obesity and eating disorders (492–500). With these abnormal senses, minds, and bodies, sociologists can thus study normal reactions to deviant conditions taken as a given. For example:

People have long recognized the blind as one of the most conspicuous groups of disabled people in society. Because the eyes
communicate much human expression, some feel extremely disturbed when they confront blind people. A blind person's gaze
does not transmit the same psychological or emotional cues as that
of a sighted person. Facial expressions provide less information to
others. Various behavioural mannerisms and other visible clues
increase the social conspicuousness of the blind, including odd
postures, rocking of the head or tilting it at odd angles, and touching objects in a groping manner, as well as distinctive paraphernalia, such as thick glasses, white canes, and guide dogs. (488)

Along with its sheer offensiveness to blind people, the
phrase 'Because the eyes communicate much ...' communi-
cates the understanding that sight, too, is seen, by normals,
as a condition interpreted as a given. However, eyesight is
not a problem condition. Those with the condition of eyesight are disturbed when they see blindness 'because' they
see that the other does not. Sighted others observe the blind
person's gaze and find lack, difference, anomaly, and conspicuous oddness. Eyesight is the condition of normalcy –
the expected, communicative, yet non-obtrusive fact of normal life. Indeed, the 'condition' of eyesight is only brought
to consciousness in the face of the 'conspicuousness of the
blind,' that is, the odd postures, rocking, tilting, angling,
touching, groping, and stigmatized paraphernalia which
signify blindness.

Despite the fact that the face of blindness has communicated the obtrusive, conspicuous, disturbing condition of
blindness, *and* has also brought the normalcy of sight to
mind, the face of blindness is still interpreted as one which
'provides less information to others.' The lesser kind of
information blind persons provide seems to be that 'the
blind' are a representation of deviance *par excellence*. What

appears as both primary and as a greater kind of information is the face of normalcy.

It is difficult, however, to come face to face with normalcy. The text encodes (Smith, 1990: 83ff) normalcy as the expected but taken-for-granted ground for the 'we-the-normals' experience, an experience, moreover, that does not usually obtrude upon one's consciousness. Instead, an unexamined position of normalcy is the unmarked viewpoint from which deviance is observed. Normalcy is typically only indirectly available to human experience as an unobtrusive background expectation. Unless we fear stigmatization, we do not usually attend to the fact of 'being normal.' Yet, the odd postures, rocking, tilting, angling, touching, groping, and stigmatized paraphernalia of disability function to bring normalcy to consciousness. This information, however, is evaluated as 'lesser.'

That this kind of information is 'lesser' is ascertained quickly and before Clinard and Meier's text displays any kind of awareness of its use of blindness to reconstitute the hegemonic normalcy of sight and able-bodiedness. Understood as lesser to the extent that blind persons lack sight, the blind person implicitly functions in the text as a kind of tribute to the greatness of normalcy. Blindness is used to make a spectacle of that which is normally the unseen taken-for-granted 'condition'of sight and able-bodiedness.

It appears as if the sociological study of disability is, as with medicine, the study of problem conditions: those who possess a body in normal working condition notice those who do not possess such a body, and what 'naturally' obtrudes is disabled persons' deviation from the normative order of normalcy. Medicine studies pathology, while sociologists study deviance, and both begin with a similar conception of the disabled body – the condition of having, and thus being, a problem.

A consequence of all this is that normal sociologists generate sociological knowledge as to why it is normal, but perhaps not necessary, to feel 'extremely disturbed' in the face of disabled persons. Note the detailed focus on the features which are assumed to deviate from the normal features of non-disability. This deviant detail 'obtrudes,' that is, is focused on, to such an extent that any interaction between attribute and stereotype is made almost invisible. Perhaps the primal scene would be better understood as the interaction between culture's dominant and unquestioned representations of difference as these interact with normal's perception and treatment of difference. But this would transform the study of disability from the study of the generation of the deviant self into the study of the genesis of the conforming 'normal' self. I turn now to a discussion of the consequences of the traditional social scientific production of knowledge about disability.

Real Consequences for Real People

This disability-knowledge, along with recounting the details of the disturbing character of blindness or disability in general, teaches much to the 'normals.' (I use 'normal' here to refer to readers of Clinard and Meier's text who accept, or conform to, the text's positioning of them as such.) In this case, it teaches much to normal teachers and normal students in the sociology of deviance. It teaches normals to attend to the primal scene *as if* the discomfort they hold in the face of disability can be attributed to disabled persons alone. It teaches normals to act *as if* this uneasiness is simply one more condition that comes from disability itself and is somehow unrelated to interpretation and interaction. It also teaches teachers and students that it is normal to act *as if* no one in their classroom, and no reader of this 1998 deviance textbook, belongs to the identity category of disability. In general, the traditional sociological approach to disability teaches normals many ways to confound the relations between normalcy and deviance, non-disability and disability, and unexamined common-sense conceptions and knowledge. The mainstream approach reproduces the illusion that disability is far removed from normal life, and it does so, in part, by communicating the improbable belief that disability is *not* a real possibility for everyone. The text makes disability 'far out,' in every sense of that term.

Disability, as the type of deviance which can be taken as a given and about which we can do nothing ('no control'), allows sociologists to study the exact way the appearance of deviance obtrudes. Thus, while 'some people live with visible physical handicaps ...,' Clinard and Meier (1998: 490, 491) conclude that 'contemporary attitudes still tend to regard people with visible physical handicaps as being apart from other human beings; many people today look on them with pity or avoid them altogether.' Given that disability is now formulated as a type of person, steeped in the condition of lack, that no one, including the disabled person, would want to be, sociology proceeds to study how the disabled self and others 'manage' this obtrusive, worthless, unexpected, unintended deviation from normalcy. The text turns to an explication of such various forms of management as rehabilitation and role socialization (500–6), passing (508), normalizing and coping (509), dissociation or avoidance, and denial and retreat (510). (There exists a massive body of literature concerning these topic areas which is cited in most sociology of deviance textbooks.)

Such a textual rendering of disability constructs disabled persons, as unexpected, and unintended[2] persons, and it

constructs normal persons as, indeed, normal to understand *them* (disabled persons) as such. As unintended,
unexpected, conditional beings, this sociological text (discourse) also constructs disability as something a disabled
person can do nothing about or exert control over. Of course,
such an understanding of disability flies in the face of the
growing disability movement and consequent legislative
changes in, for example, the United States, the United Kingdom, and Canada. Nonetheless, with this conception of
disability in hand, sociologists may learn many details about
how people become disabled, are isolated or institutionalized, how blind people are trained to make eye contact and
deaf people restricted from using sign language, how disabled people are shocked, watched, beat up, operated on,
regularized, medicated, put into therapy, locked up, controlled, helped, measured, raped, not employed, counted,
evaluated, documented, and ... studied by sociologists. Insofar as disabled people are understood as unintended,
unexpected persons conditioned by their lack of normalcy,
in regards to which they exert no control, much of what is
done to disabled persons, including sociological research,
seems rational and sensible. This way of studying disability has generated a body of knowledge that tacitly functions as a form of maintenance for the status quo while
providing exotic details on disabled people's lives.

While this may strike some of us as a social scientific
version of the 'freak show' (Thomson, 1997a, 1996) there is
no indication of such a concern: Clinard and Meier do not
provide an argument for their version of disability and do
not introduce any alternative versions. Their text obliter-
ates all signs of interpretation, *as if* interpretation is not part
of the condition of disability, as if disabled people are not
surrounded by conflicting interpretations of their identity
(Michalko and Titchkosky, 2001). Not only does this way of

conceptualizing disability occlude the possibility of any alternative sociological views regarding it, it also denies disability a politics. Thus,

> unlike homosexuals and other identified groups, however, they
> have not yet established common a [sic] sociological identity ... As
> a result, they have not successfully pressed for political power to
> remedy common concerns and problems. (Clinard and Meier, 1998:
> 482)

(Recall that the ADA was passed in 1990.) Curiously, the asocial and apolitical character of disability that this text relies upon in order to produce its knowledge about disability is not attributed to the authors of the text nor to sociological research. Instead, it is *they*, disabled persons alone, who are held to be responsible for *their* asocial and apolitical position in society.[3]

From the standpoint of conformity with the dominant point of view on disability as simply an undesired condition of lack and inability, sociologists working in the area of disability need not consider alterity (Titchkosky, 1998). For example, crime and most other topic areas in Clinard and Meier's introductory-level deviance textbook are presented in relation to competing sociological theories and debates regarding the deviant phenomena's social significance. Disability, however, is not. Disability simply is ... and what disability *is* is an indirect spectacle of the power of normalcy. Like the normals who are full of pity and avoidance, sociology, too, often avoids disability as a phenomenon in its own right (Barnes, 1998). Such a hegemonic presentation of disability is a sign of the kind of tyranny that surrounds disability as a sociological topic. There *is*, sadly, nothing new about this. Nor is there anything new about interpreting tyranny as humanistic social scientific knowledge.[4]

The *prevalence* of the sociological representation of disability as a mere spectacle in service of normalcy, stripped of any understanding of its social production, is certainly open to debate. What is not open to debate is that this is one way that academics produce 'knowledge' about 'the disabled.' It is also beyond question that since the category 'the disabled' entered Western culture there have been researchers and theorists who have resisted conformity to the dominant ideologies of their day, and, of course, others who have not. There are many empirical questions which could be raised at this point. Just exactly how dominant is this dominant ideology? Who has succumbed and who has not? How many researchers are searching for an alternative representation of disability, and how many are stuck in a freak-show mentality? What version of disability are funding agencies, publishing institutions, or university hiring committees supporting, and who is getting funded, published, and hired, and who is not? The asking and, especially, the answering of any of these questions would require that we possess some sense of the alternative representations of disability currently being proposed and employed. However, such alternatives are typically excluded by the sociological research on disability. I turn now to alternative conceptions of disability represented by those researchers who claim that there is a 'new' approach to the study of disability.

Disability: What's New?

Those who claim to be involved in the 'new' disability studies do not do so by enumerating those against whom they fight. Instead, like many other pronouncements of newness in our culture, disability studies articulates itself as qualitatively different from that which came before. For example, Simi Linton (1998: 1) begins her work by claiming,

> It was at one time seamless. There were no disjunctures between
> the dominant cultural narrative of disability and the academic
> narrative. But in the past 20 years ... [e]nter disability studies: a
> location and a means to think critically about disability, a juncture
> that can serve both academic discourse and social change ...

No one is named. Whatever is new about disability studies
is not expressed as reacting to, or deriving from, a particular person, a founding mother or father. Yet, the nature of
the mainstream approach to the study of disability is
characterized: it provided a seamless narrative that fitted
into, and reflected, taken-for-granted cultural assumptions
of disability. Linton's pronouncement of newness refers
to some kind of recent disjunction, or gap, between the
way disability is conceived academically as opposed to
commonsensically.

Still, her pronouncement is not an argument regarding
the number of years disability studies has been in existence, for Linton (1998: 3) goes on to say:

> Despite the steady growth of scholarship and courses, particularly
> in the past five years, the field of disability studies is even more
> marginal in the academic culture than disabled people are in the
> civic culture. The enormous energy society expends keeping peo-
> ple with disabilities sequestered and in subordinate positions is
> matched by the academy's effort to justify that isolation and
> oppression.

Linton passes from twenty years to five without much hesi-
tation. Whatever is deemed 'new' about disability studies,
it is not attached to a concrete historical moment of birth,
nor is it the outcome of a single transformative moment in
time.[5] Instead, 'new' appears to mark a movement, a move-

ment from a seamless unified concept of disability to disjunctive, multiple conceptions of disability. This movement is spoken of in spacial terms as well as temporal ones. The central conception of disabled people as justifiably positioned on the margins, oppressed and sequestered, gives rise to a seamless relation between everyday conceptions of disabled people and academic ones. The claim to newness is a reference to an alternative way to move within the topic of disability. Thus disability is described both as a 'location,' albeit marginal, and as a 'means' to critically analyse the mainstream academic and cultural narratives that already surround disabled people. In Simi Linton's (1998: 4) words, 'now it behooves us to demonstrate how knowledge about disability is socially produced to uphold existing practices.'

At 'one time' there was a dominant way to work on disability that was shared by sociologists, psychologists, medical practitioners, and rehabilitators. As Clinard and Meier's deviance textbook demonstrates, this time has not left us – it is present, prevalent, and powerful. For example, Mike Oliver (1990: x–xi) says,

> As a disabled sociologist, my own experience of marginalization has been more from the sociological community than from society at large. A sociologist having either a personal or a professional interest in disability will not find disability occupies a central or even a marginal place on the sociological agenda. And even where it does appear, sociology has done little except reproduce the medical approach to this issue. In recent years medical sociology has grown faster than most other areas, but even within this sub-division, medical sociologists have been unable to distinguish between illness and disability and have proceeded as if they are the same thing.

Disability is still viewed as an unexpected, undesired, asocial, apolitical, bodily condition. Oliver, too, articulates

᠁ academy's current role in seamlessly stitching together disabled people's oppression and the knowledge which justifies this state of affairs. Thus the gloss *new* does not refer to a 'paradigm shift' (Kuhn, 1962). 'New' is not a metaphor for referring to some kind of progress of, or evolution within, the production of disability knowledge.

Thus far we should possess the sense that whatever the claim to newness means, it is not an announcement of an individual's crowning achievement, or a coded reference to a discipline's birthdate; nor is it symbolic of a paradigmatic shift within the academy as a whole. Still, the claim to newness is articulated poignantly and often. For example:

> *Disability studies* is a relatively recent rubric that seeks to group research that focuses upon the historical, political, social and professional meanings ascribed to disability and disabled populations ... Disability studies takes the medicalized model of disability as its primary object of critique. (Mitchell and Snyder, 1997: 24n2; italics in the original)

And:

> Historically, disability has been the province of numerous professional and academic disciplines that concentrate upon the management, repair, and maintenance of physical and cognitive incapacity ... We rarely consider that the continual circulation of professionally sponsored stories about disabled people's limitations, dependencies, and abnormalities, proves necessary to the continuing existence of these professional fields of study. (Ibid.: 1)

What is articulated as recent is a rubric of critique. Part of that which the new disability studies has to offer is a critique of professionally generated knowledge about disability. It is a critique aimed at those forces and traditions which have functioned as the primary producers of the ascription of meaning to the lives of disabled people. The primary object of critique is the body of knowledge and practices which constitute disability as an asocial and apolitical condition of lack and inability, namely, the discourses which shape the meaning of disability in conformity to the medical model's version. It is a critique aimed at *normal* conceptions of disability that help to constitute and sustain normate culture (Thomson, 1997a). 'Normate' is a concept that references the idea of an unmarked category of persons that are culturally regarded as 'definitive human beings' (Thomson, 1997a: 8; see also Goffman, 1963: 128); for example: white, able-bodied, average height, white teeth, unblemished, athletic, married with one or two children, employed, heterosexual, male, etc., wielding authority and power, and generally expected by the normal orders of interaction, the physical environment, and the structures of knowledge. Normate is also made use of to bracket the taken-for-granted status of normalcy and to highlight normalcy as an ideological construct. *Insofar as normalcy is more of an ideological code than actual embodied beings*, 'normate culture' is a way to refer to how this ideology works to exclude, oppress, and remove definitional power from so many different types of people. The relatively recent rubric of disability studies understands disability as the location and the space to engage in a critique of normate culture.[6]

The qualitative movement to which the term 'new' implicitly refers, announces the fact that the kind of knowledge generated concerning disability has much to do with our conception of it. In so doing, the importance of perspective is asserted. Still, referring to disability studies as new does not appear to be a code word for the glorification of perspectivism or relativism. Rather, the conflict between the mainstream perspective and that of the new disability studies is treated as really Real, especially in regards to the shaping of disabled people's lives and the knowledge formed from this shaping. One would be hard-pressed to find a disability studies text that does not begin from the assumption that there are conflicting interpretations surrounding disability and that these conflicts are of essential importance.

What is new is that disability studies focuses on these conflicting interpretations and, in so doing, attests to the understanding that disability can be conceptualized and researched in at least two ways. That there are at least two ways to conceive of disability *performs* the understanding that disability is a social and not a natural category of persons. Disability studies exemplifies what Peter Berger (1963: 23) calls the first wisdom of sociology, namely, things could be otherwise. Consider, for example, how alternative and multiple conceptions of disability are being performed and brought to consciousness in the following:

> So, this reader appears at the moment that disability, always an actively repressed *memento mori* for the fate of the normal body, gains new, nonmedicalized, and positive legitimacy both as an academic discipline and as an area of political struggle. As with any new discourse, disability studies must claim space in a contested area, trace its continuities and discontinuities, argue for its existence, and justify its assertions. (Davis, 1997b: 1)

Lennard Davis asserts that the denial of the political and social constitution of disability is, nonetheless, a political and social act. Conceiving disability as simply a deviation from the natural and normal body is still a social construction. In other words, disability studies' ongoing commitment to represent a plethora of alternative and conflicting interpretations of disability is not an act of relativism. Instead, such multiplicity derives from an insistence that disability must now be seen as a sociopolitical phenomenon and not as a strictly physical or mental one. This commitment to the social character of disability leads Davis to show how disability is regarded by some as not normal; how disability is the normal fate for the normal body; how disability is conceived of as a medical phenomenon; how disability's social significance is repressed when regarded as simply bodily impairment; how disability is not regarded as a sociopolitical phenomenon; and how those engaged in disability studies must engage in the social and political work of arguing and justifying their engagement in a legitimate area of inquiry. Through these contrasting interpretations of disability, Davis asserts disability *as* a location and a means of social research and political action. Thus, disability is conceived of as a confrontation with society's ways of making up the meaning of its people. These contrasting ways of speaking and gaining knowledge about disability *are* our ways of making up the meaning of people.

As does the mainstream account of disability, Davis's text shows a growing awareness of the normative order of the normal body when in the presence of disability. But, unlike the mainstream account, becoming aware does not entail spectacular justifications for treating the standpoint of normalcy as the only place from which disability should be observed, researched, judged, evaluated, treated, and examined sociologically. While tacitly referring to the domination of the standpoint of normalcy in previous disability research, Davis also makes explicit the alternative view that such 'normal' research is engaged in the activity of repression. He suggests that others research disability so as to re-establish the primacy of normalcy, while repressing the common (and normal) fate of all of our bodies in their movement towards and within disability.

The child of Deaf parents, but not himself hearing impaired, Davis's (2000) conception of disability enables him to use the standpoint of disability as a place from which he can unpack the ideal of normalcy and deconstruct our attachment to it. The domination of the ideal of normalcy, as displayed in the construction of the physical environment, in the organization of routine interaction, *and* in the production of knowledge, requires actions which will help us to forget our common fate. If mainstream life is to remain beholden to the ideal of normalcy as the organizing standard of life and knowledge, it will require that we forget that the disabled body is the fate of the body, that the disabled body brings to mind the death, vulnerability, and mythic quality of the body conceived of as normal.

The communication of knowledge about disability through texts written *as if* no writer and no researcher, no teacher and no student, is or will ever become disabled is now understood as one way of repressing the profound social significance of disability. All of us in all probability will spend part or all of our lives as disabled people (Zola, 1982: 246). Disability, as Gadacz (1994: ix) says, 'is a social category whose membership is always open.' But what is new is more than the debunking of the mythic quality of normalcy. The critique of the ideal of normalcy, what Rosemarie Garland Thomson (1997a: 8ff) calls 'normate' culture, serves to open the way to understanding that something is

to be gained by all people from exploring the ways that the body in its variations is metaphorized, disbursed, promulgated, commodified, cathected, and de-cathected, normalized, abnormalized, formed, and deformed ... What is more representative of the human condition than the body and its vicissitudes? (Davis, 1997b: 2)

What is new is that disability is being regarded by some researchers as a place from which to speak and learn about the human condition. For example, speaking from the standpoint of blindness, Rod Michalko (1998: 4) says, 'It [blindness] has something to tell us about the human community and about what we value as individuals and as a collective.' Disability studies refutes the sense that disability is only and merely a condition to be spoken *about*. Thus Michalko (2002, 1999, 1998) gives analytic attention to ophthalmologists, rehabilitators, guide-dog trainers, genetic counsellors, and blind people as various voices in making up our culture's story of blindness, and does so as a blind sociologist. Regarding disability as a space to speak from allows the entry of another interlocutor into the conversation of the cultural constitution of the meaning and significance of disability. Disability here gains meaning as a place to reflect upon interpretive relations to the human condition.

Disability as Conversation

Giving shape to disability as a space to speak from and as a new legitimate speaker among all the others who have attributed meaning to disability leads to formulations of disability steeped in dialogue. For example:

> Although the disabled people's movement in Britain dates from the 1970's, the development of disability studies, as an academic discipline, really took off during the 1990's ... the theme of this book establishes disability as a major and neglected area of human social experience, to which it is essential and timely to devote scholarly attention. The dialogue of the collection is between the new researchers in disability studies; the political disability community; and the traditional academic approaches to disability. (Shakespeare, 1998: 1)

Or:

> This book thus begins what I hope will be a lively conversation
> within the humanities not only about the construction of disabil-
> ity through representation but also about the attendant political
> consequences. (Thomson, 1997a: 18)

There is a new and growing sense that whatever disability
is, its meaning is born of our conversations with it. These
conversations, Thomson insists, have real consequences.

Again, this more conversational view of disability positions itself in contradistinction to mainstream sociological
approaches, which typically treat most of what disabled
people have had to say and live, not as speech and life, but
instead as *symptom*. Disabled people speak and engage in
sociopolitical action, and have done so for a very long
time. Nonetheless, normate culture has easily and readily
regarded all such speech and action as a kind of symp-
tomatology, as signs of adjustment to, coping with, management of, or acceptance of disability. Thus it is possible
to interpret any or all aspects of a disabled person's life as a
series of signs and symptoms. That is, is the disabled person avowing their deviance or disavowing it? Is the disabled person adjusting to *their* bodily condition or not? Are
they overcoming or succumbing to the condition of disability? Everything disabled people say and do, from political
action to putting on make-up, from writing books to dropping out of school, has been read as symptom. Under the
hegemonic control of the medical model, disabled persons
are deciphered but not understood. Starting from the taken-
for-granted singular sense that disability is a bodily condition of lack and inability unchosen and despised, all speech
and action can be regarded as merely symptomatic of the
disabled person's healthy or ill relation to such a 'condi-

tion.' In standard and routine ways, the lived experience of disability becomes encoded as a series of signs and symptoms in need of deciphering by the experts of normate culture.

The act of regarding speech and action as symptomatic of relations to a condition may be a useful sociological technique for uncovering interpretive relations to any given phenomenon. But it is curious how rarely the 'normal' researchers of disability have turned this technique onto their own inquiry (certainly a form of speech as well as a course of action). More curious still is how this technique, which officially claims to uncover the meaningful interpretive relations people develop to the conditions of their lives, can in fact be regarded, at least in the case of disability, as a means to constitute disabled people as speechless. By claiming that there is a new disability studies, researchers are asserting that the experience of disability, the actual speech and actions of disabled people, no longer need to be read as mere symptom:

> With word and deed we insert ourselves into the human world, and this insertion is like a second birth, in which we confirm and take upon ourselves the naked fact of our original physical appearance ... its impulse springs from the beginning which came into the world when we were born and to which we respond by beginning something new on our own initiative ... This beginning is not the same as the beginning of the world; it is not the beginning of something but of somebody ... (Arendt, 1958: 176–7)

There is a common character to each and every person's first birth, including those of us who are disabled. We are brought into the world as the consequence of other people's words and deeds, and our beginning in the world is marked first and foremost with what those others have

already begun, already thought, and have already understood. We come into the world as subjects of others' interpretations of our naked physical existence. The meaning
and significance of our race, class, gender, and bodies are
inscribed and reinscribed by others from the moment of
our birth and forever onwards. Thus, our naked physical
appearance is interpreted, treated, trained, and acted upon.
In all these ways, our physical existence is a social one.
With our first birth, the *meaning* of our physical self is given
to us.

At various points, and hopefully over and over again,
we go through a second birth. Conformity with the understandings given to our first birth can be a laborious process, especially in the case of the naked fact of our physical
existence as disabled. But conformity is not the kind of
labour which gives rise to the travail of our second birth.
Nonetheless, Arendt suggests that what comes with our
first birth needs to be *'confirmed'* so as to allow for the
second. Disability studies does just this. Disability studies
has taken it upon itself to confirm the exact character of
that which is given to disabled people at birth. Such confirmation, Arendt suggests, is like a second birth inasmuch as
it requires words and deeds that insert the self into the
world of ascribed meanings that were begun before the
birth, and will continue after the death, of particular disabled people. With word and deed, we insert ourself into
the meanings already provided to us. We insert ourself in
relation to the history of disability. In these ways, we insert
into the world the possibility of beginning something new.

It is possible to read the mainstream social scientific approaches to the study of disability as a series of procedures
oriented to aborting disabled people's possibility of a second birth. Interpreting everything disabled people say and

do as nothing but a symptom or measure of their conformity to the established meaning of disability, given by normate culture, certainly does seem to eliminate the understanding that disabled people are actors and speakers. However, I do not know if this understanding holds much truth. For even if every word and deed of the new disability studies and of disabled people is taken as mere symptom of the first birth into disability, the phenomenon of confirmation and insertion remains. There is, after all, a growing sense among disability studies researchers and disabled people that the beginning of something new has been inserted into the world, most notably a confirmation and critique of normate culture, providing for the possibility that normalcy can be inserted into the world in a new way. Perhaps, what is being aborted at this time in our history is culture's own possibility of confirming itself and inserting itself into the world in a new way.

Still, I do not want to underestimate the ever present power of normate culture to arrange the life and death of the development of selfhood, and to arrange the life and death of the concrete physical existence of disabled people, or to arrange the life and death of any knowledge which does not originate from a standpoint of normalcy. Consider, for example, the following story published in a national Canadian newspaper, a story which was formally about rare diseases and disabilities whose cures were not being researched in Canada because, the article claimed, of a lack of financial incentives. The life of Courtney Popken was featured in this news report. The details of Courtney's life were used to 'put a face' on the issue of rare disease research. (Indeed, Courtney's picture was granted more space than was the printed article itself.) Part of Courtney's story as a disabled person was told by the reporter, and the telling was oriented to the need for support and protection of researchers who research rare conditions. The story included a brief mention of a hospital's ethics committee's 1993 recommendation that Courtney's parents 'extubate' the two-month-old girl because no treatment was working, and no alternative treatment could be found. 'Extubate' refers to removing Courtney's respirator, which, in her case, would mean that her lungs would collapse and that she would die. The story tells of the parents' refusal to let Courtney die. The following statement comes on the heels of the parents' refusal: 'The Doctors offered little encouragement. "She had basically no control over her future and her bodily functions, even her breathing," Dr. Cogswell said' (Evenson, 1999: B11). The doctor's statement is not treated as news. It is not regarded as a social issue. Lacking control of one's future *because* one lacks control over bodily functions and breathing is treated as part of the facts of Courtney's case. The doctor's statement is simply preceded by a detailed description of the severity of Courtney's physical condition and, of course, the need for further research. The doctor's statement does not even provoke editorial comment. In the newspaper article, the standpoint of normalcy was asserted and yet not attended to – not confirmed. Courtney's supposed lack of a future comes before a description of her deviation from the normal condition of normal people, who are normally 'in control' of bodily functions such as breathing. The imperative that disabled persons must be regarded as persons who 'exert no control' and are 'involuntary' selves is reproduced through the taken-for-granted privileging of normate culture to determine the shape and meaning of people's futures. Courtney is now five years old, is extremely debilitated, and plays, thinks, and lives in a neighbourhood. How Courtney will reconcile herself to a world that recommended her death, conceives of her as futureless, and regards her as a self who 'exerts no control' remains to be seen.

In an ironic sense, perhaps mainstream social scientists are correct – there is little that is new in our treatment of disability – but disability studies will not be extubated. Still, disability studies comes to life within an academic environment that includes philosophers who argue for the non-human status of some disabled people, and includes as well genetic researchers, engineers, ethicists, and counsellors who (on national television) speak of the 'social obligation' to eliminate 'expensive' or 'hopeless' bodily conditions. I am referring here to the recent rebirth of eugenic discourse into popular culture. The act of confirmation also needs to be achieved within an academic environment where special educators, rehabilitators, and occupational therapists can 'reasonably' speak of the problem of disability as an individual one, wherein disabled people are regarded as destined to suffer, not society, but only themselves. The act of confirmation needs to be accomplished in relation to journalism, creative writing, and policy analysis courses that stipulate that disabled people must be referred to as 'people with disabilities' (PWDs), thus reproducing the taken-for-granted sense that disabled people are 'normal' people who just happen to be troubled by an inessential add-on condition (Titchkosky, 2001). The act of confirmation also needs to be achieved among social theorists, including cultural studies and women's studies theorists, who continue to use disability only as a metaphor to express cultural inequality and processes of marginalization *for others*, while they exclude disability as itself a social and political issue. Many contemporary ideologies and ideals inscribe themselves onto the issue of disability, and the task and the promise of disability studies is to confirm and insert these disability issues into the world in a new way.

I have not sought to establish whether or not disability studies is truly new. Instead, I uncovered what the gloss 'new' means in relation to mainstream social science's rejection of such a claim and disability studies' repetitive articulation of such a claim. This chapter uncovered the values and epistemological assumptions that lie behind the social act of conceptualizing disability studies as a 'new' field of inquiry. I did this in relation to mainstream sociology's claim that there is little new in the study of disability beyond the generation of new information about particular types of disabilities in particular social contexts and in particular times and places. I have shown that the concept of 'newly emerging' is symbolic of a critical relation to much of the social scientific research on disability, and it is symbolic of an affirmation of disability as a standpoint for inquiry into the 'normate' and its culture. Such a field of inquiry is articulated as new because, at minimum, it conceives able-bodiedness as a culture in need of critical analysis and because it conceives the standpoint of disability as an opportunity to provoke such inquiry. 'New' is also a rhetorical device to highlight the traditional/normal ways to work on disability as out of fashion, backward, crude, and underdeveloped, if not completely antiquated and obsolete.

I hope, of course, that my examination of the academic discourse surrounding the study of disability serves to draw out the importance of the field in general. By examining the discourse regarding how disability is studied, we gain a lively example of the conflicting relation between mainstream social scientific organization of knowledge and marginal narratives, as well as the consequences of both. But to remain at this programmatic level of analysis could have the unintended consequence of denying the efficacy of disability studies. Thus, I now turn to an examination of normate culture as it appears in everyday life. In the next chapter, I use my experience of passing as a blind person for ten days in Toronto with Rod (a real blind person) as a way to uncover some of the structures and functions of normate culture.

CHAPTER SIX

Revealing Culture's Eye

I am not blind. I have acted, however, as though I were. I have performed the role of blindness, not in the theatre, but on the stage of everyday life. Sociologists refer to the performing of an identity in regards to which a person has no taken-for-granted connection as 'passing.' I have passed as blind in public life so as to take some share in the experience of being seen and treated as blind. While I imitated or took on collective representations of blindness so as to make others regard me as blind, I did not simulate blindness for myself – I acted as blind while I saw.

In *Bodies That Matter*, Judith Butler (1993: 225–6) reminds us that

> the discursive condition of social recognition *precedes and conditions* the formation of the subject: recognition is not conferred on a subject, but forms that subject. Further, the impossibility of a full recognition ... implies the instability and incompleteness of subject-formation.

Blindness and sightedness are achievements, and both blind and sighted people are reliant upon each other for their formation as visioned subjects. As disability studies theorists and activists have repeatedly shown, it is societal responses to bodily or sensorial impairment, and not some objective medicalized rendering of such impairment, that can teach us about the exclusion of disabled people in everyday life. What a person sees when she or he is acting blind are collective assumptions regarding what blindness looks like. Treatments of blindness, including acting blind, are an opportunity to examine how both sightedness and blindness are formed and given social meaning. This chapter will focus on blind/sighted interactions that reveal cultural assumptions regarding the appearance of the two in everyday life. First, let me set the stage of my passing as blind by providing an account of why I did so.

Seeing Blindness

The first time I passed as blind occurred quite innocently. Some years ago, my partner, Rod, was teaching government employees about human rights and disability accommodation issues. He was teaching these people in downtown Toronto on a particularly hot and humid summer day, and, for one reason or another, his workday extended into the evening. Rod was concerned that his guide dog, Smokie, was getting too hot and too tired from the long day, and asked if I would come downtown and take Smokie back home. Recall, too, that I do not drive. Smokie and I would be using public transit to arrive back home.

Smokie is a big strong dog who likes to be in charge. I left his harness on him so that we could get back home simply by my commands and his decisions about how to move through the crowds. We had a few blocks to walk until we would encounter the stairs that go underground to the platform for the home-bound subway. Rod told me that Smokie knew the route and Smokie worked well. I had received a little training in guide-dog use, and I hoped that I too was working well.

I was having fun watching how he decided which way to

move up to crowded curbs and whip around people who moved slowly. Rod had told me about this too, and I felt privileged to have some small share in Rod's guide-dog experience. As we got within thirty or forty feet of the stairs that led down into the subway, I gave Smokie the command 'Left, find the stairs.' To my surprise, Smokie went right. 'No, left, left, find the stairs,' I said. Through the tug of his harness, Smokie said, 'No, right.' Just as I realized Smokie was trying to take me to a patch of grass on the right, a man suddenly grabbed me by the arm, said 'I'll take you to the subway,' and pulled Smokie and me to the subway stairs. Down we went, and the man did not stop tugging me until he delivered me to the ticket booth.

I did protest. I said, 'I can do it. I'm fine. He just wanted to have a pee. I can do it!' Curiously enough, I did not say, 'I can see.' In fact, I did not even look the man in the face. I had just been grabbed and pulled in public by a stranger, and yet I felt ashamed to make it apparent that I was sighted. According to the stranger's treatment of me, it was clear that I was blind, and being blind meant that I was not only in need of help, but I was also not competent enough to direct this 'help.'

At the time, I thought that I did not reclaim my sighted identity because moving between blindness and sightedness is simply not a normal move. Moreover, such an identity move would reveal that I had violated a taken-for-granted norm of public life, namely, that you are who you appear to be. Having failed to look the man in the face, I sat on the subway not knowing whether or not the man was still watching me. I kept my eyes to myself – I did not gaze around. All the way home, I thought about being sighted and yet acted blind.

In my account, the words 'No, I'm sighted' are treated as if they are a magic key that I assumed would release me from the man's bodily control. Of course, living with Rod and his obvious marker of blindness (guide dog) had brought me face to face with collective assumptions regarding the magical power of sight, its ubiquitous control, and its recognition as primary, good, right, and even natural. For example, when I accompanied Rod and Smokie in public, our encounters with sighted others would often place me in the role of all-powerful and Rod in a powerless, knowledge-less, decision-less role. While I accidentally fell into passing as blind, these obvious power dichotomies, as well as the sense that it must be more complicated, provoked me to take up the performance of blindness on other occasions.

While I am sighted, I spent ten days on a trip to Toronto acting as though I were blind. Until then, I acted blind for a few minutes here, a couple of hours there, but never before for ten straight days. Rod (a real blind person) and his guide dog Smokie and I went to Toronto to visit with friends and to do some research on technology and disability. Our trip also included one more travelling companion – Cassis, a small female black Labrador retriever that I have trained to do guide-dog work. She was in harness for this trip, and I was in dark glasses. With the help of Rod, Smokie, and Cassis, I accomplished (Garfinkel, 1967) blindness and was thus treated as I appeared. This accomplishment was motivated by our concern for Cassis; Rod and I did not want Cassis to travel to Toronto in the baggage compartment of the airplane. In harness, guiding a 'blind person,' Cassis would travel with us in the cabin. As we anticipated, this passing had the serendipitous effect of allowing us to collect ethnographic data on cultural representations of blind/sighted interaction. Blind as I 'looked,' I could 'see' such interaction.[1]

In this chapter, I will take a closer 'look' at my experience of being blind as we left the Maritimes and headed for Toronto. This will help me follow through on the analytic promise held out by disability studies developed in the previous chapter, namely that the standpoint of disability is a critical space for critical inquiry. I focus specifically on those aspects of my experience which will help me think through the growing sense that disability confounds traditional modes of thought and that the boundaries between the body and society are leaky at best (Crossley, 1995; Ettorre, 1998; Frank, 1998d, 1990; Michalko, 1998; McDermott and Varene, 1995; Thomson, 1997a). The experiences that I recount in this chapter could be characterized, in many respects, as ordinary and mundane. I hope to show that even the most ordinary experience of disability can offer the rare possibility of revealing quite extraordinary cultural values, beliefs, and assumptions.

Given this aim, it is not necessary for me to give a chronological depiction of the entire ten days; instead, most of the experiences analysed here come from the first few days of our trip. I also avoid any quantification of my experiences; I do not recount how many times Rod and I were treated in this or that fashion. Thus, neither replicability nor quantifiability is a value animating this work; rather, the animating methodology of this work derives from the understanding that lived experience can be used to reveal the meaning of the social space within which lives are given shape and form.

The Question of Master Status

Our neighbours, Jason and his wife, Maggie, drove us to the Halifax Airport Hotel. The hotel is about a two-hour drive from our small town, and Jason and Maggie both knew that I would be acting blind. Arriving at the hotel parking lot, we all got out of the car, and Rod and I put the harnesses on our respective guide dogs. Jason always walks speedily ahead of us, and the dogs know that most of the time we are with Jason they are to follow him. Today was no exception, except that we were not familiar with this environment, and Jason was out of sight a little quicker than usual. Nonetheless, we arrived in the hotel lobby and went up to the counter, where we heard the clerk telling Jason that her mother too was blind. Jason must have announced the arrival of two blind people.

Hearing the clerk speak about her blind mother made me nervous. After all, she had first-hand knowledge of blindness. My first test – could I get by the clerk and stay blind? I whispered to Rod that I would stand back for the check-in. I stood quietly in the background worrying about my sightedness for what turned out to be the first of many times over the next ten days.

As Erving Goffman (1959) says, it is a normative rule of public life to treat each other as we appear. Guide dog in hand, sunglasses in place, and in the presence of Rod and Smokie, I certainly took on a unique appearance and there are but a few identities that are readily associated with such an appearance – blind person, guide-dog trainer, and the identity I feared most, fraud. My problem was to be blind and stay that way.

On this occasion, I decided to adopt a bystander participation. This technique came in handy several times over the next ten days, and it never failed me. In silence, and at a distance from those who were around me, I felt the security of appearing blind. I did not receive any interactional cues from the check-in clerk, or from any other hotel staff, that I was not doing a good job of being blind. I was not inventing blindness – I was simply reflecting some of the norms which surround disabled people. That this distanced bystander technique worked well for me demonstrates the social expectation that it is normal for blind people not to be involved. Rod and Smokie were checking in. Jason stood beside them. Maggie had not yet caught up to us. Two men, one blind, one sighted, were doing the work, and the supposed blind woman was not involved. This shows yet another cultural expectation: it is perfectly reasonable for a blind person, especially a woman, to be a bystander (Fine and Asch, 1988; Morris, 1996; Shildrick and Price, 1996).

Soon I would receive a sign that I had indeed secured my identity as a blind person. After checking in, and along with Maggie and Jason, we proceeded down the hall to our room. The room was hot. We removed the dogs' harnesses, and they explored the new but tiny space of our hotel room. Cassis's first task in a 'new home' is to locate the bathtub – I heard her pop in and out of it. Smokie's first task is to find the water bowl, which Rod always immediately provides. Smokie was slurping. In the meantime, we humans searched out the control mechanism for the air-conditioner. Maggie began tapping a wall saying, 'Tanya, it's here. Tanya, it's here on the wall next to the door.' I could, of course, see the control mechanism. Still Maggie tapped; I was doing it, I was blind.

The appearance of blindness is powerful. And on this occasion I was in possession of many powerful signs of blindness. I still had my sunglasses on, but many people wear sunglasses. Jason told Maggie that the hotel clerk did not doubt that I was blind. Maggie had just seen Cassis guiding me. She heard commands, such as right, left, find the counter, find the door. She saw Cassis doing these things, guiding me through the hotel corridors. It was clear that I was not telling my dog where we were going, but that I was telling my dog how to move me through the environment. For that moment, sighted as I was, Maggie saw me as blind.

Sociologists have called the marking of our identity by one aspect of our appearance a 'master status.' Master status is supposed to starkly contrast with the concept of 'status,' or a person's general position within society. The concept 'status' is used to represent the sum total of the rights and responsibilities that are conventionally understood to belong to that position (Linton, 1971 [1936]). Woman, partner, friend are all positions delineated by my society – their 'sum total' is supposed to represent the 'minimal' set of rights and responsibilities that I and others can expect of me. Add blindness, and the sum total changes, as do the expectations – I am now blind-woman, blind-partner, blind-hotel-patron, blind-friend.

Status is also used to refer to the social process of giving others some minimal sense of what they can expect from those with whom they interact. A 'master' status, however, refers to the social process of constituting the minimal sense of social rights and responsibilities from one status position – not their sum total. One status is regarded as lording over all other status positions; hence, it is the master status. In the face of some differences, all the other statuses and roles do not amount to much – they are at best qualifiers of one main status. My interaction with Maggie, however, makes me take a second look at this concept of master status. Maggie, my acquaintance and neighbour, is well aware of the many different statuses that make up the sum total of my self. Yet, for a moment, she thought me to be blind and recognized and treated me as such.

Being treated as blind by someone who knows that I am sighted has happened before, not with Maggie, but with Rod. Often Rod will describe the exact location of where he put the ashtray, cup, my books. When I am in close proximity to where he has placed the objects, Rod will also say, 'Oh yeah, I am treating you as if you are blind,' or 'I forgot that you can see it.' When Maggie treated me as blind, I felt humorously startled, but when Rod does so I feel a pleasurable sense of relief, as I am glad that it is not just me who forgets or ignores the other's perspective. Of course, the pleasure quickly dissipates as I realize that the consequence of my ignoring Rod's perspective is radically different from his ignoring mine. For example, if Rod tells me where he is putting a chair, I have the advantages of both his telling and my seeing where he put the chair. But, if I ignore Rod's perspective, he has no idea where I put the chair, or even that the chair has been moved. My 'inarticulate preliminary understanding' (Arendt, 1994) is that while both Rod and Maggie are engaged in the same behaviour of forgetting that I can see, the social significance of doing so is not the same and is not adequately conceptualized through the concept of 'master status.'

Representing Boundaries

Richard Dyer (1993: i) says that 'how we are seen comes from representation.' When I am 'doing blindness' in public around my sighted friends, I am doing so by relying on cultural representations of it. Blind people are not born with dark glasses, guide dogs, or white canes, and such 'signs of blindness' are not found in all cultures. Even within Western culture, glasses, dogs, and canes do not 'automatically' represent blindness. (Rod, for example, has been treated as a guide-dog trainer: 'You people sure do a good job of training those dogs' [Michalko, 1999].) The complex matrix which represents blindness extends well beyond its physical public signs.

In Toronto, my friends know that I live with a 'real' blind person and a 'real' guide dog, and that I have trained Cassis to do guide-dog work, and they know that I sometimes pass as blind. These aspects of my life also represent blindness, but they do not do so by simply offering a concrete sign of blindness that should correspond to a physical reality. Instead, I represent blindness as a relation, not only between Rod and me, but also as a relation between blindness and sight. White canes and dog guides also represent a relation between blindness and sight – see a white cane or guide dog, *see* blindness. But this relation is often forgotten. Canes and dogs are often interpreted simply as 'mobility devices' and as belonging only to a blind person. But they share a connection to sighted people, as well. White canes and guide dogs *signify* blindness – sighted people see blindness when they see canes and dogs. Such signifiers are used to constitute the subject as blind. They bring blindness to mind for sighted people, and this generates a host of expectations and conceptions of what sighted people think of blind people. This is the relationship between blindness and sightedness – one brings the other to mind.

But it is not so easy to gloss over the complex ambiguity between sight and blindness that I represent. 'Doing' blindness in public around my sighted friends, I am bringing myself and others face to face with the always present, but often hidden, interrelation between sight and blindness. I make their interrelation obvious, and yet I do so in such a way that my behaviours cannot be fitted neatly into either sight or blindness. There is no easy way to make sense of what I am doing: am I a person taking advantage of blindness, or of sightedness, or of both, or neither? Am I being unethical or helpful, a faker or someone trying to establish a close tie to blindness? Am I fooling around, playing on others' goodwill? Am I doing research, charting others' reactions? Am I taking advantage of Rod or of others? Is he taking advantage of me? And, if either of us is seeking an advantage, what would provoke us to choose such an arduous way of doing so?

Friends who notice only my sightedness while I am acting blind overlook this ambiguity, and get on with 'normal'
(sighted) interaction. Noticing only blindness, as did
Maggie, indicates some experience of this ambiguity, which
is resolved by getting on with normal interaction with a
blind person. Either way, noticing sight or blindness does
not seem to mean that one or the other, is 'mastering' my
status. Instead, a status steeped in ambiguity often calls
forth a need for mastery, to impose a definitive clarity, to
judge that a person is one or the other, but not both. What
needs to be mastered are the 'leaky boundaries' (Ettorre,
1998) between the supposedly dichotomous status positions of sightedness and blindness. Passing as blind among
those who know better, I make these leaky boundaries
obvious, and I make the ambiguity that exists between
disability and non-disability apparent.

Perhaps it is just such ambiguity that the concept 'master
status' implicitly responds to. Referring to a person as a
blind man, blind professor, blind author, or blind friend
might not simply suggest the power of an attribute, such as
blindness, to 'master' all these other status positions. It
would be rare, indeed, to refer to someone as a sighted man
or a sighted professor, even though, like blindness, sight is
a powerful attribute. We expect people to be sighted and
organize the environment and social statuses accordingly –
we expect professors or authors to see, even to be 'visionar-
ies.' But the blind man or blind professor introduces the
ambiguity of the unexpected.

Categories such as 'professor' and 'man' are often treated
as themselves clear and certain; but add the prefix blind to
either, and the clarity melds into ambiguity. The rights and
responsibilities assumed to belong to the status 'man' or
'professor,' and those assumed in the status 'blind,' may
not fit well together, may even be contradictory. During a

public discussion at a university, a young blind student, Devon, commented that he rarely thought about being a man, but always thought about being blind, even, as he put it, 'when cooking rice.' Many (sighted) people began to titter and some laughed. People told me later that Devon just doesn't realize the power of his status as man, that 'man' remains master because this status includes the fact that men do not need to attend to it: 'he does not need to see it.' Yet no one tried to articulate this argument to Devon. I asked these people why they didn't. Some responded, 'Well, he is blind.' Another (sighted) person said, 'He is probably trying to deal with blindness.' Again, 'master status,' and the mastery granted by a status, just does not seem to capture the complexity of what is going on.

In her discussion of the cultural constitution of 'freaks' and their display, Rosemarie Garland Thomson (1996: 5) says that 'bodies whose forms appeared to transgress rigid social categories such as race, gender, and personhood were particularly good grist for the freak mill.' This undoubtedly tells us something about freak mills, but it also tells us something about the body. The form of the 'disabled body' can be read as a transgression of boundaries. Such bodies threaten 'organizational principles' through their simultaneous 'excess and absence' (ibid.). In regards to the normal categories of personhood and gender, disabled bodies seem particularly able to enact a transgression. Devon's blindness makes him think of how being a man is made absent in his life; being a man makes others think that his blindness is just excess. Men today, especially in the university environment, ought to know about the organizing principles of patriarchy. Is a blind man who says he does not often think of himself as a man simply representing an excessive sign of his position and power gained from patriarchy? Or, does blindness transgress the boundaries of patriarchy? Or does patriarchy make blind men, like women, absent from its realm of power? We can add to this complexity by noting Margrit Shildrick and Janet Price's (1996: 101) claim that 'a point we would want to make about broken bodies in general' is that they are 'engendered as feminine in terms of an implied dependency and passivity.'

Such categorical ambiguity is often quickly clarified. Person-first ideology is one way to do so. Claiming that disabled people are 'persons first' manages ambiguity by seconding disability to somewhere other than the person, or forgetting about disability altogether and dealing with the 'person' (Titchkosky, 2001). Focusing solely on a person's status as disabled, as in stereotyping and discrimination, is another way to attempt to clarify the ambiguity that disabled bodies represent. In the first case, disability is cast out from some (abstract) concept of personhood; in the second, the disabled person as a whole is cast out. In both cases, the experience of ambiguity is all but annihilated.

Sighted people who treat me as blind, yet know that I am not, can be read as dealing with the ambiguity of a self, my self, who is trying to position herself between blindness and sight. Treating me as blind is a way to represent my unconventional difference in a conventional way. There are no conventions which tell people how to relate to people who are between the major status categories that serve to constitute a readily discernible identity. People, for example, who are between male and female are typically pathologized and 'remedied' by moving them into one category or the other (Butler, 1993; Gilman, 1985; Grosz, 1996). Being *between* is a problematic of both the identity and difference of disability. However, when Rod treats me as blind, I assume that my between-ness is not being denied and is, instead, being acknowledged. Every day I do many sighted things for Rod. My sight even lords over, or directs, many of the things that we do together, such as take the dogs for a run on a big open field. I also do many sighted things *to* Rod: I do move things without telling him; I do misplace objects such as the toothpaste. Everyday something happens that puts me fully in the realm of 'the sighted' and Rod fully in the realm of 'the blind,' as if there is no relation between the two. Forgetting my sight, Rod performs an absolution and allows for the possibility of my between-ness to begin again.

Staring

Soon, Maggie and Jason were on their way, and we were left to our own devices in the hotel. Down the hall, down the tiled stairs, slippery for the dogs, with one banister on the wrong side, wrong, that is, if you have a dog-guide harness in your left hand, and out a back door: we are now on a boulevard that seems to encircle the hotel. We remove the harnesses so that Smokie and Cassis can take their relief. Rod and I like to make sure that they get some time away from working in order to be just dogs. Now, my role as a sighted guide begins.

'Wait, Rod. There is a tree. The boulevard is clearer if we go this way, ah, the way your leash hand is pointed. No, I mean ... right.' My verbal rendering of this space is already complicated by my dyslexia.

'What's Smoke doing now?' asks Rod.

'Oh, his nose is stuck on sniffing the same spot. Everything but his nose looks ready to move on. Rod, if we go ahead, the way Smokie is pointed, about twenty feet and then we turn, we turn ...' Smokie is already moving along, and I feel that I need to do the same with my directions, but I falter.

'This way?' Rod points. 'To the right?'

'Yeah,' I blurt. 'If we turn there, we should end up back at the front door.'

'Okay,' says Rod.

We turn right. We are both very focused. Rod is focused on Smokie's leash and the turns, starts, and stops that Smokie is making, and I am focused on telling Rod about various obstacles on our path, such as branches at eye level. I fail to mention that we are now walking along the road beside the hotel entrance. A car passes by us, also proceeding to the front door.

'How much further?' Rod asks.

'About a hundred feet.'

'I'm going to harness him up,' says Rod, and I do the same with Cassis.

'There isn't a sidewalk, we have to go the same way that the car just did.'

'Yuck,' says Rod, as Smokie and he step off the boulevard curb onto the road and move towards the entrance. Cassis and I, as always, follow. She will not take the lead from Smokie. I hear Rod give Smokie the command 'Right, find the door.' I do the same with Cassis.

Inside we get our bearings. Our room, I tell Rod, is to the left.

'To the right,' he corrects.

The bar, I say, is 'up ahead but the other direction.' We go there. I hear voices and music coming from the bar. These sounds assure me that Rod now knows exactly where the bar is located, and I know that any directions from me would only get in the way.

Entering the bar, I am caught between blindness and sight, dyslexia and the need to give some verbal mapping of the bar's layout in order to try to make sure that we sit where Cassis and Smokie will not get stepped on. People in the bar are staring. This makes me feel more caught: I do not want to be seen as sighted. I give Rod a general verbal layout of the bar and where I would like to sit. The people staring can only observe two blind people speaking, in hushed voices, to each other, and then they hear 'Smokie, left, good boy, forward, find a chair.' They see Smokie find a chair, and they see me struggling to get my dog past the potato chips that litter a small spot on the floor.

Rod does not see this, nor does he hear that I am trying to quietly reprimand my dog and get her on the move towards the table. I see that Rod is at the table and knows that I am no longer with him. I call out, 'We'll be right there,' and finally Cassis, discouraged from having the free snack, moves towards Rod and Smokie. I know that I am doing many sighted things, but the blank stares that seem to envelope the four of us tell me that my sighted ways are not what is being stared at.

Simply sitting in a bar, having a beer, is no longer so simple. Someone in the bar is always watching, and thus everytime I reach for the glass or want to make sure Cassis is out of the way, I must do so through touch. And while my eyes still see the people staring, and still see the glass, Cassis, or whatever else I want them to see, I must still look as if I do not see. To do this, I merely keep my gaze to myself. I am watching my sighted ways. I think that I am doing a pretty good job of keeping these sighted ways from view. I know that I have been accepted as 'blind' because I am receiving the same treatment that I have observed Rod to receive, from time to time, from sighted others – ignoring, sneaking a peek, and staring.

Never before have I gone ten whole days passing as blind. Just a few hours into it, and I am tired. 'Doing' blindness is a lot of work. I tell Rod this.

He says, 'You should see what it's like when it's real and forever. You should try it from my perspective.'

I see Rod's hand, touch it, and say, 'Plus, everyone seems to be staring.'

Rod says, 'I know.'

On each of our trips around the hotel, or out to its boulevards, over this evening and the next morning, we always meet up with the airport shuttle-bus driver. Sometimes he is carrying luggage out to the van, sometimes he is waiting, and always he greets us with a 'Hello!' in a friendly distinctive voice. I appreciate his effort to give an aural shape to his presence. As we move around the hotel, we pass by the front desk, where we checked in and would be checking out. There are always people at the desk. The desk clerks, in silence, glance at us each time we pass by, but they do not stare. They seem to be watching to see if we need any help. These quiet watchful glances quickly give way, and the clerks continue with their other work.

Between stares and the unobtrusive glances, the shuttle-bus driver's friendly hellos stand out. 'Hello' no longer seems like a greeting. Between glances and stares, his hellos are welcoming and self-confirming: he makes his presence known by acknowledging ours. In so doing, we become people to greet and more than spectacle. In the morning, it is our turn to take the shuttle bus to the airport. Rod and I are relaxed. We speak freely to the driver's interest in guide dogs and their training. Again, I am fairly quiet during this exchange, but not because I fear being 'found out.' Instead, my fraudulence grates on me in relation to someone who is trying to have some sort of openness towards blindness as a way of being *in* the world. (If this openness to blindness was typical, I could not have 'been blind' for ten days.)

Saying hello is 'no big deal,' especially when it comes

from someone working in the hospitality and tourism industry. But for Rod and me, it was a big deal. We spoke about how friendly the shuttle-bus driver seemed, and we commented on how nice it was that he kept saying hello. During our short stay in the airport hotel, we, as a blind couple, were met with three basic receptions – stares, quiet watchful glances, and friendly hellos. There is some curiosity in all of these. The hotel clerks treated Rod and me like any other hotel guests. Guests need help, some more than others. Blind guests fit the latter category, and the hotel clerks kept a helpful eye on us. But Rod and I were also very different from other guests; the blindness and dogs attested to this. We were also curiosities, and the hotel clerks also kept a curious eye on us.

Staring is quite another matter, and something that I have taken a great interest in ever since the day Rod arrived home with Smokie. As I have never been able to keep pace with Rod and Smokie, and, therefore, usually walk some distance behind them, I have seen much staring on city streets. Some people suddenly come to a complete stop and stare until Rod and Smokie fade from view. I have even seen people do this on a busy city sidewalk, in front of Rod and Smokie, blocking their path. Smokie, of course, has to move quickly around these 'staring obstacles,' and a stationary person is a rather large obstacle to abruptly move around. When I catch up to Rod, he asks, 'What was *that* that Smokie whipped me around?' Rod, of course, is wondering why Smokie would have such an abrupt reaction to an obviously large obstacle. Rod wonders whether or not Smokie is paying attention. I say to Rod, 'It was a starer who stopped dead in their tracks when they saw you.' Rod is no longer unnerved that his guide dog's 'head might not be in the game,' as he puts it, but what remains?

After I began to realize that such behaviours were going

to occur on a consistent basis, I would, if I could, call out to Rod, 'It is just someone staring.' Rod would loudly reply back to me, 'Oh, just another starer!' Sometimes, I would stop and gawk at starers. If they became aware of me staring back, I would shake my head, hoping to shame them into recognition of their own public appearance. There is no helpful look in these stares: it is exaggerated curiosity, making blindness signify difference by marking it as such through the recognition embodied in the stare.

Staring Back[2]

There are many ways to stare, and there was a particular kind of stare that was present in the hotel bar and that generally follows Rod, especially in big cities. There is a different type of stare, for example, that followed Cassis and me when she was not in harness and when we used to live in Toronto. Cassis has a love of carrying things home: groceries, beer, and things that she finds. One day she found a discarded broom in a school yard, and on another occasion, a very large bucket. Both were carried home. As a result of her guide-dog training, she is a good judge of space and manoeuvres down a city sidewalk, turning her head from side to side, so that whatever she is carrying – broom, bucket, or groceries – does not touch anyone or anything. People stare, they even stop. Some say, 'Oh, my!' or 'Look at that!' or 'What a great dog.' And, whether people say anything or not, they smile, laugh, or generally look pleased. When we were getting ready to move from Toronto, I took Cassis with me to collect boxes from the liquor store. I had a large stack and so did she. Since Cassis could not see around her stack of boxes, I kept her leash slightly taut to serve as her guide, and she followed a step behind me as we walked the four blocks back home. We received many stares. People pointed at us and laughed. A person on the sidewalk, who was ahead of us, turned, saw us, smiled, moved to the side, and stared as we passed by. Street traffic slowed. An elderly man stopped his car and asked if he could take a picture. I consented, and when he was back in his car, he followed us for a while – staring. During such times, I experience a sense of confirmation, and I always smile back while agreeing with people that 'yes, she is a great dog.'

This stands in stark contrast to how people stare at Rod and Smokie, and at us in the hotel bar, and the anger I sometimes feel in response. There are no smiles. Indeed, the face and the rest of the body are quite expressionless. There are no comments. People's bodies are still, and their shoulders droop. Some people in the bar heard the command 'Find a chair' and saw Smokie proceed to an empty table and put his nose on a chair. This is surely more remarkable than my Labrador retriever carrying brooms and buckets, yet, on some occasions, no comments of wonder or astonishment accompany Rod and Smokie, just a silent, unwavering, expressionless stare.

The taken-for-granted connection between staring and curiosity is indicated by everyday expressions such as 'It's natural to stare' or 'I couldn't help it, I just stared.' The social meaning of staring is not inherent in the fixing of one's eyes. Instead, we communicate meaning through the way we fix our eyes on others (Foster, 1988; hooks, 1995; Jenks, 1995). Staring, at minimum, indicates an interest in difference, and some social theorists claim that noting the difference between self (same) and other (difference) is not only the basis for the genesis of one's identity (Lacan, 1977: 1–7), but that it is also an 'innate' ability (Dear et al., 1997: 455–7). Natural or not, the question remains as to what *type* of curiosity generates these 'dead stares' at blindness.

When we are accused of 'staring into space,' we can reasonably reply, 'Oh, sorry, I was lost in my thoughts.' By this we mean that our thoughts have become a spectacle to ourself. We have momentarily lost a sense of the normative order of daily life. This order requires us to appear oriented to the fact that we appear to others and likewise ought to be oriented to the others' appearances in the here and now with us (Cooley's 'looking-glass self'). Staring at blind people means that, like our own thoughts, blind people can be a captivating spectacle, so much so that we have momentarily lost a sense that our own staring is also making an appearance in public life.[3] If blind people are reduced to the Ones-who-do-not-see, staring at them shares yet another similarity with staring into space – space and blind people are both 'seen' as that which *cannot stare back*. Space, statues, monsters, highway accidents, and even blind people – we stare at all of them. The stare, says Rosemarie Garland Thomson (1997a: 26), 'sculpts the disabled subject into a grotesque spectacle.' Blind people are defined as 'spectacle,' but not because they are odd or disturbing. The stare formulates blindness as the 'lack of the power of vision' – blindness assumed to be the lack of the ability to stare back is thus made into an impotent reminder of 'our' shared location in social space. We are normative and moral beings, but these spectacles cannot see this. We stare, and in our staring, we lose the sense of ourselves as oriented and moral actors. These 'unsighted spectacles' are made unable to put us back into 'moral space' (Taylor, 1989: 28), and we shamelessly stare.

The deadness of the stare at blind people indicates a hardening against the social character of their appearance in public life. After all, it is more than apparent to sighted others that a starer is staring at the blind person, and this too can become a spectacle. On a small university campus one day, I was watching a blind student and his guide dog. I knew that his dog was trained in a way different from Smokie and Cassis, and I was watching for the difference. I saw that the dog was trained to sit at both up curbs and down curbs, and I was dumbfounded. How could sitting work, I wondered, in the midst of winter salt and slush, and in an environment with so many missing curbs and sidewalks? At that moment, I realized that another student was making 'bug eyes' at me, indicating to me that I appeared as someone who is staring at a blind person and this was a spectacle that had not gone unnoticed. I was ashamed. I appeared not only hardened against a blind person but also against myself. This is the irony of the dead stare: it is itself a spectacle of the monstrous character of being deadened to both self and other as social beings.

No Problem at All

The shuttle-bus ride to the airport was short. We arrived at the airport, and the driver was quite intent on making sure that we did not need any help. We said that we were okay. 'Are you sure?' the driver questioned. While we had not been to the Halifax airport before, we knew that it was small. Rod replied, 'Sure, the dogs know the command "Find the counter,"' and the driver replied, 'No kidd'n?' with an undeniable sense of wonder. Again Rod said, 'Sure, just watch.' We entered the airport and gave the command; we knew that the dogs would find a counter, the closest counter, and so long as there was a person there we could receive directions to the appropriate counter. As luck would have it (Rod never sees this as luck), Smokie proceeded to the counter where we were to check in. I turned slightly to sneak a peek at the bus driver. He was smiling. He then turned and left.

Having checked our luggage, our freedom of movement increased. We sailed to our departure gate. Nothing got in our way. Our speed, combined with the fact that most other people in the airport were focused on looking for their own gates, meant that few stares, comments, or questions followed us. Sailing along, Smokie and Rod in the lead, knowing that we simply had to proceed to the end of this very long, wide, and stairless, corridor, I closed my eyes and tried to let Cassis guide me without my sight getting in the way of her decision-making. I simply ignored the man who seemed to be trotting along after me asking me repeatedly, 'Do you need help? You need any help? Hey, lady, you want some help?' He eventually stopped. We boarded the plane. Everything went smoothly, easily, and without mishap.

Our friends, Kate and Mark, picked us up at the Toronto airport. 'How was your flight?' they asked.

I said, 'Fine.'

Rod replied, 'Uneventful.'

The ordinariness of the trip gave us both the space to 'naturally' begin to talk to Kate and Mark about other things. Moving through the social and physical environment as or with a disabled person, and having an uneventful time of it, is rare and thus a remarkable event. Landing in Toronto, heading out into a city of diversity and the potential of anonymity, as well as into the knit of friends and our old neighbourhood, into the speed of the crowd, into all that I had missed over the last two years of living in a small town, landing into all this – I thought: 'Now the adventure begins.' I was in a swirl of stimulation. I was glad that our only task was to relieve the dogs before Kate and Mark drove us to Hart House at the University of Toronto campus. This, too, all happened quickly. In a flash, we were on a highway, speeding along, with the dogs snorting noisily at the open car windows, while we were catching up with Kate and Mark in the midst of the hum of city life.

Soon, we were outside of Hart House, where we had booked a room. We had begun planning our trip some months ago, and I had thought that Hart House would be ideal. It met all of our needs: it was an inexpensive place to stay, and we were on a tight budget; it was surrounded by green lawns and campus walkways, and the dogs would enjoy this; it was near the centre of downtown, and we could be close to our friends, as well as the people we wanted to speak to about our research regarding technology and disability. Rod had phoned to book a room at Hart House and told them of the two guide dogs that would be accompanying us. He was told, 'No problem. No problem at all.' Rod phoned back a second time, to check on some other matter, again mentioning the guide dogs, and again was told by yet another person that this was 'not a problem.'

Mark helped us carry our luggage to the door of Hart House, and he and Kate proceeded on their way. We would meet up with them later that evening. We ascended the old stone staircase of Hart House. It was a grand and seemingly endless staircase, with massive decorative handrails that ran only part-way along the stairs. Rod, with suitcase in one hand, a guide dog in the other, proceeded up these stairs. He had no reason to notice the useless banisters, but his feet noticed how unevenly each stair was spaced. Smokie edged up to yet another set of stairs and then almost stutter-stepped in place as he waited for Rod to say, 'Forward.' Cassis was attempting to keep pace with them, and thus I was being jostled along while imagining going up and down these stairs many times every day – I began to scope out alternative routes. I spotted none, but I did imagine many. Having gone up two such flights of stairs, we reached the main floor and approached the check-in counter.

I was becoming anxious about the location of the only available room that we had booked. It was on the third floor. Arriving now at the check-in counter, my only greeting was the exclamation, 'Where is the elevator?'

There is none, we were told. 'You've got to be kidding!' Rod and I simultaneously replied.

'No elevator, but student council has been trying to raise money for one.'

The words 'no problem at all' echoed in my mind. For whom, I wondered? Still, we proceeded. Up more and more stairs. I did not care if everyone could see that I could see, and I was horrified by what I saw. The next flights of stairs were the same as the first: spaciously set, very wide stone, accompanied with useless banisters, but now they also included a turn with no banister at all. Up we proceeded. The final flight was very steep and very narrow, with a wrought-iron handrail on one side and nothing but a brick wall on the other. These, too, were built of smooth stone and included a turn. At the turn, the staircase narrowed, too narrow for Rod, the suitcase, and Smokie. He had to let go of Smokie's harness. Suitcase in hand, Rod proceeded to the top with the guidance of each foot finding the stairs. Smokie stood at the top of the stairs watching Rod.

Coming up these stairs was certainly difficult, but going down was definitely going to be a problem. The banister was on the left of the stairs, and Smokie and Cassis were also on our left sides. Thus far, our adventure in Toronto consisted of negotiating stairs with a mounting sense of anxiety. Our tiny third-floor garret was suddenly filled with simultaneous exchanges of 'This is impossible' and 'I'm sorry' and, of course, the sound of Cassis hopping in and out of the bathtub. We fed and watered Smokie and Cassis while commenting to each other that 'no problem' had quickly become one. Hart House was vigorously inaccessible. It was dangerous. Anchored to this room, more than wary about moving, I found a phone book and Rod began calling hotels.

Could we find a place to stay, for ten consecutive days, starting immediately, that met our needs? Rod was very specific in his detailing of our needs to each place that he called.[4] It was two hours later before we secured a place to stay. Neither of us was disgruntled by the long search for accommodation – it was all that we had between us and our descent of the stairs.

Having secured a hotel room, and after coaxing Cassis out of the bathtub, we descended the stairs. Hesitantly and breathlessly, we worked our way down to where we had checked in. Smokie and Cassis seemed just as worried as we were. Neither of them could get traction on the first and steepest flight of stone stairs, and as the momentum of the downward slide began to quicken their speed, they would awkwardly come to a complete stop before continuing down a few more steps. The sound of their nails against the stone was a little bit like chalk screeching against a chalkboard. Reaching the bottom of the steepest flight, Cassis began to jump up on me, as she usually does when she is nervous or afraid, and we did not proceed until I calmed her. The remaining sets of stairs were not as steep, but they were no less treacherous as a result of their useless handrails. Rod reached and reached for the banister and finally gave up only to find his arm rubbing against the banister part-way through the descent, at which point the stairs turned, and the handrail that he had just found, disappeared. I watched all this happening as if in slow motion. I watched in silence, as there was nothing I could say about what I was seeing that would make our descent any easier. Finally, I uttered,

'This is the last flight.' Again the half-way turn, again no banister, and the final few steps, which we did in full view of everyone at the counter where we had checked in and where we were about to check out.

Neither helpfulness nor curiosity was written on the watchers' gaze. I would like to think that their gaze was inscribed with a hopefulness that we would be okay. I would like to think that this is why they were frozen in place as we lumbered across the smooth flat floor between the stairwell and the counter.

To the left of the counter, I spotted a sliver of a doorway. In fact, it may not have been a door but, rather, an elongated, yet screenless, window. Whatever the case, on the other side of it there was a grassy courtyard. I told Rod of the courtyard and, heedless of our luggage as well as the people at the counter, we squeezed through the narrow opening. Unhappy and stressed as we were, at least Smokie and Cassis could run around and relax before we proceeded. This done, we clambered back through the window-door.

Like the making of our reservation, our abrupt departure was 'no problem.' 'Oh, but it is a problem,' said Rod.

The clerk, who had witnessed both our ascent and descent through these hallowed halls, looked down and, while ripping up our credit-card imprint, said, 'I know.' Soon, we really were no problem for Hart House. We hoisted our luggage and began our descent of the final two flights of stairs. On solid ground, we waited for a taxi to come and deliver us to a more promising locale. Fifteen minutes later, we were outside of a hotel where an employee not only took our luggage, but showed us to the elevator, described the keypad, and took us up to our room on the eighteenth floor. Here we were greeted by a living room, a small kitchen, bedroom, balcony, and air-conditioning. From this locale, we daily trotted through the streets of Toronto, book shopping, visiting with friends, and interviewing people for our research, and during this time our sleeping accommodations did not wear us out. Disability as the experience of ambiguous difference within a social and physical environment that often finds the presence of disabled people startling, if not questionable, took on a subtler or more manageable form, once we had secured a decent place to stay.

Beyond Minority Status: The Problem of Meaning

René Gadacz (1994: 4–5) says that

> disability can mean many things. Disability is a socially created category rather than an attribute of individuals. At the same time, disability is a formal administrative category ... The essence of disability is the social and economic consequences of being different from the 'majority' ... Disability can be viewed as a relationship between a person with a physical or mental impairment and the social and physical environment around him or her.

That 'disability can mean many things' suggests that every move a disabled person makes is done in the midst of the many meanings disability holds. In a single day, Rod and I had moved from a hotel, to the Halifax airport, to an airplane, to the Toronto airport, into a friend's car, up and down the stairs of Hart House, and then to another hotel. We moved through various locales, all of which imbue disability with meanings. The 'attribute' of being blind is clearly but one part of this mixture, and this mixture of meanings makes the experience of disability quite diverse and complex.

Moving through the social, economic, administrative, and

physical environment, and doing so in the way that the 'majority' do not, is, for Gadacz, definitive of disability. However, it is more than likely that Rod and I shared much in common with the majority of people who that day also made use of the Halifax airport, rode in a car with friends, or decided to rent a room at Hart House. Moving through the wide stairless airport corridors, with both aural and visual announcements indicating the way to go, meant that the majority of wheelchair users, deaf people, or non-disabled people would have, as the saying goes, no problem at all. Similarly, getting up to one's third-floor room at Hart House would necessarily be a problem for the majority of people who attempted it that day. Hart House would be a problem, for example, for people who were not wearing running shoes, who had an inner ear infection, or a sore ankle. It would be a problem for people who smoke, who had had a few drinks, or who were overweight. It would be a problem for people who were tired from a long journey or from illness, for people carrying awkward or heavy luggage, or who were afraid of heights. Hart House would be a problem for all kinds of people. Thus, the essence of disability does not seem to lie in an experience of the environment that only a minority of people share. What, then, might Gadacz be referring to when he claims that 'the essence of disability is the social and economic consequences of being different from the "majority" ...'? Addressing this question requires that closer attention be paid to the fact that disability can mean many things and that this has consequences.

For Gadacz, disability's meaning is constituted in relation to the social and physical environment: in its physical layout, in its social and administrative categories, and in the interrelation of its participants. At an airport, for example, all the different participants, be they passengers or airport employees, come to this locale with pre-established conceptions of disability. More than a physical, mental, or sensory impairment, these conceptions of disability themselves can get in one's way of moving through the environment. Disability conceived of as spectacle, as the need for unsolicited help, or as unintended participation, can impede disabled people's movement through the environment, no matter how well endowed it is with accommodative measures (Zola, 1982). Disability is an administrative category for the airline industry, which is addressed by federal and provincial law and included in employee training (Bickenbach, 1993). By law, for example, guide dogs are allowed to accompany their handlers everywhere (but zoos). While our fellow travellers asked us, even as we boarded the plane, when the dogs would be put into baggage, such a question never arose for any airport employees. Instead, seating arrangements were rearranged so that we and the dogs would have more room in the bulkhead seats.

The plethora of interpretations of disability influences the most profound and the most prosaic of everyday activities; these interpretations influence whether or not disabled persons can get where they intend to go, sleep where or when they intend to sleep, eat, move, pee, speak, or be heard. All these interpretations are inscribed (Foucault, 1979) upon disabled bodies. So pointed, obvious, and mixed are these interpretations, at the administrative, social, economic, and physical levels, that *ambiguity* becomes the consequential experience of disability. Hence, 'no problem at all' is a serious problem. At Hart House, for example, we were, in the eyes of the law and perhaps even in the minds of the staff, 'no problem.' Yet, we were. We were imagined as no problem, but seen as a serious one. We reserved a room at Hart House, no problem at all; we arrived, big problem; we then left, no problem (?); we were the ambiguous 'no-problem-problem.'

While we shared with the majority the fact that moving through Hart House is very difficult, Rod's blindness and my imitation of it symbolized the necessity of alternatives: we embodied this necessity; we were no mere suggestion of it. The embodiment of the necessity of alternatives, also, strikes people in many different ways. Necessary alternatives, for example, could make a hotel clerk astonished, worried, or angry – either at us or even (hopefully) at the inaccessible building. Or, holding firm to the belief that disabled people are no problem and should be treated no differently from the majority, a clerk could have charged us for our time in the room at Hart House or for the phone calls that we made. Disabled people not only move among various interpretations of who they are, but they also negotiate these meanings while mediating some sense of alterity. As Rosemarie Garland Thomson (1997a: 24) says, 'disability confounds any notion of a generalizable, stable physical subject ... Disability is the unorthodox made flesh.' Disability, as embodied alternatives mixing with and mediating the plethora of alternative interpretations, brings ambiguity to life in a way that conceptions of disability such as 'exclusion from the majority' or 'deviation from the norm' cannot quite capture.

Nevertheless, physical, economic, and ideological forces impinge upon disabled people (Hogan, 1999; Oliver, 1996) and make the presence of disabled people questionable. Not only is the presence of disabled people put into question by such forces, but also disabled people, once present, are surrounded by vigorously disparate interpretations. After a few days in Toronto, we began to have a stretch of 'bad luck' hailing taxis. There were plenty of taxis around, but none would stop for us. One hot afternoon, when we were eager to get back to our air-conditioned hotel room, not only were taxi drivers passing us by, but one driver even waved at us. He waved while laughing and glancing around to see if anyone else had spotted the hilarity of waving at 'blind people.' I removed my sunglasses and began a sighted version of hailing taxis, making eye contact with the drivers. Eventually, a taxi stopped. After a bit of small talk with this driver about the heat of the day, the driver said, 'I wasn't going to pick you up.'

'Oh?' I replied and readied myself for some comment about dogs, or blind people, or incompetence, or being in a rush, or a story about the last time the driver picked up a blind person, or ...

'Yes,' said the driver, 'I knew he was blind and I knew I could trust his dog – but you, you looked right at me, I didn't know what to make of you and your dog.' Then Rod told the driver of all the problems that he was having hailing a taxi as a blind person. The driver was very angry with this: 'That is not right. That is illegal. Every taxi has a number on the back, get the number and report them ...' There was a pause, then we all laughed. 'Any way you look at it,' said the driver, 'you've got a problem.' The problem that Rod has is that there are so 'many ways' to look at disability that 'many problems' are generated. While Rod's appearance (looking blind) appears certain to all involved, all involved nonetheless make it murky and ambiguous each time he moves out into the environment. It seems clear that disability is always seen, but how it is 'looked at' is not so clear. Any way you look at it, disability can be made a problem.

The consequence of all this is that disability is an ambiguous experience for everyone involved. When Rod said to the Hart House clerk, 'Oh, but it is a problem,' and she looked down and said, 'I know' there is no doubt that she did not want to see us as a problem. She had expressed no ill will, yet there she was firmly positioned within an environment so ill conceived. For a moment, disability positioned her in a liminal position – she could not play her role as clerk, and yet she could not *not* play it. The taxi driver who did eventually pick us up, after many others passed us by, was fairly certain that he felt confident and comfortable dealing with blind customers; he also expressed perplexity and suspicion towards me as a sighted person with a guide dog by my side. Yet, upon hearing of the unequal treatment received by Rod, his blind customer, 'sight' (get the number and report them) was the only thing he could think of recommending in order to remedy the situation. Driving through the city blocks that lie between Bloor and Bathurst to Church and Dundas, the driver, too, had moved through various interpretations of the ambiguous interrelation between sightedness and blindness.

Disability is essentially a radically mixed set of interpretations striking at the level of a person's presence in an environment. This, of course, has real social and economic consequences. Our accommodation in Toronto tripled in cost. The students from Nova Scotia who were also travelling to Toronto and were going to contact us at Hart House, now could not do so. Rod and I were too worn out to meet up with Kate and Mark later that first night in Toronto, as we had planned. We had to take more taxis and subways than we had initially planned. These are some of the concrete economic and social consequences that are born of what Gadacz glosses by the phrase 'a difference from the majority.' But, is the nature of disability's 'difference' tied only to lack and exclusion: lack of economic resources, exclusion from social contact, lack of an ability to fulfil normal role expectations? Is disability's significance – its social substance – '*only* a consequence of material relations' (Darke, 1998: 223; italics in the original)?

Every person, disabled or not, confronts a complex milieu of interpretation, especially at the level of *who or what* they are – are you rich or poor, woman or man, Black or White, friendly or distanced, a pleasure to serve or a real grump? People are 'usually' and 'normally' assigned to one side or the other of these sets of dichotomous categories used to constitute identity (Scott, 1998, 1995). Indeed, being a normal person usually means allowing or enabling others to so place oneself. What disabled people represent, more so than does the 'majority,' is a vivid and complex stream of interpretation, not simply at the level of who a disabled person is, but also at the level of how a disabled person's embodied presence is organized as ambiguity incarnate.

Economic, physical, and administrative forces impinge upon all people, and thereby inclusion, exclusion, or control is enacted. But the matter is different with disabled people, or disabled people mediate or symbolize an important aspect of this process. *The difference, which truly belongs to a minority of people, is the blatant and unambiguous ambiguity that comes with the disability experience.* The presence of disability throws into question what being in or out, marginalized or mainstreamed, controlled or empowered means. Disability raises the question of being 'in-between' (Asenjo, 1988; Corker and French, 1999b: 2–6; Mitchell and Snyder, 1997; Titchkosky, 2001b, 1997). Will it ever be clear, for example, whether our abrupt departure from Hart House was a sign of its control over us or of our power over it? It certainly felt like both and neither, all at once. According to Thomson (1997a: 114), it is 'within this liminal space the disabled person must constitute something akin to identity.'

'Liminal' is a term used by anthropologists in order to describe events like initiation rituals or community rituals of, for example, birth, death, and harvest. The liminal refers to that space within individual or collective life where people, as Arendt (1955: 3–15) says, are 'no longer and not yet.' As a person moves from the identity of 'girl' to 'woman,' the community makes use of segregation, symbolism, and ceremony, and thereby provides a ritual-filled marker of the individual's time as neither. Being liminal, says Victor Turner (1985: 151–73), is a dangerous or uncertain phenomenon that communities have traditionally both marked off and transformed. In Western(ized) cultures, the tradition of medicine seems to envelope most newly disabled people; that is, it moves one back into the position of able-bodiedness through remedial or rehabilitative practices, or it confirms one's identity *as* disabled. But once disabled ... limbo. As the glosses 'minority status' and 'master status' indicate, 'disability' can disrupt and make questionable all identity positions. Into the plethora of conflicting and ambiguous cultural interpretations of disabled people, a disabled person negotiates 'something akin' to an identity.

Subjectively Problematic

The body can be explained, says Alan Radley (1995: 3), as the 'object of the actions and interests of others.' This is how René Gadacz understands the essence of disability; it is a socially constructed category built from the actions of non-disabled others. But is there not more? Is there not something about disability, as it is lived and performed in the midst of others, within exclusionary and oppressive environments, that adds to or acts upon mainstream life and 'normal' identity? Radley insists that there is: '... the body is a key expressive medium and, in its material aspect, the basis upon which we symbolize our relationship to the world of which we are a part' (ibid.: 4). The disabled body brings this expressivity to the fore. While signs of empowerment and control are not clear, Rod and I with guide dogs in hand did express alternative relationships to the world of which we are a part. What all our comings and goings mean will never be clear and certain; but we certainly *expressed and performed* such uncertainty, and we did so in many different ways.

This uncertainty was brought home to me during the return flight to Nova Scotia. Our seats were in the middle row; I sat at the outer edge, and Cassis and Smokie, very tired now, were tucked in as safely as was possible within the confines of the bulkhead seating area. Across the isle from me, an elderly woman was seated. Part-way through the flight, the woman got my attention and said, 'I am going blind, when did you go blind?'

Hoping beyond hope that none of the flight crew would hear me, and hoping also that the woman would not see that I was wearing sunglasses in the plane, I replied, 'I am not blind, I'm just training this dog.' Disappointment was writ large on the woman's face, and I quickly introduced her to Rod as a 'real blind person.' They attempted a conversation over the hum of the plane's engines and the space of the isle. I sat still, struck by an extreme sense of my fraudulence, combined with sadness at a broken connection, and disappointment in myself for ever passing as blind. In the face of the woman's question, I resolved to never pass again. Before this moment, passing signified two main sets of relations: a kind of private intimacy with Rod; and an ironic distance to my sighted culture. The woman's question made me realize that the ambiguity expressed within my passing project was loaded with more meaning and contradiction than I had attempted to see in it. The realization that passing is something more than merely catching the reflections of cultural attitudes towards blindness served to eliminate my desire to ever do it again.

Radley refers to the expressiveness of the body as the 'body-subject'; this is the body that is always more than what others make of it. The body-subject, he says, plays 'a special role in the configuration of meaning, a meaning whose significance is bound up with its ... elusory nature.' (1995: 7) This elusory nature is tied to the fact that disability embodies 'illegitimate fusion[s] of cultural categories' (Thomson, 1997a: 114). Through engagement with the stuff of culture (interpretive categories) and through the process of illegitimate fusions, disabled people constitute something akin to identity. The accessible airport allowed for confident and competent movement, yet people offered assistance. 'Competent/blind person' is then one such illegitimate fusion of cultural categories, which the offer of unnecessary help intends to set straight. Hopefully, the refusal or renegotiation of such 'help' maintains the fusion of competence and disability, a fusion that this particular offer of help sought to destroy. Hart House put terror-ific barriers between us and our movement through it. My sense of incompetence was substantial. Still, moving through Hart House in this 'incompetent' way provided a 'running commentary' to the staff of its inaccessibility, and, in this, I found some pleasure. The illegitimate fusions between terror/pleasure, mobility/immobility, and incompetency/commentary were ubiquitous. Rosemarie Garland Thomson (1997a: 44, 41, 114, 112) suggests that disability as 'violated wholeness, unbounded incompleteness, unregulated particularity, dependent subjugation, disordered intractability' symbolizes the ambiguous mixing of a not-me and me, of normal and abnormal, of uniqueness and uniformity, of known and unknown.

Disability is not only a sign of deviation from the majority, a deviation which that same majority attempts to control. To claim that this is all that disability is 'renders the body so docile, so pliable as to be nothing more than a passive mirror in which to catch the reflections of social action' (Radley, 1995: 7). The disabled body described by Gadacz, and others who focus on disability as the consequence of others' actions and material relations, represents the docility of the 'body-object.' But this focus need not obliterate the possibility of considering the expressiveness of the 'body-subject' (Crossley, 1995: 45–8). Understanding the body as object needs to be done in such a way so as to allow us to take into account what the disabled body as subject is inserting into the world in the here and now.

Still, insists Radley, it would do us little good to 'make-believe' that the body-subject is 'merely a vehicle for departing from social norms, for escaping from the strictures of moral codes.' The body-subject is, in its positive aspects, the 'grounds for configuring an alternative way of being that eludes the grasp of power' (Radley, 1995: 9) by opening up a space between all the dichotomous categories which normally organize the normal self in normal everyday life and its ordinary representations. Such an understanding of the body allows us to conceive of disability experience as infusing new significance, disturbing the picture of the everyday reality of the 'majority,' and as making a comment upon society, and it is this body that can elude the control of societal powers (ibid.: 11).

The body may certainly be treated as a sign of a deviation from the norm, or even as a sign of exclusion from the majority, but it symbolizes more. Disability is always more than stigmatized deviation (master status) and oppressive minoritization (minority status). It is more insofar as it is the embodiment of an alternative way of being steeped in the fact that the disabled body is situated *between* all the stuff a culture gives to its people. In this between-ness, disability can make us rethink the meaning of identity formed and pre-formed through unexamined assumptions regarding the stability of the self.

I turn now, in the final chapter, to this between-ness, symbolized by disability as the marginal figure of mainstream life; and I do so as a way to draw out the sense in which disability is a teacher that makes us rethink the meaning of identity formed in relation to a body that both violates and resists assumptions regarding the stability of the self.

CHAPTER SEVEN

Betwixt and Between: Disability Is No-Thing

In *Waist-High in the World: A Life among the Nondisabled* (1996), Nancy Mairs says:

> As one of my idiosyncrasies, I prefer to call myself a cripple ... 'Mobility impaired,' the euphemizers would call me, as though a surfeit of syllables could soften my reality. No such luck. I still can't sit up in bed, can't take an unaided step, can't dress myself, can't open doors ...
>
> My [name] choice may reflect a desire for accuracy more than anything else. In truth, although I am severely crippled, I am hardly disabled at all, since, thanks to technology and my relatively advantaged circumstances, I'm not prevented from engaging in meaningful activity. (12–13)

Twenty pages later, I read:

> Like many young women of my generation, the first to aspire to 'have it all,' I vastly overextended myself when I was younger, and by the time of my diagnosis [MS], I wore so many hats I could hardly hold my head up: wife, mother, teacher, graduate student, political activist, not to mention cook, housekeeper, family correspondent, redecorator, needlewoman, digger of pet graves ... Over the years, I've had to pare back this list; and relinquishing, or at least revising each role has wounded and shamed me. (34)

But, continues Mairs,

> I always write, consciously, as a body ... And it is this – my –
> crippled female body that my work struggles to redeem through
> that most figurative of human tools: language. Because language
> substitutes a no-thing for a thing whereas a body is pure thing
> through and through, this task must fail. But inevitable disap-
> pointment does not deprive labor of its authenticity.
>
> And so I use inscription to insert my embodied self into a world
> with which, over time, I have less and less in common. Part of my
> effort entails reshaping both that self and that world in order to
> reconcile the two. (60)

Disability as Contradiction?

When I first read Mairs's book, I was captivated. Yet, I felt
slapped in the face – I read her book as inscribing her lived
experience of disability with contradiction. Mairs calls herself a cripple yet claims that she is hardly disabled at all.
When I read that thanks to technology and privilege the
name 'disability' barely fits her, and read this in the context
of Mairs's having just provided a long list of what she can
no longer do, I was surprised, startled, perplexed.

I attempted to resolve this contradiction by positing an
ideological subtext: because of one ideology or another,
Mairs contradicts herself, I reasoned. Perhaps Mairs was
displaying an ideological adherence to the idea that the
body and self can be fully split in two – the body could thus
be crippled and the self 'hardly disabled at all.' Such a split,
born of Enlightenment thought, reconfigures self (mind,
reason, intellect) over and against body conceived of as
nature in need of human control.

Mairs follows her claim that she is hardly disabled at all
by saying that she is not 'putting on a brave face here, and
I'm not denying the seriousness of my situation' (ibid.: 13).

I began to realize that this was not a book about the 'strength of human spirit' – the most common and powerful ideology that surrounds disability (Robillard, 1999: 119). This ideology holds that what is newsworthy, interesting, and important about disability is to be found in its ability to serve as an occasion for the strength of the human mind to shine bright and strong. This strength is supposed to overcome, or so the story goes, the fragility of the body. It feeds into the modern conception of the individual as 'rational, autonomous, centered and stable' (Poster, 1995: 80). The euphemism 'mobility impaired' softens bodily experience, taming it down so that the mind can shine forth, but Mairs disengages herself from such a project. Mairs rejects the idea that mind is the only thing of interest in disability experience, and her raw descriptions of her life in her body attest to the fact that her book is no mere reiteration of the mind/body split. As she says, 'This is not ... a "feel good" book' (ibid.: 18); this is not a book about autonomous-independent-transcendent-mind mythically overcoming the gritty groundedness of the body.

In a few paragraphs, Mairs strips me of the ways that I typically make sense of contradictory renderings of disability. Still, I insist, this work is full of contradiction. Being 'hardly disabled,' while preferring to call herself 'crippled,' still feels like a slap in the face. I remain perplexed. 'Crippled' resonates with a sense of the past, an old-fashioned word. It is a word that the UN, the Canadian and U.S. governments, newspaper editors, and even North American sociology of deviance textbooks say should no longer be used. But 'crippled' is what this articulate, well-read, feminist activist calls herself. Crippled is what she wants her readers to face even while we must also face the notion that she is 'hardly disabled' because she is not prevented from engaging in meaningful activity.

Mairs goes on to say that she suffers the loss or revision

of her meaningful roles, as wife, mother, student, teacher. Of mothering, indeed a meaningful activity, Mairs says, 'When my children were growing up, for instance, I was often wracked by guilt that they didn't have a "normal" mother. I was convinced, in fact, that my disability was traumatizing them.' The self proclaimed 'hardly disabled cripple' now conceives of herself as the disabled person potentially crippling the lives of her children. Still another surprise, she concludes the discussion of her own mothering by exclaiming, 'Such arrogance!' Her pairing of worries about not being a 'normal mother' with 'arrogance' is unexpected and highly unusual. She does not struggle to redeem herself as 'normal.' Mairs does not even struggle to maintain a 'normal' conception of normal as necessary and good. It is, rather, her 'crippled female body' that Mairs struggles to redeem both for herself and for the world of which she is a part, and a world in relation to which she holds less and less in common. Disability seems to be everywhere in Mairs's life while being no-thing that she or her reader can know and be done with once and for all.

My 'enlightened' mind reads Mairs's account as overflowing with a surfeit of contradictions. I am struck with perplexity, and these contradictions tingle my nerves. But as Mairs begins to reflect upon her project of writing, I too am provoked to do the same with my project of reading: I have to rethink and reflect upon my reading of her. What does it mean to 'always write, consciously, as a body ...'? What does it mean to redeem the body through 'that most figurative of human tools: language'? What does it mean that in this project of writing consciously as body, Mairs is certain of the inevitable disappointment of failure, which she nonetheless calls 'authentic'? Initially, I answered all these questions with the stipulation that the meaning Mairs's work holds is *simply* contradiction. My culture has taught me, usually through 'compare and contrast' exercises aimed at developing the rational mind, to face contradiction and dissolve it by privileging one side over and against the other side of any contradictory pairing. In the light of such reasoning, a person does not write consciously as a body, because the conscious mind and the not-so-conscious body are opposites, and the mind is what matters and what writes. We have also been taught that the body is not redeemed and refigured by language because the body is simply a thing that language, at best, describes. Or, inasmuch as failure and authenticity are opposites, surely authenticity is the higher good of the two.

Yet, I could not deny that something much more powerful than dissolved contradictions stayed with me after reading Mairs. She had inscribed, in a sense, her body on my mind; this made me quiver, and the experience of reading Mairs's work has stayed with me for a very long time.

Uncommon Experience

Mairs did not provide me with a common experience of disability. In everyday life, disability is often rendered as a personal tragedy, which can only be overcome by the strength of the human spirit. This ideology emphasizes the person's triumph over the disabled body, and it usually leads to a reiteration of humanness as somehow distinct, different, and detached from disability, if not from the body in general. Disability is typically depicted as a problematic thing inserted into a person's life. Of course, everyday life also has plenty of images of disability as a personal tragedy which some people do not 'overcome.' Lately, this description of disability foregrounds the ongoing debates about whether or not such people should even be allowed to live (Hubbard, 1997; Rifkins, 1998; Russell, 1998; Singer 1995,

1993). In academic life, disability is commonly rendered as a thing susceptible to research regarding its cause and its effect on both disabled and non-disabled people (see chapter 5). Whether in the academy or in everyday life, disability is most commonly represented (mapped, as in chapters 2 and 3) as a problem-thing, causing more problems which affect both self and others, and thereby causing more problems. These *common* ways of both reading and writing disability do not seem to be Mairs's ways.

Mairs says that she writes in a world with which she has less and less in common, and I have been struck by the fact that she also writes disability in an uncommon way. Her inscription of disability does not fit neatly into any of the ways that my culture has given me to conceive of it. Perhaps, what I initially read as contradiction, what got 'under my skin' and 'got on my nerves,' was this uncommonness. After all, a sense of contradiction is dependent upon taken-for-granted beliefs regarding what 'belongs' together. Since Descartes, the mind and redemption belong together; similarly, the body, nature, and the necessity of transcendence have been conceived of as belonging together. From these beliefs, we can generate the 'rational' understanding that it is only by transcending the encumbrance of the body that the redeeming qualities of mind can shine forth and secure our stance in humanity. It is, however, uncommon that disability is presented stripped of a thing-like character; it is uncommon that disability is remade into a no-thing which must be faced, which must be rethought; and it is uncommon to question whether or not the project of seeking to overcome disability is a worthwhile one. I have read many academic accounts of disability, and it is uncommon that disability is narrated as something as raw and as redeemable as Mairs renders it.

The project of bodily redemption, however, only goes so

far, as Mairs insists that '... the truth is that regardless of structural and attitudinal modifications, I am never going to be entirely at ease in the world' (1996: 105). Mairs neither redeems nor describes herself as 'at one' with the world. No amount of personal privilege, or structural and attitudinal transformation, is going to make her 'entirely at ease' with the world. Still, she seeks a reconciliation between self and world. The world has its ways of making ideas and things, minds and bodies, belong together, and Mairs has hers. Mairs seeks to reconcile herself, and her world, to the differences that lie between the two. Mairs writes consciously as a body and tries to put into words how she is positioned between and in the midst of these differences. The world seeks to redeem her mind. Mairs seeks to redeem her body. Yet Mairs's mind and body exist in-between these redemptive projects.

To recognize that one will never be entirely at ease in the world is to begin to articulate one's self as marginal. To be marginal, through disability, is to recognize the fact that the world inscribes itself upon the body, the body inscribes itself upon the world (Frank, 1998d: 209), and the self is positioned in-between these inscriptions. Confirmation and reconciliation is one possible (albeit uncommon) relation to this situation of between-ness.

Of her marginality, Mairs has this to say:

Postmodern criticism, feminist and otherwise, makes a good deal of the concept of wall-hugging, or marginality ... regardless of the way marginality is conceived, it is never taken to mean that those on the margin occupy a physical space literally outside the field of vision of those in the center, so that the latter trip unawares and fall into the laps of those they have banished from consciousness unless these scoot safely out of the way. 'Marginality' ... is no metaphor for the power relations between one group of human

beings and another but a literal description of where I stand (figuratively speaking): over here, on the edge, out of bounds, beneath
your notice. I embody the metaphors. (1996: 59)

As of late, a good deal has been made of the marginality
that accompanies gender, race, class, and sexuality (Adam
and Allan, 1995; Ferguson et al., 1990; Gergen and Davis,
1997; hooks 1990; Rajchman, 1995). Mairs sounds perturbed
as she discusses marginality, but not only with the people
who trip unawares into her lap as she occupies a place on
the margins in her wheelchair. She also seems perturbed
with postmodern criticism, feminist and otherwise, that
has attended to and theorized marginality and yet trips
unawares past, over, on top of disability. In the academy, as
in everyday life, disability is *'beneath notice,'* and yet able-
bodied theory and non-disabled people fall into the lap of
disability. Mairs exists in-between a radical awareness of
the social significance of marginality and theorists' general
lack of awareness of disability as the embodiment of this
same marginality. This, too, makes up the world of which
Mairs is a part, and from which she is separated.

In her wheelchair, in her body, Mairs claims that she
literally embodies marginality. This marginality does not
signify that she is 'outside' of social space; after all, non-
disabled people do end up on Mairs's lap, and complex
theories of marginality have ended up in her life. She represents her marginality as being connected to the world
through a separation from it, and being separated from the
world through some unusual connection to it (Titchkosky,
1998: 490–8; 1997: 1–20). In writing consciously as a body
and in being embodied in the ways that she is, Mairs represents this marginality just as much as she lives it.

The Enlightened mind, with its adherence to cause/effect
rationality, and thus at ease with much of the world (which

is no surprise since this rationality created it), can read Mairs's book as 'only' contradiction. Initially, I had read with just such a common mindset. Mairs has failed to make disability thing-like. Its boundaries are neither clear nor certain; its meaning floats and wanders through her life and her writing. In this 'failure' to approach and then define, and thereby confine disability, resides an authenticity. Mairs seeks to author some reconciliation between how the world inscribes meaning on her body and her life and how her body inscribes meaning on her life and her world. It is this project of reconciliation which successfully disrupted my Enlightened mentality, a mentality that had only sought to render disability, her crippled body, into yet one more object upon which to exercise a cause/effect rationality and dissolve her contradictions.

Marginality as Between-ness

'Actually,' says the phenomenologist F.G. Asenjo (1988: 65), '... we commit a major error when we force ourselves to choose just one side in a many-sided contradictory situation.' Asenjo is asking us to rethink situations, such as personal accounts of disability, that are full of many-sided contradictions. He is saying that we can deal with contradiction as if it is simply an error, but if we do so, we are committing a major error. What is the major error behind my unexamined inclination to choose mind over body, authenticity over failure, normal over abnormal, or, even, disabled over crippled?

Asenjo is not arguing that through such an inclination I make an egregious slight against 'relativism' *as if* the values of mind, body, authenticity, and failure are all the same. He is not making the relativist claim that to regard something as more choice-worthy than something else is only an act of denying the relative character of the world. It is not relativism that grounds Asenjo's major worry about the major error.

Asenjo is focused on the *meanings* of the word, of language, of these contradictions,[1] and such meaning, for him, is more precise and nuanced than pre-existing interpretive schemes such as 'relativism,' 'plurality,' or 'power.' Asenjo (ibid.: 61) says, for example, that a word is 'primarily a decantation of meaning.' 'Crippled' certainly decants a plethora of meanings, and if the word has meaning, it cannot be relative to any other word. But Asenjo (ibid.: 62) insists there is more: there is a '... crisscrossed, back-and-forth process of shifting and floating in the fluid in-between of words.' Something happens for us as we read Mairs, something between the words 'crippled' and 'disabled,' between normalcy and arrogance. Attending to that which exists in-between words, Asenjo says:

> The spark that flashes between two words is ... a factor not fully explained by the words themselves. Not only is the spark unpredictable but it also has the power to burn away any cliché, and in so doing illuminates the context, whose existence – like that of every whole – is dependent on how it is reflected in its parts ... [In-between words] we are continually being surprised by combinations that articulate the seemingly unsayable. For this reason, strictly speaking there are no synonyms ... (ibid.)

A word is not merely a word, and one word is never just as good as any other. The words through which we insert ourselves into the world are always made use of in relation to other words, words chosen and not chosen, words said and sometimes left unsaid, words that fit us well and words that we must struggle to claim for ourselves. Between hardly being disabled and being crippled a contradiction flashes into reality; it is a flash that illuminates disability as unpredictable and never captured fully by cliché or ideology. 'Crippled' and 'disabled' are part of the world, and they are words ubiquitously used; sometimes they are used to denote the same thing, and sometimes to differentiate people from one another. These words not only indicate a person's difference, they also marginalize this difference. 'Crippled,' 'disabled,' 'handicapped,' 'impaired' ... Mairs exists, as do all disabled people, betwixt and between these words. *In the middle* of all these words and the things that they produce, disabled people find themselves marginalized, embodying a plethora of conceptualizations that are packed full of contradictory meanings. Yet, living in the midst of all these concepts means that every disabled person represents the possibility of combining these words, these concepts, in a new way and thereby forging some reconciliation with the world.

The reconciliation is not the feel-good harmony of being at one with the world. Activism, writing, theorizing, or getting on with one's day – consciously as a disabled person – means inserting into the world the possible flash of new meaning. Just as Mairs must reckon with a world that makes her a marginal figure, her writing, her crippled body that is hardly disabled, and the people who fall onto her lap must reckon with the meaning Mairs has brought into the world. Again, it is doubtful that this will make people at ease with Mairs.

Lennard Davis (1997: 1) says that disability is always an 'actively repressed *memento mori* for the fate of the normal body.' That disability puts others in mind of the death of the normal body may be but one extreme expression of how the life of disability always holds open the possibility of inserting alternative meaning into the world.[2] Between life and death, the disabled person can embody alternative relations to, and interpretations of, both. These alternatives are not just for 'them' because even while 'they' are on the edge, out of bounds, and beneath the notice of non-disabled people, everyone can fall into the lap of alterity, from time to time. And if we recognize the importance of marginalized people, combining words, lives, and bodies in unexpected and extraordinary ways, we may begin to fall into the midst of alterity a little more willingly, a little more often, and with some awareness of the necessity of doing so. This does not necessarily make anyone at ease with very much, not even with one's own body, mind, or senses. Nonetheless, this alterity, with all its possible promises and calamities, is what disability can teach us ... if we are open to such lessons. It is the context of alternative possibilities for life, embodiment, and thought that is illuminated by the literal marginalization of the figure of disability, who is beneath our notice even as we fall into her lap. This is the context in which the possibility of what Asenjo (1988: 62) calls the 'seemingly unsayable' is born.

The Seemingly Unsayable

In the 'shifting and floating in the fluid in-between of words ... we are continually being surprised by combinations that articulate the seemingly unsayable' (Asenjo, 1988: 62). Articulations of disability that attempt to speak outside the boundaries of ideology, as well as the appearance of disabled people in the course of everyday life, in environments and situations which do not expect us, seem to have a particular power to give rise to the 'seemingly unsayable.' There are at least two versions of the seemingly unsayable that arise in the face of disability. There are many times when I hear people speak of disability, and I am shocked. It seems impossible to me that people today could say what they do:

- During a class discussion of cultural conceptions of disabled people, including examples from my own life as a dyslexic professor, a student appears frustrated and exclaims: 'Look, what's important is that they are just like us.'
- In a deviance textbook, I read: 'The central difference between a physical disability and another form of deviance is ... [that] a disabled person exerts no control over this condition' (Clinard and Meier, 1998: 482).
- Rod and I go for dinner at a friend's house, where we are sitting side-by-side. Looking only at me, the host asks, 'Will he have potatoes?'
- In an interprovincial newsletter regarding government initiatives to increase the 'employability' of disabled people, provinces proudly announce that they have begun to offer 'assertiveness training for persons with disabilities so as to address their increased numbers among the ranks of the unemployed.'

My shock and my sense of the seemingly unsayable are grounded upon a simple wish: I wish people would not utter such absurd and banal things. This is a concrete rendering of Asenjo's idea of the 'seemingly unsayable'; it 'seems' that these things should not be 'sayable.' I simply wish that there was more room in the world for the alternatives that disability represents and that people were more open to engaging such alterity. Being closed to alterity, whether perpetrated by me or by others, is unseemly to me, and I think such utterances unsayable only because they *ought* to be.

But thankfully this concrete version of the seemingly unsayable is not the only one that exists. The above situations express that which I wish was not sayable, and they give off the deceiving appearance of a final certainty. 'Will he have potatoes?' may put the eating of potatoes into question, but it does so by forcefully asserting a finalizing and totalizing delineation of disability as some-thing. In this case, blindness is that thing which makes someone know nothing, not even what they may or may not like to eat. There is a common desire for finality that lies behind all of the above expressions and there is a common neglect of the interactional production of contrasts between us/them, abled/disabled, inclusion/exclusion. However, Asenjo (1988: 64) insists that one can still find the generation of the 'seemingly unsayable' – there is still the possibility of new content between these words and sentences. For example, between 'Will he have potatoes?' and my blank stare, or 'Oh my, you better ask Rod,' or Rod's rejoinder 'Yes, The Blind eat potatoes,' the content of who is in the know and who is not shifts and moves.

This version of the seemingly unsayable of disability is grounded in the in-between of words used to articulate disability and the in-between of bodily experiences which make an appearance in everyday life. Disability powerfully represents the possibility of beginning something new from the position of being betwixt and between. At one and the same time, a disabled person is excluded by the structure of the environment and yet can be disturbed by therapeutic practices oriented to implementing some version of inclusion. Needing to find one's way into this environment and these practices can lead to new thoughts and new meaning. Consider the words of Leonard Kriegel (1997: 40):

When I think back to those two years in the [polio] ward ... rehabilitation ... was ahistorical, a future devoid of any significant claim on the past ... its purpose was to teach one how to steal a touch of the normal from an existence that would be striking in its abnormality.

Between stealing a touch of the normal and being struck by the touch of abnormality, disability is made present as a complex relation that is neither one nor the other. Even if policy and law someday ensure that the touch of normal life is not as far out of reach for disabled people as it is currently, the fact will remain that people will need to think about what it means to move and live in normate culture in a non-typical way. It will always be the case that being able to 'get on with life' and 'just do it' will always be different for disabled people. Disability brings to the fore the complex set of meanings that surround such doings and goings-on.

Recognizing that one is a part of the world through some separation from it and that one is separate from the world through some unique connection to it can give rise to a perplexing sense of self, one that is necessarily provocative of new thoughts. Sally French (1999: 21) says:

> As a small child I had a dislike of going out on windy days. My mother, no doubt exasperated, asked me why this was so, to which I replied 'The wind gets in my way' ... A common feature of life as a visually disabled person, which starts very early, is having constantly to explain oneself and yet rarely having one's experiences confirmed.

Being constantly asked to explain oneself means that others are recognizing you as one who experiences the world in ways that may not be commonly shared. While everyone may experience the wind, not everyone experiences it as getting in the way. Ironically, the noticing of one's alterity by non-disabled others can also serve to put one on notice that such differences will be discounted, and left unconfirmed. Similarly, the current drive to understand disabled people as 'just like' the non-disabled, that is, as people 'with' disabilities (PWDs), may in fact confirm some shared stance in an abstract version of humanness. At the same time, however, a confirmation of being a human, just like any other, may remove that most basic of human necessities, namely, to have an experience of the world that others confirm. As Dorothy Smith (1990: 107–38) argues, the first social step that must be taken if we are to treat someone as mentally incompetent is to deny him or her a confirmation of her or his experience of the world. What lies in-between Sally French's words is this complex interrelation amongst mind, body, society, and self.

Within an educational environment, learning-disabled people learn that learning is difficult and sometimes impossible. But it is easy for us (learning-disabled people) to learn that no one wants to learn anything about us. It is easy to learn what does not count as knowledge and what does not even count as learning:

> If you found out what they're not good at and put a label on them they would feel real low because you are messing around with their weakness. And no one wants you to play with their weakness because if it is your weakness you can say too much about it. (High school student quoted in Peters, 1999: 103)

Or, consider the words of a girl in grade five whom I interviewed:

> I use to go, I don't any more, I use to go to a special reading class. I don't go anymore. I hated it. I didn't learn noth'n. Everyone knew I was going to the dumb class. Now I take my books home, I read every night. I don't let anybody know if I have any problems. (Quoted in Titchkosky, 1995: 53)

Situated between power and knowledge (Foucault, 1973), learning-disabled students embody both power and knowledge in their full complexity, and bring to the fore new articulations of what counts as knowing and what does not, in new ways. These students with learning difficulties vividly draw out what it means to live between knowledge that counts and knowledge that does not. Between our knowledge of *different types* of knowing arises the flash of self-understanding as it is constituted between one's self and others.

Between words, bodies, and lives, we are continually being surprised by combinations that articulate the seemingly unsayable. Consider how Rod (Michalko, 1999: 160) describes an experience with his guide dog:

> we were on our way home on a familiar subway line, one on which we both knew all the stops. Someone sat down next to us and after a few seconds asked, 'Do you know where you are?' This was the first time I had ever been asked such a question, and it took me by surprise. I was sitting on the subway, Smokie was lying beside me, and we had three stops to go. What is more, the names of the stops are announced over the subway's public address system ... I decided to find out how far this person would go in her assumptions about blindness. 'Where?' I asked. The person surprised me again as she proceeded to tell me which subway line we were on, the direction in which the train was going, and the name of the next stop. The woman seriously assumed that I did not know where I was. What she thought Smokie and I were doing on that subway ... I asked, 'What city?' After a few seconds of silence, she began to laugh. She then apologized ... she said, 'I think your dog is smarter than me.'

Even in the face of that which we *wish* was indeed unsayable, new meanings, new conceptions, and new relations arise. The pushing of the question 'Do you know where you are?' forced the gaze of the woman from blindness to herself. She began to examine the seemingly unsayable which allowed her to say only too clearly her beliefs regarding the effects blindness had on people. The question 'What city?' produces a flash of recognition found in her laughter and in her comment that 'I think your dog is smarter than me.' The sighted subway patron's essentializing of blindness as that thing which produces a radical lack of knowledge becomes unfixed and uncertain. Saying 'What city?' situates the blind person in-between a cultural conception of blindness as that which disallows knowledge and the artful wisdom necessary to disrupt such conceptions. 'What city?' performs the understanding that sighted people's ways and beliefs are also subject to scrutiny. The sight/knowledge connection is torn asunder and something new comes of this.

Sometimes, the seemingly unsayable rises up in the most extreme fashion, as in Robert Murphy's introduction to his book *The Body Silent*:

> My wife Yolanda and I are now engaged in a long-term study of quadriplegics having little or no movement below the neck, reducing their address on life to thought and speech. We are asking of these people: What sustains your rage to live and to stay in the mainstream of life? (1987: vii)

Between sustaining a rage to live and staying in the mainstream of life there is a gap, a disjuncture, a spark of meaning. The rage to shop, road rage, or a rage against those who get in our way are certainly part of mainstream life. But a rage to live? Rarely do we hear such passion paired with the ordinary order of daily life. It would seem that having a rage to live would throw one out of the mainstream of life. Perhaps it does. But in their research, in Murphy's own life with quadriplegia, and when he and Yolanda Murphy pose their question to other quadriplegics, they open up disability as a space between a rage to live and mainstream life. While mainstream life may inscribe an outsider quality on anyone who develops a rage to live, the Murphys have made mainstream life into something that must reckon with those bodies, lives, and thoughts that represent this rage. It may always be the case that mainstream life rejects the inclusion of the rage to live as one of its orienting values, preferring instead the values of profit, progress, proficiency, and power. Murphy indicates that this is likely the case and mentions that he began raising his research question during the brutality of Reaganism (ibid.). The fact remains that disability has inserted the possibility of alternative orienting values into the world. Yet, a quadriplegic person is *not* totally reduced to addressing life through thought and speech, as Murphy suggests. In a body that has little or no movement below the neck, Murphy articulates and represents the significance of living between a rage to live and the mundane ordinary order of mainstream life.

The articulations of all of these disabled people cited above may be regarded by some people as strictly signs of oppression. It certainly is oppressive to be regarded as simply that thing which lacks knowledge or as that thing which must be remedied or rehabilitated or as that thing whose existence has been excluded by the built physical reality of everyday life. Traditional disciplines within the social sciences may regard what disabled people have to say as mere data which delineates human deviation from the norm. And, certainly it is deviant to possess a body that does not work in, or look, the same way as does the 'average' body. Furthermore, it is more than possible, and relatively easy, to interpret what disabled people have to say as nothing but a negotiation of their deviant status within the land of the normals. Finally, from the standpoint of psychology, rehabilitation, and other medicalized stances, all of the above articulations of life in disability can be readily interpreted as part of the symptomology of the necessity for self-acceptance, the development of coping mechanisms, and the need for training and other adaptive techniques and technology: if you don't see well, get a guide dog, and what happens along the way in using this technique is not as important as the fact that you are moving and living among the normals; if your body does not move below the neck, you must presevere – there are always things which you can do, after all, there is your mind; if you have a problem learning, seek help from a professional and don't try to go it alone. From a medical standpoint, all disabled people, and every aspect of our lives, can be read as displaying 'healthy' or 'ill' relations to being disabled.

Indeed, these ways of interpreting disability are both very normal and very common; and they seem to always find exactly what they are looking for. There is no surprise. Sociologists, rehabilitators, or psychologists often find exactly what they are looking for when they observe disabled people – they find deviance, the need for technical training, or the need for medical remedy. But is there something to be gained through the attempt to seek the 'seemingly unsayable' – the flash of new meaning which elucidates the context of disability – in the words and bodies of people who live in the midst of disability?

Disability as Between-ness

Disability, then, can be painful, comfortable, familiar, alienating, bonding, isolating, disturbing, endearing, challenging, infuriating, or ordinary. Embedded in the complexity of actual human relations, it is always more than the disabled figure can signify. (Thomson, 1997a: 14)

Disability is always more than the disabled figure can signify or even say, but not simply because others possess a plethora of interpretations regarding what disability is; nor is it because these interpretations often conflict. A multiplicity of interpretive positions is a key feature of all aspects of everyday life. Disability is always more because it powerfully represents, embodies, and brings to the fore the complexity of the alterity which arises between cultural values and assumptions, societal conceptions and expectations. Disabled people, as the marginal figures of everyday life, academic research, and bodily experience, are positioned betwixt and between contrasting values, conflicting assumptions, painful conceptions, and infuriating and ordinary expectations; and, yet, they are never actually reducible to any of these. It is rare that disabled people escape the signification of this alterity, the same alterity that is downplayed or ignored in the normal order of things.

For Thomson (1997a: 114), this situation of between-ness means that

> the disabled person always fuses the physically typical with the physically atypical ... [It] is also experienced as a transformation, or a violation, of self, creating classification dilemmas, ambiguous status, or questioning assumptions about wholeness. All persons with physical disabilities thus embody the 'illegitimate fusion' of the cultural categories 'normal,' which qualifies people for human status, and 'abnormal,' which disqualifies them. Within this liminal space the disabled person must constitute something akin to identity.

This fusion does not simply make for the extraordinary or the exotic; indeed, it may not even be a solid 'fusion.' A relation between dichotomous identity categories certainly does constitute the figure of difference in all its current categorical manifestations (e.g., gender, class, race, and disability). But fusion does not deliver us to the specific difference that disability makes. What is specific to disability is its ability to highlight the precarious partiality and incompleteness of such a fusion – the apparent fusion is really a gap. Disability represents the gaps between self and world, body and society, which nonetheless connect the unexpected.

This book has been about these apparent fusions that are really gaps that indicate that the power of disability, its promise and its suffering, lies in the essential significance of the social rendering of disability as a form of marginality. I began this book from the sense that I am situated between blindness and dyslexia. I am not blind, but I share my life with someone who is. Rod is not dyslexic, but I am. Together, we are situated between two radically different kinds of disability: one visible, one invisible; one often marked as a 'severe disability,' the other as 'mild.' Our life is spent in these mixtures of disabilities, which also position us differently in the social worlds of which we are a part and from which we are often separated. Rod is almost always seen as blind. I am almost never seen as dyslexic. Seeing blindness and overlooking dyslexia are social acts tied to an awesome diversity of cultural conceptions of both disabilities. These conceptions interact with our separate lived experiences of 'being disabled,' and all of this interacts with our need to think about the social significance of disability. Any examination of these conceptions and experiences is only possible, however, if I claim my marginality as a valid place from which to begin inquiry. This book would remain unsayable and unwriteable if I did not examine these conceptions as they interact with my lived experience of being situated between a variety of bodily experiences and cultural expectations. Both literally and figuratively, this book grows out of this experience of between-ness. Every word on these pages has been related through me, a dyslexic writer, putting my unique word order into 'normal' grammar, and I have read every word aloud to Rod, in his blindness, and all of this has occurred in a life steeped in various experiences of, and relations to, disability. I have drawn upon my lived experience of being situated between dyslexia and blindness so as to vividly address what the standpoint of disability has to offer to an examination of identity formed on the margins of mainstream life. Claiming disability as one's place betwixt and between raises the possibility of inserting into the world alternative ways of being and alternative ways of knowing. In this, the possibility of beginning something new arises.

Disabled people have fought, are fighting, and will continue to fight for our inclusion in the set-up and workings of society. This fight necessarily includes the making and remaking, the revision and rescinding, of policy and law, even though the fight for concrete pragmatic accommodation alone cannot unite disabled people. Bodily experience and the needs of each disabled person are highly diverse and distinct. Gently sloped curb cuts is but one case in point: this serves mobility-impaired people well, blind people not at all, and may be approached with indifference by learning-disabled people until we need to articulate possible paths for movement to other people. Nonetheless, the oppressive exclusion from the material environment and the oppressive entrapment of disabled people by the ideologies of personal tragedy and medicine remain commonalities amongst all disabled people. These structural and attitudinal environments make up the world of which disabled people are a part and yet within which we remain marginal. It is upon this shared experience of oppression that a politics of disablement has been grounded. This politics, however, has paid little attention to the overloaded social significance of the fact that disabled people exist as quintessential marginal figures within mainstream life.

There is, therefore, also a politics to claiming disability as a between-ness and attempting to speak, act, and think from that position. But this is a politics that needs a pedagogy and not merely a policy or law. In the face of a world that often acts as if it holds a singular conception of disability as that problematic thing in need of remedy, seeking to understand disability as that which can teach us about human alterity in the midst of common doings and ordinary thought is a radical socio-political interpretive stance. But to receive an education on and from the margins requires something more than a collection of details about those lives that are typically beneath notice. It requires something more than a recipe of how to properly move and live with disabled people. It even requires something more than a recitation of the mainstream's powerful ability to oppress and devalue the lives of disabled people. What *is* required is that the experience of the marginal existence of disability be observed, heard, responded to, and understood *as* teacher. This is one of the most difficult tasks and responsibilities that faces all those who are engaged in disability studies today.

Part of the extreme difficulty of orienting to disability as teacher is tied, yet again, to the fact that disability is necessarily an experience of marginality. Disabled people are not 'fully outside' of mainstream life. Instead, we are marginal; therefore, we are connected to all the ways that our culture has taught us to attend to disability and to produce what counts as knowledge of it. It is easy to attend to and gather knowledge about disability that in no way indicates that disability is being situated as teacher. 'It' can be studied just like class, race, gender, illness, medicine, etc. – but such studies do not necessarily treat disability as a teacher. Indeed, disability studies programs and literature, especially as they gain some academic recognition and acceptance, must face the problem of conforming to the dominant inclination to treat disability as simply one more object for knowledge production. The special task and responsibility of disability studies today is to encourage all people to regard the existence of disability as a unique teacher of human alterity within a culture committed to maintaining a singular sense of the ordinary and normal as unexamined values.

The promise of disability studies does not lie in the ability of researchers to give us details. We now live in a time when it is acceptable to know how the ancient Greeks treated the deaf members of their society, or how modern America diagnoses and manages learning-disabled children, or how contemporary rehabilitative practices enforce a sense of normalcy upon their clients, or in what year we shifted away from saying 'handicapped' and towards saying 'person with a disability,' or that computer technology is highly desired yet rarely accessible, etc., etc. All these 'teachables' ought to be part of any curriculum regarding human difference and diversity. However, none of these details will necessarily teach anybody about how to orient to their concrete experience of disability as teacher.

Every time disability is treated as an 'object for thought,' instead of as a marginal experience of existence which can speak to the character of that existence, we can miss the opportunity to understand disability as that which is teacher *par excellence*. The existence of disability, its social treatment and organization, is especially able to teach us about culture's means of knowledge production, cultural values regarding the relation between mind and body, as well as the place of alterity within contemporary times. Detailing the oppression which disabled people face, or detailing the

disabled body in a culture that neither anticipates nor wel-
comes disabled people, does not necessarily make disability a teacher. Learning, for example, that the unemployment
and non–labour force participation rate among disabled
people is over 50 per cent and rises higher in relation to the
perceived severity of a disability, is a factual detail that fits
well with innumerable interpretive paradigms. Such a 'fact'
can be used as one more sign of disabled people's oppression, or as a sign of disabled people's general inability, or as
a sign of the psychological devastation of having a disability and thus of the supposed necessity of rehabilitative
practices, counselling, or assertiveness training. These different interpretive paradigms share in common the fact
that they all regularly make *use* of the same disability details in order to put flesh around what is already known
about disability as this knowledge is given by one privileged interpretive paradigm or another. With the right argument, such details can be used to affirm multiple and
even conflicting interpretations of disability. Detailed descriptions of disability have been with us for a very long
time and have come through a great many different disciplines (Canguilhem, 1991). The extremely unjust rate of
employment among disabled people exists in a culture that
has a number of ways to interpret this rate, and it exists in
the lives of disabled people who live with unemployment
and those who do not. It is only from between these
details – how they are used, how they impact upon the
lives of disabled people – that we can begin to rethink
the relation of disability and, in this case, employment or
the lack thereof.

On their own, details and facts will not teach others how
to orient to disability as teacher. Details, no less and no
more than repudiation or neglect, will not deliver us into a

consideration of the radical social significance of disability for culture nor for how culture makes up the ambiguous meaning of its disabled people.

Disability Studies as Quest and Promise

But there is the possibility of a different interpretive quest in the face of disability, different, that is, than the *use* of disabled bodies and lives in order to put flesh on an interpretive scheme or give weight and substance to the various paradigms through which disability is rendered into a problematic *thing*. This book was my attempt to exemplify the possibility of this different interpretive quest. I have attempted not to get stuck in a relation to disability that can only make use of it for the sake of supporting some pre-established model of disability. My problem throughout has been to make disability make me think. Every rendering of disability into a problematic thing needs neither to be rejected nor accepted. Instead, every 'objective' rendering of disability needs to be treated as *pointing* to the significance of disability, and not as the empirical reality of disability. I have attempted, in other words, to take up marginality as a political commitment. Such commitment requires that I regard myself as marginal even to the meaning and significance of disability itself. (This is why disability studies can be pursued by both disabled and non-disabled people.) Being situated in the midst of intersubjective relations with cultural renderings of disability as a problematic thing can, and ought to, be treated as a marginal position that allows for an inquiry into the possible meaning that disability holds out to disabled and currently non-disabled people. This quest requires us to treat the on-going objectification of disability, as it interacts with the lived experience of disabled people, as being no-thing at all, but rather a gap or space within which the social significance of disability can be examined and explored.

The promise of disability studies lies in confirming the Really real interpretations, assumptions, and experiences which surround and marginalize disabled people. But, such confirmation needs to occur from a marginal position that is committed to understanding disability as no-one-thing while at the same time treating it as the occasion that allows for a consideration of what disability might mean and what meaning disability brings into the world. This kind of confirmation can be accomplished from the experience of marginality that accompanies disability. This is what is difficult and rare. How can the ways in which a disabled existence interacts with the culture that surrounds and organizes it be listened to for the whisper of that seemingly unsayable that resonates with new content, new meaning, inserting itself into our understanding of the social significance of the situation of disability? Culture needs to be confirmed from the situation of disability, from that place where disability talks back to how it is spoken about by others. To 'confirm' is not merely to provide details, nor is it to accept or reject automatically what culture says and how it maps out the lives of disabled people. To confirm is to recognize one's position in the world as marginal, as a stranger, as 'beneath notice,' and use this space of marginality, this situation of being between all that culture gives to its disabled members, as a way to recognize one's distinction from what has been given. Clearly, culture organizes the lives of disabled people in a devalued way. The task now is to seek some *reconciliation* (Arendt, 1994: 307–27) with a world that has almost no interest in, and sometimes would rather kill, alternative ways of being-in-the-world.

Understanding what disability means in all its complexity is political action insofar as such understanding ' is essentially always the beginning of something new' (ibid.: 320).

This task of being able to respond to a world that would rather see disabled people as objects in need of treatment, incarceration, or annihilation requires us to place ourselves in the midst of these object-like details so as to address what the standpoint of disability has to offer to an examination of identity formed on the margins of mainstream life. This is to actualize the promise of disability studies: disability is not one more thing to be studied; it is a place from which we can study the meaning of our world and its people. This is why one of the themes coursing through this entire book is that disability constitutes the self as a marginal identity and that the social significance of such an identity cannot be grasped through the cultural inclination to define disability simply through negation: as something missing, something lacking, something not working, or as impaired bodies leading to deviant identities. Disabled people are defined as things which lack, and thus we (disabled people) often do not notice how we as marginal figures represent, articulate, and embody the potentially radical space of between-ness. Marginal identities always offer people the experience of being positioned between knowledge of what culture typically values and the knowledge that they do not embody these values. Marginal people embody alternative ways of being-in-the-world and act as living depictions of the possibility that things could be otherwise. This is why disability studies needs to attend to the concrete ways that disabled people insert themselves into a world through word and deed.

Just as meaning and significance arise between the unique combination of words, meaning and significance also arise between the unique combination of bodies, lives, and envi-

ronments. Critical awareness, and the possibility of deconstructing and reconstructing the significance of embodied
existence, is what the marginality of disability offers to us
all.

I began this book with a commitment to the understanding that disability is a teacher and ought to be regarded and
studied as such. Throughout, this teacher has had much to
say about being 'between.' This between-ness is just as
worthy of study as are the stigmatization, deviance, oppression, and need for humane response of those whose
needs differ from ordinary others. Moreover, the space of
between-ness offers some relief from the constant no-win
situations of the double binds that come with the study of
stigma, oppression, deviance, and the 'helping' of disabled
others. The untypical body's subjection to the words and
deeds of others is but part of the story of disability. The
other part of the story is what disability – its concrete existence in the lives of people – says back and does to the
doings and sayings of others. We can study disability as a
stigmatized identity, and we can try to fight our stigmatization; we can study disability as societal oppression, and we
can fight for our liberation; we can do the same with the
medical version of disability. But alongside this fight there
is still one more possibility: one which lies between the
recognition of what is born out of the relation between
disabled people and what culture gives to us, and what
meaning is born in the midst of our fight against the power
of these 'cultural gifts.' We say, 'Here we are,' devalued by
culture as stigmatized, deviant, and oppressed people. Of
course, this, we say, must be fought. But both the fight and
the recognition are born of our unique position of being
situated between all that culture gives and what we say
back and do to culture. Here, in-between all this, lies both
our creativity and our constraint. Thus, in the between-

ness, within which every disabled person lives, we find the symbolic power of disability. Disability inserts the ambiguity of between-ness into the world, and this ambiguity ironically clarifies our understanding of the body and how it might speak to the human condition. This book is my attempt at such an insertion.

Notes

1. Disability: A Social Phenomenon

1 On 4 June 2001, Rod's guide dog, Smokie, died.
2 Saramago (1997) calls his fictional epidemic of blindness the 'white sickness' because the people who go blind see nothing but a milky white world.
3 Suspending remedy is meant here as a suspension of the dominant version of disability such remedy requires. Disability is not merely an individual problem requiring remedy, nor is it only a problem of inaccessible environments also requiring remedy. As Williams (1998: 240) says, 'disability as a social reality of people's experiences is caused neither by the externalities of the environment nor by any "facts" of biological trauma or deterioration, but emerges out of the relations between persons and society.' I intend the suspension of remedy as a methodological device that serves to uncover the version of disability and of societal responses to it that generates disability merely and only as a remedial problem.
4 For discussions of what coming out as disabled might mean, especially as it relates to the order of normalcy, see Brueggemann, 1997; Swain and Cameron, 1999; Thomson, 1996: xvii; and Titchkosky, 2001b.
5 The complexity of this definitional process can be observed in both medical discourse on learning disabilities (Dalby et al., 1998; Gersons-Wolfensberger and Ruijssenaars, 1997; Hammill et al., 1987; Padget, 1998; Shaw et al., 1995) and within social discourse (Hicks-Coolick and Kurtz, 1997; Palombo, 1996; Zuriff, 1996). Few are researching the consequences of either form of definition of learning disabilities (for an exception, see Jenkins, 1998; Simpson, 1996: 96).

6 For a discussion of documentary reality, see Smith, 1999: 61–80.

7 I am not referring here to the hegemonic cliché "We're all disabled in one way or another." Instead, I am referring to the fact that disabled people are in society, while often marginalized and oppressed by interactional norms, intellectualized stereotypes, and inaccessible environments.

8 Within the field of disability research there are many who make claims to pursuing a kind of disability studies. Here I am making use of the term in a way similar to how the terms 'cultural studies' and 'women's studies' are currently used. These are all fields of study which problematize the traditional or mainstream ways in which culture, women, or disabled people have been studied. For discussions of disability studies, see Corker and French, 1998: 1–11; Corker and Shakespeare, 2002; Davis, 1997b; Wilson and Lewiecki-Wilson, 2001; Linton, 1998; Mitchell and Snyder, 1997a: 1, 24, esp., footnote 2; Oliver, 1996; Thomson, 1997a: 5, 140–1, esp., footnote 1; Titchkosky, 2000; Michalko, 2002.

2. Situating Disability: Mapping the Outer Limits

1 Not noticing the language of the body is a part of everyday life and also a phenomenon in which the discipline of sociology engages. The work of Shilling (1993), Synnott (1993), and Linton (1998) traces how the body has been ignored by sociology. Even within cultural studies, those who theorize identity and the body usually make disability matter only as a metaphor for the oppression of race, class, and gender, and disability is excluded as an identity category. For example, see the collection *Out There: Marginalization and Contemporary Cultures* (Ferguson et al., 1990), where disability is never imagined as an identity category even when long lists of marginalized people are generated. This omission leads to the cultural reproduction of disability as simply a metaphor for lack. For example, West (ibid.: 25–6) describes the 'New World *bricoleurs*' of the cultural politics of difference as 'persons from all countries, cultures, genders, sexual orientations, ages and regions with protean identities who avoid ethnic chauvinism and faceless universalisms.' These are the *'flexible'* (ibid.) people who avoided the *'silences and blindnesses'* (ibid.: 26, 35) of male WASP hegemony (my italics). Marking the limits of traditional knowledge systems through the metaphorical use of 'disability' while at the same time speaking of bodies and

identities as they are constituted through race, class, and gender, serves only to hyper-marginalize disabled people even within the academic analysis of marginality and exclusion. Moreover, many cultural critics' uncritical use of disability as a metaphor for a tradition's lack and ineptitude, shows these critics to be in conformity with Western culture's dominant conceptualization of disability as *not* there, *not* right, *not* working, *not* able. Such work offers a necessary deconstruction of the social processes that organize our knowledge of the Other but reconstructs disability as 'really' out there (e.g., Minnich, 1990; Nussbaum, 1997; Rajchman, 1995).

2 For example, there are different ways to define blindness – an inability to see the big *E* on an eye chart, as 10 per cent or less of normal acuity, or inability to read the print of ordinary newspapers. Still, these various definitions share in common the fact that they conceive of blindness essentially as a measurable thing of lack. Arguments regarding the appropriate definition of disability usually only question the contours and shape of the object. Thus, despite contested definitions of disability, and thereby different measurements and different statistical figures, disabled persons in Canada, the United States, Britain, and around the rest of the world are concretized, typed, and counted. These counts are then used to make arguments which will support a variety of policies and procedures all of which subscribe to the belief that disability is an object of lack which needs to be managed as such.

3. Mapping Normalcy: A Social Topography of Passing

1 We can say with Simi Linton (1998: 24–5) that 'the *normal* and the *abnormal* depend on each other for their existence and depend on the maintenance of the opposition for their meaning.' Insofar as language gives us blindness and sight as opposites, the distinction between the normal and abnormal is maintained. Yet, continues Linton, there is an 'instability and relational nature of the designations *normal* and *abnormal*.' This lesson is, however, at least as old as Socrates and his teacher Diotimia, who spoke it through the language of sameness and difference, as told in the *Symposium* (206d–208d). The problem seems to be that this is a lesson which generation after generation forgets. Disability studies can be read as an attempt to recollect this lesson for humanity once more, as if for the first time.

2 Rod's second book, *The Two in One: Walking with Smokie, Walking with Blindness* (1999), gives a detailed account of this movement into blindness, and his final jump into the identity of a blind person, through the acquisition of a dramatic cultural symbol of blindness.

3 Every verbal command that a guide dog learns is accompanied with a hand signal. A verbal 'left' has a short swift swoosh of the hand to the left; the verbal 'right' has the same hand movement, but to the right. After Cassis had learned many other things, such as helping to put on the harness, leading out, and stopping at curbs, she was ready to learn left and right, but only one at a time. This allowed me to make sure that I knew that I had the correct hand in mind to accompany the verbal command. Eventually the day arrived when I set out to use both left and right commands. We proceeded to a curb. Cassis stopped to indicate it. I gave a verbal and hand command. She did not move. As she stood there staring at me, I realized that I had given a verbal left and a hand-signal right.

4. The Expected and the Unexpected

1 I am referring here to the fact that built environments are often inaccessible to disabled people. For example, stairs in the absence of ramps make it impossible for a wheelchair user to move in that environment, thus making the wheelchair user vulnerable. The vulnerability of such a body is not located in the body itself, but in the social construction of the environment. Thus, the 'socially vulnerable body.'

2 See 'Building Standards for the Handicapped 1970: Supplement No. 5 to the National Building Code of Canada.' The supplement 'recommends,' but does not require, measures 'to allow handicapped persons to enter and use buildings without assistance' (1.1).

3 In 'Putting Disability in Its Place: It's Not a Joking Matter' (2001), Michalko and I provide separate analyses of the experience documented here, and do so from the vantage of different theoretic interests. This part of the chapter draws on my earlier analysis.

4 In the context of this interaction, 'little things' refers to possible accommodations which are inexpensive and not too difficult to accomplish. However, 'little things' are no small matter from the point of view of someone who is disabled. For example, placing Braille markings on an elevator keypad could make a massive

difference to blind persons. It could make the difference between getting to where one intends to go or not. 'Little things' are only little in relation to currently non-disabled persons' concern about expense, level of difficulty, etc.

5 This occurred until one of the 'bigger guys' dropped the student. The student began attending an off-campus church that was more accessible and did not return to campus the following academic year.

6 Many established members of the university, including faculty and administrators, have told me about the other university. For example: 'That University, twenty years ago, decided to become accessible' or 'That University receives all the funding for disability issues.' (In regards to this latter point, it is interesting to note that many students have insisted it is a myth.) Even if true, it is also true that moving, living, and working with disabled people on this university campus inevitably leads to stories about St Elsewhere. The story of 'St Elsewhere' is the story of a 'little utopia' which does not intend to exclude disabled people. At the same time, this story functions as a morality tale *for* disabled people and not *for* the non-disabled members of this university. The moral of the story is that all reasonable and rational disabled people *ought* to go to St Elsewhere.

7 Disabled students represent an additional expense to a university only when such students are not understood as essential to the university. Whether or not the day will come when our society understands accommodations to disabled people as a routine part of organizational life, and thus not as an additional expense, is difficult to say since disability may always be viewed as an 'unfortunate' aspect of human life.

8 The *Chronicle of Higher Education* (http://chronicle.com/colloquy/99/disabled/background.htm) ran an on-line colloquy which expressed great anxiety regarding learning-disabled students and their growing numbers. See also Zuriff, 1996.

9 This university's Senate Committee on Disability was established in 1991. I am referring to the 1996 revised policy approved by the senate. In practice, the Committee on Disability functions as part of 'Student Services.' The university's 'Policy for Students with Disabilities – Statement of Intent' includes the stipulation that 'students with disabilities who are judged academically qualified should be admitted except for the most compelling reasons.' The

document then describes the administrative chain of command which will 'attempt' to implement 'special arrangements' for these students with 'special needs' who have self-identified on the admission application form. Thus, in relation to accommodation, the university is committed to only making an *attempt*. Further, the policy does not describe what a 'compelling reason' for *not* admitting a disabled student would look like. The resulting uncertain status of a disabled student's admission and accommodation is correlative with his or her status as 'unintended' participant.

10 The government (*In Unison*, 2000: 17) documents the disability rate of the working-age population at 17.7 per cent. Zola (1982: 242–3), working with U.S. data, says that illness may be a 'statistical *norm*' and that any American 'is at best momentarily able-bodied [and] ... will at some point, suffer from one or more chronic diseases and be disabled, temporarily or permanently, for a significant portion of their lives.' Gadacz (1994), working with Canadian data, comes close to the same conclusion.

11 Karen Anderson (1996: 381–402) has produced one of the few introductory sociological textbooks that includes disability as a major topic area. Her chapter on disability, written with Gary Woodill, critiques the hegemony of the medical model. However, the alternative models (humanitarian, social investment, conflict, social control, and even the disabled consumers' movement) are all tacitly depicted by the authors as relying upon 'pragmatism' as a dominant and unquestioned value (see, especially, 401).

5. Disability Studies: The Old and the New

1 In Canada, the official rate of disability among the working age (15–65) population is 17.7 per cent, or well over two million persons (Gadacz, 1994: 27–33). The non-employment rate, which includes the underemployed and the unemployed, among disabled persons is 52 per cent, which means that over one million working-age adults with disabilities in Canada are not in the labour force (Canada, *In Unison*, 2000). A recent report released from the Canadian Human Rights Commission (CHRC, 6 March 1999: 1) states: 'The Commission welcomed the latest amendments to the Canadian Human Rights Act recognizing that accommodation, short of undue hardship, is a right, not a privilege.' Yet, despite this legal support, the report went on to say that '... the situation of people with dis-

abilities in the workforce is abysmal. "It is most disturbing that the already deplorable situation of people with disabilities has further deteriorated," stated the Commission. In the federally regulated private sector, disabled peoples representation deteriorated from 2.7 per cent in 1996 to 2.3 per cent in 1997 ...' (CHRC, 6 March 1999: 1). The U.S. Department of Commerce, Economics and Statistics Administration (1997) brief on disability states: 'About 1 in 5 Americans have some kind of disability, and 1 in 10 have a severe disability.' As in Canada, the U.S. rate of unemployment and labour force non-participation among disabled persons is huge. The United Nations (1996) says that 'more than half a billion persons are disabled as a result of mental, physical or sensory impairment and no matter which part of the world they are in, their lives are often limited by physical or social barriers.' The United Nations calls the state and fate of disabled persons worldwide a 'silent crisis.' These numerical depictions of disability are startling, but more startling is the obvious absence of disability as a major social issue within the discipline of sociology. More startling still is that the sociological interest in inequality employs the triad 'race, class, and gender,' but often excludes 'disability.'

2 See the previous chapter, as well as Michalko and Titchkosky, 2001.

3 Bauman (1990: 37–53) discusses the 'us/them' dichotomy as it is used in everyday life. In his introductory sociology text, he presents this theme as a topic area for sociological research. It is curious that while first-year sociology students may be introduced to sociological thought on the us/them dichotomy, deviance research and texts often pay no attention to their own employment of it in the production of knowledge about disability.

4 The connection between the generation of knowledge and power has an extensive literature. The work of Foucault (1980, 1979, 1973) is very influential in this regard. I rely heavily upon phenomenology's contribution to the knowledge/power connection. See, for example, Arendt, 1994 (especially 'Understanding and Politics': 307–27); 1954; 1951. Smith (1999, 1990, 1987) also has done extensive work in the knowledge/power connection, steeped in feminist standpoint theory and drawing upon the work of Marx, phenomenology, Bakhtin, and the version of the sociology of knowledge that flows from Mannheim's work. The sense in which marginality may indeed be a site for critical inquiry into the power/knowledge connection is also developed by Harding (1996) and by many au-

thors within cultural studies, for example, Cornel West (1995, 1990), hooks (1995, 1990), and Scott (1995). Hermeneutics has also been influential in my development of an analytic approach to the episte- mological assumptions behind the study of disability. See Gadamer, 1996, 1975; and Ricoeur, 1974.

5 In the United Kingdom there is another story of the development of disability studies. The story does have founding fathers, Michael Oliver and Vic Finkelstein, and it does have a birthdate, 1973, with the Union of the Physically Impaired against Segregation (UPIAS) document that delineates the 'Social Model of Disability.' The Social Model is understood by some to represent a paradigmatic shift in that it is taken as a rejection of the World Health Organization's (WHO) medicalized conception of impairment/disability/handi- cap. The Social Model claims that while there is the problem of bodily impairment best managed by medicine and technology, the focus of disability research should be on how societies disable their impaired members. There is another genesis story in Canada with the founding of the Independent Living Movement and the estab- lishment of the Coalition of Provincial Organizations of the Handi- capped (COPOH) in 1976 (Driedger, 1989: 22). In this case, the founding father seems to be Henry Enns. These interpretive takes on disability were instrumental in the establishment of Disabled Persons International (DPI) in 1980. The U.K. model has led to much research regarding the isolation and oppression of disabled people, usually published by Open University Press and The Dis- ability Press, and in the journal *Disability and Society*. The Canadian model has led to research that begins from a 'consumeristic' slant (see Gadacz, 1994) and has also led to the establishment of the Canadian Centre for Studies in Disability (CCSD, formally estab- lished in 1995). Because my concern here is to address a multiplicity of perspectives on disability which come from disability researchers who also reflect the power of such plurality, I do no more here than mention these organizations. Along with fighting for the rights and needs of disabled persons, these organizations have also been en- gaged in fights for the primacy of their singular conceptions of disability. See, for example, many of the footnotes in Driedger, 1989, and her exclusion of Oliver from her history; and Oliver's and Barnes's critique of disability research that does not follow their work (Oliver, 1999; Barnes and Oliver, 1995; Barnes, 1998).

6 For an examination of the relation between the production of

knowledge as it depends upon taken-for-granted conceptions of 'normal man,' see Minnich, 1990. However, her examination demonstrates how disability is used to reference negativity, which she explicitly announces in her frontispiece, which reads: 'It is not the intelligent woman vs. the ignorant woman, nor the white woman vs. the black, the brown, and the red, – it is not even the cause of woman vs. man. Nay, 'tis woman's strongest vindication for speaking that the world needs to hear her voice ... The world has had to limp along with the wobbling gait and the one-sided hesitancy of a man with one eye. Suddenly the bandage is removed from the other eye and the whole body is filled with light. It sees a circle where before it saw a segment. The darkened eye restored, every member rejoices with it.'

6. Revealing Culture's Eye

1 It is illegal to pass as blind. Whether it is unethical is a different question. How one answers this question of ethics will reveal a conception of disability that should be examined as much as should the question of the ethics of passing.
2 I borrow this provocative phrase from Kenny Fries (1997).
3 Levin (1988: 69) says, 'Staring is an attempt to dominate; but, in the end, it always compels us to see spontaneous, uncontrollable changes in the field of visibility: changes that occur whether we will them or not.' Ironically, the starer can become an 'uncontrollable change in the field of visibility' when another person makes visible the starer's staring by 'staring back.' This irony is artfully captured in *Staring Back: The Disability Experience from the Inside Out* (Fries, 1997).
4 Rod (Michalko, 2002) provides an analysis of these phone calls (one of which included the proprietor saying, 'We don't rent to blind people') as they relate to conceptions of disability as 'useless difference.'

7. Betwixt and Between: Disability Is No-Thing

1 Ricoeur (1974: 19, 23) also speaks of the necessity of situating ourselves between conflicting interpretations if we are to think: '... it is only in a conflict of rival hermeneutics that we perceive something of the being to be interpreted ... [Meaning] is given nowhere but in this dialectic of interpretations ... '

2 Robillard (1999: 72) offers yet another interpretation of the belief
that disability is a reminder of the death of the normal body: 'It is
said that witnessing a disabled person is equivalent to seeing one's
own mortality. I think these reasons have little to do with the deri-
sion [faced by disabled people]. I surmise that in the perception of
others one sees the full range of bodily instrumentalities and potential instrumentalities, calling out and institutionalizing, moment by
moment, one's own bodily capacities and opportunities; the sight of
the paralyzed, the crippled, the lame is a sharp denial of the com-
monsense, reciprocal knowledge. But this is a topic for another time.'
In problematizing the belief that disability is the *memento mori* for
the fate of the normal body, Robillard raises the issue of disability
as a marginal figure; disability represents the extreme margins of
common-sense knowledge regarding the body. Disability puts us in
mind of the limits and character of that which counts as 'reciprocal'
relations.

References

Abberley, Paul. 1987. 'The Concept of Oppression and the Development of a Social Theory of Disability.' *Disability, Handicap and Society* 2(1): 5–19.

– 1998. 'The Spectre at the Feast: Disabled People and Social Theory.' Pp. 79–93 in *The Disability Reader: Social Science Perspectives*. Ed. Tom Shakespeare. London: Cassell Academic.

Adam, Barbara, and Stuart Allan, eds. 1995. *Theorizing Culture: An Interdisciplinary Critique after Postmodernism*. New York: New York University Press.

Albrecht, Gary. 1992. *The Disability Business: Rehabilitation in America*. London: Sage.

– 1997. Review of *Disability and the City: International Perspectives*, by Rob Imrie. *American Journal of Sociology*. 103(2): 515–17.

Anderson, Karen. 1996. *Sociology: A Critical Introduction*. Toronto: Nelson Canada.

Arendt, Hannah. 1951. *The Origins of Totalitarianism: Part Three*. New York: Harcourt Brace Jovanovich.

– 1954. *Between Past and Future: Eight Exercises in Political Thought*. New York: Penguin Books.

– 1955. *Men in Dark Times*. New York: Harcourt Brace Jovanovich.

– 1958. *The Human Condition*. Chicago: University of Chicago Press.

– 1963. *Eichmann in Jerusalem: A Report on the Banality of Evil*. New York: Penguin.

– 1994. *Arendt: Essays in Understanding, 1930–1954*. New York: Harcourt Brace and Company.

Arokiasamy, Charles. 1993. 'A Theory for Rehabilitation?' *Rehabilitation Education* 7: 77–98.

Aronowitz, Robert A. 1998. *Making Sense of Illness: Science, Society, and Disease*. Cambridge: Cambridge University Press.

Aronowitz, Stanley. 1995. 'Reflections on Identity.' Pp. 111–27 in *The Identity Question*. Ed. John Rajchman. New York: Routledge.

Asenjo, F.G. 1988. *In-Between: An Essay on Categories*. Lanham, MD: The Center for Advanced Research in Phenomenology, Inc. and the University Press of America, Inc.

Atkinson, Karen, and Rob Middlehurst. 1995. 'Representing AIDS: The Textual Politics of Health Discourse.' Pp. 113–28 in *Theorizing Culture: An Interdisciplinary Critique after Postmodernism*. Ed. Barbara Adam and Stuart Allan. New York: New York University Press.

Bakhtin, Mikhail Mikhailovich. 1986. Trans. Vern W. McGee. *Speech Genres and Other Late Essays*. Austin: University of Texas Press.

Barnes, Colin. 1996. 'Visual Impairment and Disability.' Pp. 37–44 in *Beyond Disability: Towards an Enabling Society*. London: Sage Publications.

– 1998. 'The Social Model of Disability: A Sociological Phenomenon Ignored by Sociologists?' Pp. 66–78 in *The Disability Reader: Social Science Perspectives*. Ed. Tom Shakespeare. London: Cassell Academic.

Barnes, Colin, and Geoff Mercer, eds. 1996. *Exploring the Divide: Illness and Disability*. Leeds: The Disability Press.

– 1997. *Doing Disability Research*. Leeds: The Disability Press.

Barnes, Colin, and Mike Oliver. 1995. 'Disability Rights: Rhetoric and Reality in the UK.' *Disability and Society* 10(1): 111–16.

Barton, Ellen. 1996. 'Negotiating Expertise in Discourse of Disability.' *Text*. 16(3): 299–322.

Barton, Len, and Mike Oliver, eds. 1997. *Disability Studies: Past, Present and Future*. Leeds: The Disability Press.

Bauman, Zygmunt. 1990. *Thinking Sociologically*. Oxford: Blackwell Publishing.

Beauvoir, Simone de. 1952. *The Second Sex*. Trans. H.M. Parshley. New York: Vintage Books.

Beckwith, J.B., and J.M. Matthews. 1995. 'Measurement of Attitudes of Trainee Professionals to People with Disabilities.' *Journal of Intellectual Disability Research* 39(4): 255–62.

Berger, Peter. 1963. *Invitation to Sociology: A Humanistic Perspective*. New York: Doubleday.

Bickenbach, Jerome. 1993. *Physical Disability and Social Policy*. Toronto: University of Toronto Press.

Bloom, Allan. 1987. *The Closing of the American Mind*. New York: Simon and Schuster.

Blum, Alan. 1994. 'The Ethical Face of Commonplace Malice: Convolutions of the Divided Subject.' *Studies in Symbolic Interactionism* 16: 215–49.

Booth, Tim, and Wendy Booth. 1998. 'Risk, Resilience and Competence: Parents with Learning Difficulties and Their Children.' Pp. 76–101 in *Questions of Competence: Culture, Classification and Intellectual Disability*. Ed. Richard Jenkins. New York: Cambridge University Press.

Bordo, Susan. 1993. *Unbearable Weight: Feminism, Western Culture, and the Body*. Berkeley: University of California Press.

Brueggemann, Brenda Jo. 1997. 'On (Almost) Passing.' *College English* 59(6): 647–60.

Butler, Judith. 1993. *Bodies That Matter*. New York: Routledge.

Butler, Ruth, and Hester Parr, eds. 1999. *Mind and Body Spaces: Geographies of Illness, Impairment and Disability*. New York: Routledge.

Cahill, Spencer E., and Robin Eggleston. 1998. 'Wheelchair Users' Interpersonal Management of Emotions.' Pp. 140–50 in *Inside Social Life: Readings in Sociological Psychology and Microsociology*. Ed. Spencer Cahill. Los Angeles: Roxbury Publishing Company.

Canada. 1996. *Equal Citizenship for Canadians with Disabilities: The Will to Act*. Federal Task Force on Disability Issues. Ottawa: Ministry of Public Works and Government Services Canada.

– 1998. *In Unison: A Canadian Approach to Disability Issues: A Vision Paper*. Federal/Provincial/Territorial Ministers Responsible for Social Services. Hull: Human Resources Development Canada.

– 2000. *In Unison 2000: Persons with Disabilities in Canada*. Federal/Provincial/Territorial Ministers Responsible for Social Services. Hull: Human Resources Development Canada.

Canada. Canada Pension Plan Advisory Board. Committee on Disability Issues. 18 Dec. 1994. *A Report to the Minister of Human Resources Development from the Canada Pension Plan Advisory Board*.

Canada. Human Resources Development. 1998. *Estimates: Performance Report for Period Ending March 31, 1998*. Ottawa: Ministry of Public Works and Government Services.

Canada. Information from the National Clearinghouse on Family Violence. 1998. *Family Violence against Women with Disabilities*. Ottawa: Health Canada.

Canada. Library of Parliament Research Branch. 1996. *Disability: Socio-*

Economic Aspects and Proposals for Reform (95–4E). Ottawa: Minister of Supply and Services Canada.

Canada. Office of the Minister of Human Resources Development Canada. 1995. *Vocational Rehabilitation and Disabled Persons Act: Annual Report 1994–1995*. Ottawa: Human Resources Development Canada.

Canada. Parliamentary Special Committee on the Disabled and the Handicapped. 1981. *Obstacles*. Ottawa: Minister of Supply and Services Canada.

Canadian Human Rights Commission (CHRC). 1999. 'Canadians with Disabilities Still Denied Equal Opportunities' [on line]. 6 March. http://www.chrc-ccdp.ca/ar-ra/ar98-ra98/rndis-cpdef.asp.

Canguilhem, Georges. 1991 [1966]. *The Normal and the Pathological*. Trans. Carolyn Fawcett and Robert Cohen. New York: Zone Books.

Charlton, James I. 1998. *Nothing about Us without Us: Disability Oppression and Empowerment*. Berkeley: University of California Press.

Chronicle of Higher Education. 1999. Colloquy [on line]. May. http://chronicle.com/colloquy/99/disabled/background.htm.

Clements, John, Isabel Clare, and Lesley Anne Ezelle. 1995. 'Real Men, Real Women, Real Lives? Gender Issues in Learning Disabilities and Challenging Behaviour.' *Disability and Society* 10(4): 425–35.

Clinard, B. Marshall, and Robert F. Meier. 1998 [1957]. *Sociology of Deviant Behavior*. 10th edn. Fort Worth: Harcourt Brace College Publishers.

Cooley, Charles Horton. 1909. *Social Organization*. New York: Schocken Books.

Corker, Mairian. 1998a. *Deaf and Disabled or Deafness Disabled?* Buckingham: Open University Press.

– 1998b. 'Disability Discourse in a Postmodern World.' Pp. 221–33 in *The Disability Reader*. Ed. Tom Shakespeare. London: Cassell Academic.

– 1999. 'New Disability Discourse, the Principle of Optimization and Social Change.' Pp. 192–209 in *Disability Discourse*. Ed. Mairian Corker and Sally French. Buckingham: Open University Press.

Corker, Mairian, and Sally French, eds. 1999a. *Disability Discourse*. Buckingham: Open University Press.

– 1999b. 'Reclaiming Discourse in Disability Studies.' Pp. 1–11 in *Disability Discourse*. Ed. Mairian Corker and Sally French. Buckingham: Open University Press.

Corker, Mairian, and Tom Shakespeare, eds. 2002. *Disability/*

Postmodernity: Embodying Disability Theory. London: Continuum Press.

Crawford, Robert. 1980. 'Healthism and the Medicalization of Everyday Life.' *Journal of Health and Sciences* 10 (3): 365–88.

Crossley, Nick. 1995. 'Merleau-Ponty, the Elusive Body and Carnal Sociology.' *Body and Society* 1(1): 43–63.

Crutchfield, Susan, and Marcy Epstein, eds. 2000. *Points of Contact: Disability, Art and Culture*. Ann Arbor: University of Michigan Press.

Dalby, Mogens A., Carten Elbro, and Hans Stodkilde-Jorgensen. 1998. 'Temporal Lobe Asymmetry and Dyslexia: An In Vivo Study Using MRI.' *Brain and Behavior* 62(1): 51–69.

Darke, Anthony. 1998. Review of *Disability and the City*, by Rob Imrie. *Sociology* 32(1): 223–34.

Davis, Fred. 1961. 'Deviance Disavowal: The Management of Strained Interaction by the Visibly Handicapped.' *Social Problems* 9: 120–32.

Davis, Ken. 1996. 'Disability and Legislation: Rights and Equality.' Pp. 124–33 in *Beyond Disability: Towards an Enabling Society*. London: Sage Publications.

Davis, Lennard J. 1995. *Enforcing Normalcy: Disability, Deafness and the Body*. London: Verso Press.

– 1997a. *The Disability Studies Reader*. New York: Routledge.

– 1997b. 'The Need for Disability Studies.' Pp. 1–6 in *The Disability Studies Reader*. New York: Routledge.

– 1997c. 'Constructing Normalcy: The Bell Curve, the Novel, and the Invention of the Disabled Body in the Nineteenth Century.' Pp. 9–28 in *The Disability Studies Reader*. New York: Routledge.

– 2000. *My Sense of Silence: Memoirs of Childhood with Deafness*. Urbana: University of Illinois Press.

Dear, Michael, Robert Wilton, Sharon Lord Gaber, and Lois Takhashi. 1997. 'Seeing People Differently: The Sociospatial Construction of Disability.' *Environment and Planning D: Society and Space* 15: 455–80.

Delos, Kelly H. 1996. *Deviant Behavior: A Text-Reader in the Sociology of Deviance*. New York: St Martin's Press.

Deutsch, Helen, and Felicity Nussbaum, eds. 2000. *'Defects': Engendering the Modern Body*. Ann Arbor: University of Michigan Press.

Disabled Persons Commission. 1995. *Persons with Disabilities in Nova Scotia: A Statistical Handbook*. Halifax: Disabled Persons Commission.

Driedger, Diane. 1989. *The Last Civil Rights Movement: Disabled People's International*. New York: St Martin's Press.

Durkheim, Emile. 1915. *The Elementary Forms of Religious Life*. New York: George Allen and Unwin.

Dyer, Richard. 1993. *The Matter of Images: Essays on Representations*. London: Routledge.

Emberley, Peter C. 1996. *Zero Tolerance: Hot Button Politics in Canada's Universities*. Toronto: Penguin Books.

Enns, Ruth. 1999. *A Voice Unheard: The Latimer Case and People with Disabilities*. Halifax: Fernwood Publishing.

Ettorre, Elizabeth. 1998. 'Re-shaping the Space between Bodies and Culture.' *Sociology of Health and Illness* 20(4): 458–555.

Evenson, Brad. 1999. 'The Only Case in the World: Courtney Popken's Disease May Be Unique, but Finding a Cure for Her Could Strengthen Us All.' *National Post*, 6 March, p. B11.

Farrington, D.P. 1993. 'Childhood Origins of Teenage Antisocial Behavior and Adult Social Dysfunction.' *Journal of the Royal Society of Medicine* 86: 13–17.

Fawcett, Gail. 1996. *Living with Disability in Canada: An Economic Portrait*. Hull: Office for Disability Issues, Human Resources Development Canada.

Featherstone, Mike, Mike Hepworth, and Bryan S. Turner, eds. 1991. *The Body: Social Process and Cultural Theory*. London: Sage Publications.

Fekete, John. 1994. *Moral Panic: Biopolitics Rising*. Montreal: Robert Davies Publishing.

Ferguson, Russel, Martha Gever, Trinh T. Minh-ha, and Cornel West, eds. 1990. *Out There: Marginalization and Contemporary Cultures*. New York: The New Museum of Contemporary Art; Cambridge: MIT Press.

Fine, Michelle, and Adrienne Asch. 1988. *Women with Disabilities: Essays in Psychology, Culture, and Politics*. Philadelphia: Temple University Press.

Finkelstein, Vic. 1998. 'Emancipating Disability Studies.' In *The Disability Reader*. Ed. Tom Shakespeare. London: Cassell Academic. 28–49.

Fleischer, Doris Zames, and Frieda Zames. 2001. *The Disability Rights Movement: From Charity to Confrontation*. Philadelphia: Temple University Press.

Foster, Hal, ed. 1988. *Vision and Visuality: Discussions in Contemporary Culture*. Seattle: Bay Press.

Foucault, Michel. 1973. *The Birth of the Clinic: An Archaeology of Medical Perception*. Trans. A.M. Sheridan Smith. New York: Vintage Books / Random House.

- 1979. *Discipline and Punish: The Birth of the Prison*. Trans. Alan Sheridan. New York: Vintage Books.
- 1980. *The History of Sexuality*. Volume 1. *An Introduction*. New York: Vintage Books.
Frank, Arthur. 1990. 'Bringing Bodies Back In: A Decade Review.' *Theory, Culture and Society* 7(1): 131–62.
- 1995. *The Wounded Story Teller: Body, Illness, and Ethics*. Chicago: University of Chicago Press.
- 1998a. 'Bodies, Sex and Death.' *Theory, Culture and Society* 15 (3–4): 417–25.
- 1998b. 'Enacting Illness Stories When, What and Why.' Pp. 31–49 in *Stories and Their Limits: Narrative Approaches to Bioethics*. Ed. Hilde L. Nelson. New York: Routledge.
- 1998c. 'From Disappearance to Hyperappearance: Sliding Boundaries of Illness and Bodies.' Pp. 205–32 in *The Body of Psychology*. Ed. Henderickus J. Stam. London: Sage Publications.
Frank, Geyla. 1988. 'Beyond Stigma: Visibility and Self-Empowerment of Persons with Congenital Limb Deficiencies.' *Journal of Social Issues* 44(1): 95–115.
- 2000. *Venus on Wheels: Two Decades of Dialogue on Disability, Biogra-phy and Being Female in America*. Berkeley: University of California Press.
French, Sally. 1999. 'The Wind Gets in My Way.' Pp. 21–7 in *Disability Discourse*. Ed. Mairian Corker and Sally French. Buckingham: Open University Press.
Freud, Sigmund. 1973. *Introductory Lectures on Psychoanalysis*. London: Penguin.
Fries, Kenny, ed. 1997. *Staring Back: The Disability Experience from the Inside Out*. New York: Penguin.
Gadacz, René. 1994. *Re-Thinking Dis-Ability: New Structures, New Relationships*. Edmonton: University of Alberta Press.
Gadamer, Hans-Georg. 1975. *Truth and Method*. New York: Crossroad Publishing Company.
- 1996. *The Enigma of Health: The Art of Healing in a Scientific Age*. Trans. Gaiger and Walker. Stanford: Stanford University Press.
Garfinkel, Harold. 1967. *Studies in Ethnomethodology*. Englewood Cliffs, NJ: Prentice-Hall.
Gartner, A., and T. Joe., eds. 1986. *Images of the Disabled, Disabling Images*. New York: Praeger Books.

Gergen, Mary M., and Sara N. Davis, eds. 1997. *Toward a New Psychology of Gender: A Reader*. New York: Routledge.

Gersons-Wolfensberger, D.C.M., and A.J.J.M. Ruijssenaars. 1997. 'Definition and Treatment of Dyslexia: A Report by the Committee on Dyslexia of the Health Council of the Netherlands.' *Journal of Learning Disabilities* 30(2): 209–13.

Gilman, Sander. 1985. *Difference and Pathology*. New York: Cornell University Press.

Giroux, Henry A., and Patrick Shannon, eds. 1997. *Education and Cultural Studies: Toward a Performative Practice*. New York: Routledge.

Gleeson, Brendan. 1999. Geographies of Disability. London: Routledge.

Gliedman, John, and William Roth. 1980. *The Unexpected Minority: Handicapped Children in America*. New York: Harcourt, Brace, Jovanovich.

Goffman, Erving. 1959. *The Presentation of Self in Everyday Life*. New York: Doubleday Anchor Books.

– 1963 *Stigma: Notes on the Management of Spoiled Identity*. Englewood Cliffs, NJ: Prentice-Hall.

Goode, David A. 1992. 'Who Is Bobby? Ideology and Method in the Discovery of Down Syndrome Person's Competence.' Pp. 197–212 in *Interpreting Disability: A Qualitative Reader*. Ed. Philip M. Ferguson, Dianne L. Ferguson, and Steven J. Tayor. New York: Teachers College Press.

Goode, Erich, ed. 1996. *Social Deviance*. Boston: Allyn and Bacon.

Gowman, Alan G. 1956. 'Blindness and the Role of the Companion.' *Social Problems* 4 (July): 68–75.

Grosz, Elizabeth. 1995. *Space, Time and Perversion*. New York: Routledge.

– 1996. 'Intolerable Ambiguity: Freaks as/at the Limits.' Pp. 55–66 in *Freakery: Cultural Spectacles of Extraordinary Body*. Ed. Rose-marie Garland Thomson. New York: New York University Press.

Hales, Gerald. 1996. *Beyond Disability: Towards an Enabling Society*. London: Sage Publications in association with the Open University Press.

Hammill, Donald D., James E. Leigh, Gaye McNutt, and Stephen C. Larsen. 1987. 'A New Definition of Learning Disabilities.' *Journal of Learning Disabilities* 20(2): 109–13.

Hansen, Carl, and Leonard Perlman. 1989. 'Technology: A Vital Tool for Persons with Disabilities.' *Journal of Rehabilitation* 55: 18–21.

Harding, Sandra. 1996. 'Standpoint Epistemology (a Feminist Ver-

sion): How Social Disadvantage Creates Epistemic Advantage.'
Pp. 146–60 in *Social Theory and Sociology: The Classics and Beyond*.
Ed. Stephen P. Turner. Cambridge, MA: Blackwell Publishers Ltd.

Harrison, Felicity, and Mary Crow. 1993. *Living and Learning with Blind Children: A Guide for Parents and Teachers of Visually Impaired Children*. Toronto: University of Toronto Press.

Hartsock, Nancy. 1997. 'Comment on Heckman's "Truth and Method: Feminist Standpoint Theory Revisited."' *Signs: Journal of Women in Culture and Society* 22(2): 367–73.

Heitzeg, Nancy A. 1996. *Deviance: Rulemakers and Rulebreakers*. Minneapolis: West Publishing Company.

Herman, Nancy, and Charlene Miall. 1990. 'The Positive Consequences of Stigma: Two Case Studies in Mental and Physical Disability.' *Qualitative Sociology* 13(3): 251–69.

Heyman, Bob, et al. 1997. 'Alone in the Crowd: How Adults with Learning Difficulties Cope with Social Network Problems.' *Social Science and Medicine* 44(1): 41–53.

Hicks-Coolick, Anne, and David Kurtz. 1997. 'Preparing Students with Learning Disabilities for Success in Postsecondary Education: Needs and Services.' *Social Work in Education* 19(1): 31–42.

Higgins, Paul C. 1996. 'Outsiders in a Hearing World.' Pp. 335–44 in *Deviance: The Interactionist Perspective*. 6th edn. Ed. Earl Rubington and Martin S. Weinberg. Boston: Allyn and Bacon.

Hillyer, Barbara. 1993. *Feminism and Disability*. Norman: University of Oklahoma Press.

Hogan, Anthony. 1999. 'Carving Out a Place to Act: Acquired Impairment and Contested Identity.' Pp. 79–91 in *Disability Discourse*. Ed. Mairian Corker and Sally French. Buckingham: Open University Press.

Holzer, Brigitte, Arthur Vreede, Gabriele Wiegt, eds. 1999. *Disability in Different Cultures: Reflections on Local Concepts*. Bielefeld, Germany: Transcript Verlag.

hooks, bell. 1990. 'Marginality As Site of Resistance.' Pp. 341–5 in *Out There: Marginalization and Contemporary Cultures*. Ed. Russel Ferguson, Martha Gever, Trinh T. Minh-ha, and Cornel West. New York: The New Museum of Contemporary Art; Cambridge: MIT Press.

– 1995. 'The Oppositional Gaze: Black Female Spectators.' Pp. 142–59 in *Feminism and Tradition in Aesthetics*. Ed. Peggy Zegglin Brand and Carolyn Korsmeyer. University Park: Pennsylvania University Press.

Howes, David, ed. 1991. *The Variety of Sensory Experience: A Sourcebook in the Anthropology of the Senses*. Toronto: University of Toronto Press.

Hubbard, Ruth. 1997. 'Abortion and Disability.' Pp. 187–200 in *The Disability Studies Reader*. Ed. Lennard Davis. New York: Routledge.

Hughes, Bill, and Kevin Paterson. 1997. 'The Social Model of Disability and the Disappearing Body: Towards a Sociology of Impairment.' *Disability and Society* 12(3): 325–40.

Imrie, Rob. 1996. *Disability and the City: International Perspectives*. New York: St Martin's Press.

Ingstad, Benedicte, and Susan Reynolds Whyte, eds. 1995. *Disability and Culture*. Berkeley: University of California Press.

Jenkins, Richard, ed. 1998. *Questions of Competence: Culture, Classification and Intellectual Disability*. Cambridge: Cambridge University Press.

Jenks, Chris, ed. 1995. *Visual Culture*. London: Routledge.

Johnstone, David. 1998. *An Introduction to Disability Studies*. London: David Fulton Publishers.

Jones, Colin, and Roy Porter, eds. 1994. *Reassessing Foucault: Power, Medicine and the Body*. New York: Routledge.

Jones, Edward E., Amerigo Farina, Alberta H. Hastorf, Hazel Markus, Dale T. Miller, and Robert A. Scott. 1984. *Social Stigma: The Psychology of Marked Relationships*. New York: W.H. Freeman and Company.

Jones, Ruth J.E. 1994. *Their Rightful Place: Society and Disability*. Toronto: Canadian Academy of the Arts.

Kantowitz, Barbara, and C. Kalb. 1998. 'Boys Will Be Boys.' *Newsweek*, 11 May, pp. 54–60.

Kessler, Suzanne, and Wendy McKenna. 1978. *Gender*. Chicago: University of Chicago Press.

Kleck, Robert, Hiroshi Ono, and Albert H. Hastorf. 1966. 'The Effects of Physical Deviance upon Face-to-Face Interaction.' *Journal of Human Relations* 19: 425–36.

Kleege, Georgina. 1999. *Sight Unseen*. New Haven: Yale University Press.

Kleinman, Arthur. 1995. *Writing at the Margin: Discourse between Anthropology and Medicine*. Berkeley: University of California Press.

Kleinman, Arthur, and Joan Kleinman. 1997. 'The Appeal of Experience; the Dismay of Images: Cultural Appropriations of Suffering in Our Times.' Pp. 1–24 in *Social Suffering*. Ed. Arthur Kleinman, Veena Das, and Margaret Lock. Berkeley: University of California Press.

Kriegel, Leonard. 1997. 'Falling into Life.' In *Staring Back: The Disability Experience from the Inside Out*. Ed. Kenny Fries. New York: Plume.

Kuhn, Thomas S. 1962. *The Structure of Scientific Revolutions*. Chicago: University of Chicago Press.

Kuusisto, Stephen. 1998. *The Planet of the Blind*. New York: Dial Press.

Lacan, Jacques. 1977. *Ecrits: A Selection*. Trans. Alan Sheridan. New York: Tavistock Publications.

Langer, Lawrence L. 1997. 'The Alarmed Vision: Social Suffering and Holocaust Atrocity.' Pp. 47–65 in *Social Suffering*. Ed. Arthur Kleinman, Veena Das, and Margaret Lock. Berkeley: University of California Press.

Levin, David Michael, ed. 1988. *The Opening of Vision: Nihilism and the Postmodern Situation*. New York: Routledge.

– 1993. *Modernity and the Hegemony of Vision*. Berkeley: University of California Press.

Liachowitz, Claire H. 1988. *Disability As a Social Construct: Legislative Roots*. Philadelphia: University of Pennsylvania Press.

Liggett, Helen. 1988. 'Stars Are Not Born: An Interpretive Approach to the Politics of Disability.' *Disability, Handicap and Society* 3(3): 263–75.

Linton, Ralph. 1971 [1936]. 'On Status and Role.' Pp. 90–7 in *Sociology: The Classic Statements*. Ed. Marcello Truzzi. New York: Random House.

Linton, Simi. 1998. *Claiming Disability: Knowledge and Identity*. New York: New York University Press.

Linton, Simi, Susan Mello, and John O'Neill. 1995. 'Disability Studies: Expanding the Parameters of Diversity.' *Radical Teacher* 47: 4–10.

Longmore, Paul, and Lauri Umansky, eds. 2001. *The New Disability History: American Perspectives*. New York: New York University Press.

Low, Jacqueline. 1996. 'Negotiating Identities, Negotiating Environments: An Interpretation of the Experiences of Students with Disabilities.' *Disability and Society* 11(2): 235–48.

MacNaughten, Phil, and John Urry. 1995. 'Towards a Sociology of Nature.' *Sociology* 29: 203–20.

Mairs, Nancy. 1996. *Waist-High in the World: A Life among the Nondisabled*. Boston: Beacon Press.

Manning, Philip. 1992. *Erving Goffman and Modern Sociology*. Stanford: Stanford University Press.

Margalit, Malka. 1995. 'Social Skills Learning for Students with Learning Disabilities and Students with Behavior Disorders.' *Educational Psychology* 15(4): 445–56.

Marks, Deborah. 1999. *Disability: Controversial Debates and Psychological Perspectives*. London: Routledge.

Matthews, Gwyneth Ferguson. 1983. *Voices from the Shadows: Women with Disabilities Speak Out*. Toronto: Women's Press.

McDermott, Ray, and Hervé Varene. 1995. 'Culture As Disability.' *Anthropology and Education Quarterly* 26(3): 324–48.

Mead, George Herbert. *Mind, Self, and Society: From the Standpoint of a Social Behaviourist*. Ed. Charles W. Morris. Chicago: University of Chicago Press.

Merleau-Ponty, Maurice. 1962. *Phenomenology of Perception*. Trans. Colin Smith. London: Routledge and Kegan Paul.

– 1964. *The Primacy of Perception: And Other Essays on Phenomenological Psychology, the Philosophy of Art, History and Politics*. Evanston, IL: Northwestern University Press.

Michalko, Rod. 1998. *The Mystery of the Eye and the Shadow of Blindness*. Toronto: University of Toronto Press.

– 1999. *The Two in One: Walking with Smokie, Walking with Blindness*. Philadelphia: Temple University Press.

– 2001. 'Blindness Enters the Classroom.' *Disability and Society* 16(3): 349–59.

– 2002a. *The Difference That Disability Makes*. Philadelphia: Temple University Press.

– 2002b. 'Estranged Familiarity.' Pp. 246–58 in *Disability/Post-modernity: Embodying Disability Theory*. Ed. Mairian Corker and Tom Shakespeare. London: Continuum Press.

Michalko, Rod, and Tanya Titchkosky. 2001. 'Putting Disability in Its Place: It's Not a Joking Matter.' Pp. 200–28 in *Embodied Rhetorics: Disability in Language and Culture*. Ed. James C. Wilson and Cynthia Lewiecki-Wilson. Carbondale: Southern Illinois University Press.

Minnich, E.K. 1990. *Transforming Knowledge*. Philadelphia: Temple University Press.

Mitchell, David T., and Sharon L. Snyder. 1997. 'Disability Studies and the Double Bind of Representation.' Pp. 1–31 in *The Body and Physical Difference: Discourses of Disability*. Ed. David T. Mitchell and Sharon L. Snyder. Ann Arbor: University of Michigan Press.

– 2000. *Narrative Prosthesis: Disability and the Dependencies of Discourse*. Ann Arbor: University of Michigan Press.

Morris, Jenny, ed. 1991. *Pride against Prejudice: Transforming Attitudes to Disability*. Philadelphia: New Society.

– 1996. *Encounters with Strangers: Feminism and Disability*. London: Women's Press.

Murphy, R., J. Scheer, Y. Murphy, and R. Mack. 1988. 'Physical Disability and Social Liminality: A Study in the Rituals of Adversity.' *Social Science and Medicine* 26(2): 235–42.

Murphy, Robert. 1987. *The Body Silent*. New York: W.W. Norton.

Nijhof, Gerhard. 1998. 'Heterogeneity in the Interpretation of Epilepsy.' *Qualitative Health Research* 8(1): 95–105.

Norwich, Brahm. 1997. 'Exploring the Perspectives of Adolescents with Modern Learning Difficulties on Their Special Schooling and Themselves: Stigma and Self-Perceptions.' *European Journal of Special Needs Education* 12(1): 38–53.

Nussbaum, Martha C. 1997. *Cultivating Humanity: A Classical Defence of Reform in Liberal Education*. Cambridge: Harvard University Press.

Oliver, Michael. 1990. *The Politics of Disablement*. London: Macmillan.

– 1996. *Understanding Disability: From Theory to Practice*. New York: St Martin's Press.

– 1999. 'Final Accounts and the Parasite People.' Pp. 183–91 in *Disability Discourse*. Ed. Mairian Corker, and Sally French. Buckingham: Open University Press.

Overboe, James. 1999. '"Difference in Itself": Validating Disabled People's Lived Experience.' *Body and Society* 5(4): 17–29.

Padget, Yancey S. 1998. 'Lessons from Research on Dyslexia: Implications for a Classification System for Learning Disabilities.' *Learning Disabilities Quarterly* 21(2): 167–78.

Palombo, Joseph. 1996. 'The Diagnosis and Treatment of Children with Nonverbal Learning Disabilities.' *Child and Adolescent Social Work Journal* 13(4): 311–32.

Parens, Erik, ed. 1998. *Enhancing Human Traits: Ethical and Social Implications*. Washington, DC: Georgetown University Press.

Peters, Susan. 1999. 'Transforming Disability Identity through Critical Literacy and the Cultural Politics of Language.' Pp. 103–15 in *Disability Discourse*. Ed. Mairian Corker and Sally French. Buckingham: Open University Press.

Phillips, Marilyn. 1990. 'Damaged Goods: Oral Narratives of the Experience of Disability in American Culture.' *Social Science and Medicine* 30(8): 849–57.

Pile, Steve, and Nigel Thrift, eds. 1995. *Mapping the Subject: Geographies of Cultural Transformation*. London: Routledge.

Pontell, Henry N., ed. 1996. *Social Deviance: Readings in Theory and Research*. Upper Saddle River, NJ: Prentice-Hall.

Poster, Mark. 1995. 'Postmodern Virtualities.' *Body and Society* 1(3–4): 79–95.

Priestley, Mark, ed. 2001. *Disability and the Life Course: Global Perspectives*. Cambridge: Cambridge University Press.

Radley, Alan. 1995. 'The Elusory Body and Social Constructionist Theory.' *Body and Society* 1(2): 3–23.

– 1997. 'The Triumph of Narrative? A Reply to Arthur Frank.' *Body and Society* 3(3): 93–101.

Rajchman, John, ed. 1995. *The Identity in Question*. New York: Routledge.

Richardson, Stephen A., et al. 1961. 'Cultural Uniformity in Reaction to Physical Disabilities.' *American Sociological Review* 26(1–6): 241–7.

Ricoeur, Paul. 1974. *The Conflict of Interpretations: Essays in Hermeneutics*. Evanston, IL: Northwestern University Press.

Rifkin, Jeremy. 1998. *The Biotech Century: Harnessing the Gene and Remaking the World*. New York: Penguin Putnam.

Robillard, Albert. 1999. *Meaning of a Disability: The Lived Experience of Paralysis*. Philadelphia: Temple University Press.

Rogers, Linda, and Beth Blue Swadener, eds. 2001. *Semiotics and Dis/ability: Interrogating Categories of Difference*. New York: State University of New York Press.

Roth, William. 1983. 'Handicap As a Social Construct.' *Society* 20: 56–61.

Rubington, Earl, and Martin S. Weinberg, eds. 1999. *Deviance: The Interactionist Perspective*. 7th edn. Boston: Allyn and Bacon.

Russell, Marta. 1998. *Beyond Ramps: Disability at the End of the Social Contract*. Monroe, ME: Common Courage Press.

Sagarin, Edward. 1975. 'The Disabled As Involuntary Deviants.' In *Deviants and Deviance: An Introduction to Disvalued People and Behavior*. New York: Praeger. 210–13.

Saint Francis Xavier University. 1998. *Students with Disabilities at 'X.'* Antigonish: St Francis Xavier University Health and Counselling Centre.

Saramago, Jose. 1997. *Blindness*. Trans. Giovanni Pontiero. New York: Harcourt Brace.

Schissel, Benard, and Linda Mahood, eds. 1996. *Social Control in Canada: Issues in the Social Construction of Deviance*. Toronto: Oxford University Press.

Schutz, Alfred. 1973. *Collected Papers I: The Problem of Social Reality*. The Hague: Martinus Nijhoff.

Scotch, Richard. 1994. 'Making Disability: Exploring the Social Transformation of Human Variation.' *Contemporary Sociology* 23(1): 145–6.

Scott, Joan. 1995. 'Multiculturalism and the Politics of Identity.' Pp. 3–12 in *The Identity in Question*. Ed. John Rajchman. New York: Routledge.

– 1998. 'Deconstructing Equality-Versus-Difference: Or the Uses of Postcolonial Structuralist Theory for Feminism.' *Feminist Studies* 14(1): 32–50.

Scott, Robert A. 1969. *The Making of Blind Men: A Study of Adult Socialization*. New York: Russell Sage Foundation.

Scott, Sue, and David Morgan, eds. 1993. *Body Matters: Essays on the Sociology of the Body*. Washington: DC: Falmer Press.

Shakespeare, Tom, ed. 1994. 'Cultural Representations of Disabled People: Dustbin for Disapproval?' *Disability and Society* 9(3): 283–300.

– 1998. *The Disability Reader: Social Science Perspectives*. London: Cassell Academic.

Shakespeare, Tom, and Nicholas Watson. 1997. 'Defending the Social Model.' *Disability and Society* 12(2): 293–300.

Shapiro, Joseph P. 1993. *No Pity: People with Disabilities Forging a New Civil Rights Movement*. New York: Times Books.

Shaw, Stan F. , Joseph P. Cullen, Joan M. McGuire, and Loring C. Brinckerhoff. 1995. 'Operationalizing a Definition of Learning Disabilities.' *Journal of Learning Disabilities* 28(9): 586–97.

Shildrick, Margrit, and Janet Price. 1996. 'Breaking the Boundaries of the Broken Body.' *Body and Society* 2(4): 93–113.

Shilling, Chris. 1993. *The Body and Social Theory*. London: Sage Publications.

– 1997. 'The Body and Difference.' Pp. 63–120 in *Identity and Difference*. Ed. Kathryn Woodward. London: Sage Publications.

Shogan, Debra. 1998. 'The Social Construction of Disability: The Impact of Statistics and Technology.' *Adapted Physical Activity Quarterly* 15: 269–77.

Shur Edwin, M. 1979. *Interpreting Deviance: A Sociological Introduction*. New York: Harper and Row.

Simpson, Murray. 1996. 'The Sociology of "Competence" in Learning Disability Services.' *Social Work and Social Sciences Review* 6(2): 85–97.

Singer, Peter. 1993. *Practical Ethics*. Cambridge: Cambridge University Press.

– 1995. *How Are We to Live? Ethics in an Age of Self-Interest*. Amherst, NY: Prometheus Books.

Slatin, John M. 1986. 'Blindness and Self-Perception: The Autobiographies of Ved Mehta.' *Mosaic: A Journal for the Interdisciplinary Study of Literature* 19(1): 173–93.

Smith, Dorothy E. 1987. *The Everyday World As Problematic: A Feminist Sociology*. Toronto: University of Toronto Press.

– 1990. *The Conceptual Practices of Power: A Feminist Sociology of Knowledge*. Toronto: University of Toronto Press.

– 1993. 'A Peculiar Eclipsing: Women's Exclusion from Man's Culture.' Pp. 347–70 in *Sociology: An Introduction: From the Classics to Contemporary Feminists*. Ed. Gordon Bailey and Nolga Gayle. Toronto: Oxford University Press.

– 1999. *Writing the Social: Critique, Theory, and Investigations*. Toronto: University of Toronto Press.

Spivak, Gayatri Chakravorty. 1982. 'The Politics of Interpretations.' *Critical Inquiry* 9(1): 259–78.

Statistics Canada. 1991. http://www.statcan.ca/english/Pgdb/People/Health/health12a.html and http://www.hrdc-drhc.gc.ca/sommon/news/ 9821b3.html

Stiker, Henri-Jacques. 1999. *A History of Disability*. Trans. William Sayers. Ann Arbor: University of Michigan Press.

Stone, Deborah A. 1984. *The Disabled State*. Philadelphia: Temple University Press.

Stone, Emma, ed. 1999. *Disability and Development: Learning from Action and Research on Disability in the Majority World*. Leeds: The Disability Press.

Susman, Joan. 1994. 'Disability, Stigma and Deviance.' *Social Science and Medicine* 38(1): 15–22.

Swain, John, and Colin Cameron. 1999. 'Unless Otherwise Stated: Discourses of Labelling and Identity in Coming Out.' Pp. 68–78 in *Disability Discourse*. Ed. Mairian Corker and Sally French. Buckingham: Open University Press.

Synnott, Anthony. 1993. *The Body Social: Symbolism, Self and Society*. London: Routledge.

Taussig, Michael. 1980. 'Reification and the Consciousness of the Patient.' *Social Science and Medicine* 4(1B): 3–13.

Taylor, Charles. 1989. *Sources of the Self: The Making of the Modern Identity*. Cambridge: Harvard University Press.

Thomas, W.I. 1971 [1923]. 'On the Definition of the Situation.' Pp. 274–

7 in *Sociology: The Classic Statements*. Ed. Marcello Truzzi. New York: Random House.

Thomson, Rosemarie Garland, ed. 1996. *Freakery: Cultural Spectacles of Extraordinary Body*. New York: New York University Press.

– 1997a. *Extraordinary Bodies: Figuring Physical Disability in American Culture and Literature*. New York: Columbia University Press.

– 1997b. 'Feminist Theory, the Body, and the Disabled Figure.' Pp. 279–92 in *The Disability Studies Reader*. Ed. Lennard Davis. New York: Routledge.

Titchkosky, Tanya. 1992. 'Learning to Read: Desire and the Economy of Reading.' MA thesis, York University, Toronto.

– 1997. 'The Primacy of Betweenness: Marginality and Art.' PhD diss., York University, Toronto.

– 1998. 'Anorexia, Women, and Change.' *Journal of Dharma* 23(4): 479–500.

– 2000. 'Disability Studies: The Old and the New.' *Canadian Journal of Sociology* 25(2): 197–224.

– 2001a. 'Disability – a Rose by Any Other Name? People-First Language in Canadian Society.' *Canadian Review of Sociology and Anthropology* 38:(2) 125–40.

– 2001b. 'Coming Out Disabled: The Politics of Understanding.' *Disability Studies Quarterly* 21(4): 131–9. http://www.cds.hawaii.edu

– 2002. 'Cultural Maps: Which Way to Disability?' Pp. 145–60 in *Disability and Postmodernity*. Ed. Mairian Corker and Tom Shakespeare. London: Continuum.

– Forthcoming. 'Acting Blind: A Revelation of Culture's Eye.' In *Bodies in Commotion: Disability and Performance*. Ed. Philip Auslander and Carrie Sandahl. Ann Arbor: University of Michigan Press.

Turner, Bryan S. 1996. *The Body and Society: Explorations in Social Theory*. London: Sage.

Turner, Victor. 1985. *On the Edge of the Bush: Anthropology As Experience*. Arizona: University of Arizona Press.

United Nations. 1996. *Information Note Prepared by the United Nations Secretariat*. Gopher://gopher.un.org/00/sec/dpcsd/dspd/disabled/DIS96 or Http://www.un.org/dpcsd/

U.S. Department of Commerce, Economics and Statistics Administration. 1997. *Census Brief: Disabilities Affect One-Fifth of All Americans*. Bureau of Census: Dec. Cenbr/97–5.

Vaughan, Edwin C. 1998. *Social and Cultural Perspectives on Blindness:*

Barriers to Community Integration. Springfield, IL: Charles C. Thomas Publisher.

Wendell, Susan. 1996. *The Rejected Body: Feminist Philosophical Reflections on Disability*. New York: Routledge.

West, Candace. 1996. 'Goffman in Feminist Perspective.' *Sociological Perspectives* 39(3): 353–69.

West, Cornel. 1990. 'The New Cultural Politics of Difference.' Pp. 19–36 in *Out There: Marginalization and Contemporary Cultures*. Ed. Russel Ferguson, Martha Gever, Trinh T. Minh-ha, and Cornel West. New York: The New Museum of Contemporary Art; Cambridge: MIT Press.

– 1995. 'A Matter of Life and Death.' Pp. 15–32 in *The Identity in Question*. Ed. John Rajchman. New York: Routledge.

Williams, Gareth. 1998. 'The Sociology of Disability: Towards a Materialist Phenomenology.' Pp. 234–44 in *The Disability Reader*. Ed. Tom Shakespeare. London: Cassell Academic.

Wilson, James C., and Cynthia Lewiecki-Wilson, eds. 2001. *Embodied Rhetorics: Disability in Language and Culture*. Carbondale: Southern Illinois University Press.

Wittgenstein, Ludwig. 1980. *Remarks on the Philosophy of Psychology*. Volume 2. Chicago: University of Chicago Press.

Zola, Irving Kenneth. 1982. *Missing Pieces: A Chronicle of Living with a Disability*. Philadelphia: Temple University Press.

– 1985. 'Depictions of Disability – Metaphor, Message, and Medium in the Media: A Research and Political Agenda.' *Social Science Journal* 22(4): 5–17.

– 1988. 'Whose Voice Is This Anyway?' *Medical Humanities Review* 2(1): 6–15.

Zuriff, G.E. 1996. 'The Myths of Learning Disabilities: The Social Construction of a Disorder.' *Public Affairs Quarterly* 10(4): 395–405.

Index